The Sociological Souls of Black Folk

The Sociological Souls of Black Folk

Essays by
W.E.B. Du Bois

Introduction, Reconstructed Essay, and
Additional Editing by
Robert A. Wortham

LEXINGTON BOOKS
Lanham • Boulder • New York • Toronto • Plymouth, UK

Published by Lexington Books
A wholly owned subsidiary of The Rowman & Littlefield Publishing Group, Inc.
4501 Forbes Boulevard, Suite 200, Lanham, Maryland 20706
http://www.lexingtonbooks.com

Estover Road, Plymouth PL6 7PY, United Kingdom

British Library Cataloguing in Publication Information Available

Library of Congress Cataloging-in-Publication Data
Du Bois, W. E. B. (William Edward Burghardt), 1868–1963.
  The sociological souls of Black folk : essays / by W.E.B. Du Bois ;
introduction, reconstructed essay, and additional editing by Robert A. Wortham.
      p. cm.
  Includes bibliographical references and index.
  ISBN 978-0-7391-5073-3 (cloth : alk. paper)
  1. African Americans. I. Wortham, Robert (Robert A.) II. Title.
  E185.6.D796 2011
  305.896'073—dc22   2011013885

Printed in the United States of America

Contents

List of Figures

List of Tables

The Sociological Souls of Black Folk: Editor's Introduction

The Souls of Black Folk is W.E.B. Du Bois' most famous work. Numerous editions of the book have been published since the book's initial release in 1903. While the work is often viewed as a classic in African American literature and the history of the African American experience, the sociological significance of the work has been understated. Provenzo (2005) briefly addresses the sociological significance of the work in his "Introduction" to *The Illustrated Souls of Black Folk*. During his initial discussions with the original publisher, A.C. McClurg & Company, in 1900, Du Bois proposed to prepare a volume that would showcase his ongoing sociological work on "the Negro problems." The publisher responded by asking for a volume that would appeal to a more general audience. Du Bois met the publisher's request by combining several previously published sociological essays with a few new essays. In the preface to the fiftieth anniversary edition to *The Souls of Black Folk*, Du Bois expressed his reservations about this decision. Here he maintained that he had hesitated to proceed "because I was sure that with more time and thought I could do a better job; in so many respects this was incomplete and unsatisfactory ([1903a] 1953, ix)."

What eventually emerged as *The Souls of Black Folk* was a collection of fourteen essays with an added "Forethought" and an "Afterthought." Each essay was introduced with a quote from a European author and a strain from one of the African American "Sorrow Songs." The prefacing of each essay with the word "Of" appears to be modeled after *The Thirty-Nine Articles of Religion* of the Church of England (see Articles of Religion 2007).[1] Utilizing these literary techniques, Du Bois was able to frame each essay within the African American community's experience of "double consciousness" and life "within the veil." Nine of the fourteen essays were based on eight sociological studies previously published between 1897 and 1902. Herein one discovers the "Sociological Souls of Black Folk" and the showcasing of Du Bois' sociological work on "the Negro problems."

While many editions of Du Bois' classic text have appeared, there has never been an edition that has focused primarily on the eight previously published essays in their original form and in chronological order. This fact alone makes *The Sociological Souls of Black Folk* unique. This introductory essay addresses the sociological significance of the original essays by providing commentary on the major themes contained in each of the eight essays comprising the "Sociological Souls of Black Folk." This section is followed by a discussion of the main sociological issues addressed in eight additional sociological essays originally published between 1897 and 1900. These studies have been included in this volume to showcase the richness of Du Bois' early sociological work. These eight additional essays address such topics as "the Negro problems," business, crime, race relations, liberal arts education, the Black Church, and the quality of life in the Southern Black Belt. Hopefully, the essays included in *The Sociological Souls of Black Folk*, will enable the reader to first gain a greater appreciation for Du Bois' early sociological work and second to recognize that Du Bois is indeed one of the pioneering figures in the development of sociology in the United States.

The Previously Published Sociological Essays

The eight previously published studies represent the sociological core of *The Souls of Black Folk* and reflect Du Bois' original intent for the work. These essays form "The Sociological Souls of Black Folk." These original essays are presented in the order they were published in Figure I.1. The placement of the essays and the title employed in *The Souls of Black Folk* are included in parentheses.

The eight previously published essays address such important sociological issues as:

- The concept of the self and racial identity.
- Race relations in the South.
- Quality of life in the Southern Black Belt.
- The economic transformation of the South.
- Social structure and social change.
- Social disorganization and crime.
- Education, employment, voting rights, social status, and social mobility.
- The role of the Black Church as an integrative mechanism promoting social stability and social reform.
- The emergence of a leadership class (the "Talented Tenth").
- The use of ethnographic data to validate experiences of racial inequality.

Several of these themes are developed further by Du Bois in the 1903 Atlanta University Conference study, *The Negro Church*, his 1903 essay on "The Talented Tenth," the 1904 Atlanta University Conference study, *Some Notes on Crime Particularly in Georgia*, his 1906 article, "The Negro Question in the United States," two essays in the 1907 volume with Booker T. Washington on *The Negro in the South*, and *The Quest of the Silver Fleece*, his 1911 novel on

Figure I.1. The Sociological Souls of Black Folk

Reading 1. "Strivings of the Negro People"
            The Atlantic Monthly, Volume 80, Issue 478 (August 1897a): 194–98.
            (*The Souls of Black Folk*: Chapter 1, "Of Our Spiritual Strivings")

Reading 2. "A Negro Schoolmaster in the New South"
            The Atlantic Monthly, Volume 83, Issue 495 (January 1899a): 99–105.
            (*The Souls of Black Folk*: Chapter 4, "Of the Meaning of Progress")

Reading 3. "The Religion of the American Negro"
            New World 9 (December 1900a): 614–625.
            (*The Souls of Black Folk*: Chapter 10, "Of the Faith of the Fathers")

Reading 4. "The Freedman's Bureau"
            The Atlantic Monthly, Volume 87, Issue 521 (March 1901a): 354–65.
            (*The Souls of Black Folk*: Chapter 2, "Of the Dawn of Freedom")

Reading 5. "The Negro as He Really Is"
            The World's Work 2 (June 1901b):846–66.
            (*The Souls of Black Folk*: Chapter 7, "Of the Black Belt" and Chapter 8,
            "Of the Quest of the Golden Fleece")

Reading 6. "The Evolution of Negro Leadership"[a]
            The Dial 31 (July 16, 1901c): 53–55.
            (*The Souls of Black Folk*: Chapter 3, "Of Mr. Booker T. Washington and
            Others")

Reading 7. "The Relation of the Negroes to the Whites in the South"
            Annals of the American Academy of Political and Social Science, 18 (July
            1901d): 121–40.
            (*The Souls of Black Folk*: Chapter 9, "Of the Sons of Master and Man")

Reading 8. "Of the Training of Black Men"
            The Atlantic Monthly, Volume 90 (September 1902): 289–97.
            (*The Souls of Black Folk*: Chapter 6, "Of the Training of Black Men")

Note: [a] This is a review of Booker T. Washington's *Up from Slavery* ([1901] 2003).

life in the Black Belt and the status of African American women. This last volume was also originally published by A.C. McClurg & Company.

To gain a better understanding of the sociological significance of each of the eight original articles, the major themes of each article are now discussed. These readings are referenced as Readings1–8. This represents the order in which they appear in *The Sociological Souls of Black Folk*. The "Strivings of the Negro People" (Reading 1) is the first of four articles included in *The Sociologi-*

cal Souls of Black Folk that were originally published in *The Atlantic Monthly*. In the middle and at the end of the first paragraph of this essay, Du Bois (1897a, 194) raised the now famous question, "How does it feel to be a problem." Here Du Bois addressed the issue of African American identity. In books like Carroll's *The Negro A Beast or In the Image of God* (1900) and Dixon's *The Leopard's Spots: A Romance of the White Man's Burden, 1865-1900* ([1902] 1967), the very humanity of African Americans was questioned. It is in response to racist ideologies at the time like these that Du Bois presents his 1903 collection of revised and new essays known as *The Souls of Black Folk*. In this first essay, one sees that as early as 1897 he was very much aware of the double nature of African American self-consciousness.

Addressing the issue of double consciousness, Du Bois talked about life "within the veil" and the "two-ness" of soul and thought. Rather than simply being defined by others, an early expression of the concept of the significant other,[2] and conforming to the expectations of others, Du Bois maintained that it was important for African Americans to be both Americans and African Americans. Rather than supporting racial assimilation, Du Bois supported racial accommodation. Double consciousness was based on maintaining a both/and rather than an either/or identity. The concept also did not promote a synthesis of the two identities. Rather than being polar opposites, the two identities were held in dialectical tension.

Some have argued that Du Bois' concept was grounded in the work of William James and Alfred Binet (Bruce 1999). In the first volume of *The Principles of Psychology* ([1890] 2007), James included a chapter on the cohesive nature of the self. Here he distinguished among the empirical self (the me), the material self, the social self, and the rivalries and conflicts that exist among the different selves. Likewise, Binet, in *Alterations of Personality* ([1892] 1896), devoted the entire second section of this work to "coexistent personalities." Consequently, for Du Bois, African American identity within the veil was defined by a fundamental "two-ness" of experiences that were held in tension.

In "Strivings of the Negro People," Du Bois identified poverty, ignorance, and slavery as the roots of prejudice. He also believed that ignorance could be addressed through empirical research and a quest for the truth and facts. Here it appears that Du Bois had been heavily influenced by the pragmatist approach of Williams James and Gustav Schmoller's inductive approach to research which insisted on focusing on *what is* rather than *what ought* to be (Wortham 2009a). In an 1898 essay, "The Study of the Negro Problems," Du Bois outlined further his approach to the study of social factors impacting African American quality of life. Here he argued that a social group should be studied in its own particular social environment and that the aim of sociology is the discovery of the truth. This truth could be discovered through a multidisciplinary approach to research that integrated findings from history, statistical study, sociology, and anthropology. Again, the influence of Schmoller and the interdisciplinary *Staatswissenschaften* perspective on Du Bois, which he encountered during his doctoral studies in Germany, are apparent (Wortham 2010a). The University of Berlin experience provided one of the cornerstones of Du Bois' sociological perspective. At Berlin he was also introduced to the work of Adolph Wagner and Max Weber.

While Du Bois was an undergraduate at Fisk University from 1885–88, he spent part of the summers of 1886 and 1887 teaching at a small rural school outside of Nashville near Alexandria, TN. Here Du Bois directly encountered the poverty of the Southern Black Belt. In June of 1898 Du Bois gave the commencement address for the graduates of Fisk University. This address, "Careers Open to College-Bred Negroes," is included as Reading 13 in this volume. Following this address Du Bois took time to revisit the African American community near Alexandria. "A Negro Schoolmaster in the New South" (Reading 2), originally published in January of 1899 in *The Atlantic Monthly*, provided a first-hand ethnographic account of these experiences.

During his early sociological period (1897–1914), Du Bois routinely employed a triangular methodological approach to the study of "the Negro Problems." Often this approach involved integrating findings from census data, survey data, and ethnographic data. By the time Du Bois published this study based on his experiences as a rural school teacher, he had completed two major social studies employing a triangular methodology. One study addressed the quality of African American life in Philadelphia, a major urban city (Du Bois [1899] 1996), while the other was an in-depth study of rural life in Farmville, VA (Du Bois [1898b]). Du Bois' essay on his teaching experiences in rural Tennessee reads like a travelogue and is thus similar to Harriet Martineau's *Society in America* ([1837] 2009).

Integrating participant observation, with thick description, Du Bois invites the reader to experience African American rural life within the veil. Josie, Wheeler's "corn shelter" schoolhouse, the Dowells, Fat Reuben, and Doc Burke's farm were all crucial players and props on a stage depicting poverty, depleted land, and low wages. This slice of life characterizes the realities of the Southern Black Belt. Structural inequalities were brought closer to home by being given human faces. Within this context Du Bois (1899a, 104) raised the all important question, "How shall man measure Progress there where the dark-faced Josie lies?" For Du Bois the veil of poverty, sorrow, strife, and hard labor blocked the path to opportunity. This is what Du Bois invites the reader to see and experience.

On a more personal note, Du Bois described two of his experiences which further underscored the quality of life of African Americans in the Jim Crow South. The first experience involved a diner experience after presenting the commissioner with his teaching credentials for his summer job. Du Bois assumed that when he was invited to eat, he would be eating with the other candidate and the commissioner. Rather, he discovered that he was to eat afterwards, alone. The second experience involved his ride home in 1898 after revisiting the rural community a little more than ten years later. Du Bois returned to Nashville by riding in the Jim Crow car.

In the 1897 essay, "The Problem of Amusement" (Reading 14), Du Bois maintained that the Black Church was the social, economic, and religious center of African American life. This point was restated in the 1900 essay, "The Religion of the American Negro" (Reading 3). Du Bois wrote extensively on religion and the Black Church throughout his early sociological period. In addition to including this essay in *The Souls of Black Folk*, the 1903 collection of essays also included a tribute to Alexander Crummell, a noted African American minister and founder of the American Negro Academy, and an essay on the African American sorrow songs. These songs, an example of qualitative data, preserved the African American experiences of inequality as a result of the legacy of slavery, the color line, and the veil. In 1903 Du Bois also edited *The Negro Church*. This ground breaking Atlanta University Conference study represents the first book-length empirically based sociological study of a religious group (Wortham 2005; Zuckerman, Barnes, and Cady 2003). In *The Negro and the South* (1907), Du Bois and Booker T. Washington each contribute an essay, within an opposing viewpoints fashion, on economic conditions in the South and on religion in the South respectively. Du Bois also composed a series of prayers for the students of Atlanta University from January 1909 through May 1910. Here Du Bois was able to utilize the prayer form to raise social awareness among a younger audience (Wortham 2010b). These prayers were published posthumously in 1980 by Herbert Aptheker as *Prayers for Dark People*. The final early sociological study of religion by Du Bois was the 1913 Atlanta University Conference study, *Morals and Manners among Negro Americans*. This study was the sequel to *The Negro Church* and was co-edited with Augustus Dill. The study was based on a survey of African American morals. The data provided in this conference report have been content analyzed recently, and the report has been reissued (Wortham 2010a; Du Bois and Dill, [1914] 2010).

Du Bois begins "The Religion of the American Negro" by identifying three primary characteristics of slave religion. These characteristics are the preacher, the music, and the frenzy. Within the African American community, the preacher functioned as a leader and a politician. The music captured the African American community's experiences of hope, sorrow, and despair while the frenzy represented the expression of religious emotion through shouting and stomping. Du Bois goes on to describe the current role of the Black Church as strengthening moral character, supporting family life, providing benevolent aid, and serving as a community center addressing social, economic, religious, and intellectual needs. In this essay one observes Du Bois providing an early functional analysis of a religious institution.

Reference is also made to the 1890 *Census of Religious Bodies* data. Here Du Bois noted that within the African American community, there were ten church members to every twenty-eight persons. Two points are worthy of note here. First, until recently, researchers had either forgotten or failed to recognize that the census data on religion were a valid source of data for the study of the changing U.S. religious economy (Finke and Stark 2005). The census published volumes on religion on a decennial basis from 1850–90 and then from 1906–36. Second, Du Bois suggested that in the South almost everyone was a church member. Perhaps Du Bois was aware that in the South religious participation was expected and thus semi-involuntary. This point was reaffirmed almost one hundred years later by Ellison and Sherkat (1995) in their study of African American religious participation.

Du Bois identified the Negro Church as the first African American social institution, even predating the African American family. He had great respect for the African Methodist Episcopal Church, but he did criticize the church as being self-serving and failing to address the needs of the community. Du Bois identified the challenges of the Black Church as: the Negro Problems, enhancing the status of women, supporting the home and childrearing, wealth accumulation, and crime.

One of the classic quotes from *The Souls of Black Folk* is "The problem of the twentieth century is the problem of the color-line . . ." (Du Bois [1903a] 2007, 8). Segregation was formally identified as a social structure characterizing American society, but this was not the first time Du Bois utilized this expression. It appears earlier in "The Freedman's Bureau" (Reading 4), an essay published in *The Atlantic Monthly* two years earlier in 1901. Here Du Bois used the expression as a framing device to begin and conclude the essay. This framing device is dropped in "Of the Dawn of Freedom," the revised version of the essay for *The Souls of Black Folk*.

However, Du Bois was employing this expression to describe the global nature of racial inequality as early as 1900. In "To the Nations of the World," an address given on July 25, 1900 to the Pan-African Conference in London, Du Bois (1900b, 10) wrote:

> In the metropolis of the modern world, in this closing year of the nineteenth-century, there has been assembled a congress of men and women of African blood, to deliberate solemnly upon the present situation and outlook of the darker races of mankind. The problem of the twentieth century is the problem of the colour line, the question as to how far differences of race, which show themselves chiefly in the colour of the skin and the texture of the hair, are going to be made, hereafter, the basis of denying to over half the world the right of sharing to their utmost ability the opportunities and privileges of modern civilization.

The phrase also appeared on the first page of "The Georgia Negro: A Social Study" (Reading 16). This 1900 study was part of the Exhibit of the American Negroes at the 1900 Paris International Exhibition. On the title page of the exhibit Du Bois included the following two statements to describe the purpose of the exhibit: "This case is devoted to a series of charts, maps and other devices designed to illustrate the development of the American Negro in a single typical state of the United States. The problem of the 20th century is the problem of the color-line." The second statement was enclosed in quotation marks, and the focus has now shifted to racial inequality locally. In this case the local context is the state of Georgia, the state with the largest African American population at the time.

Returning to the essay on the Freedman's Bureau (Reading 4), Du Bois identified the accomplishments and failures of the organization in its attempt to promote the social and economic reconstruction of the South. By highlighting some of the positive actions of the Freedman's Bureau, Du Bois laid the foundation for his massive 1935 study, *Black Reconstruction.* Du Bois' split labor market theory was developed in this massive work. Du Bois believed that dividing workers on the basis of race was a mechanism of social control utilized by groups with power. In "The Freedman's Bureau," Du Bois credited the bureau with promoting a system of free labor and encouraging peasant proprietorship. The organization was a strong advocate for the official recognition of African American rights in courts of law and the provision of free common school education throughout the South. In fact, the provision of common school education (grades one to eight) was acknowledged as the bureau's most significant contribution to reconstruction.

The failures of the Freedman's Bureau were noted also. Three specific failures were highlighted. First, the bureau was unsuccessful in promoting good-will among former slaves and former masters. Second, the organization was also viewed as having encouraged economic dependence rather than promoting self-reliance. Third, the freedmen were not furnished with land. This coupled with the current system of disfranchisement limited the degree of social change brought about by the Freedman's Bureau and by Reconstruction.

Du Bois provided another social study on the quality of African American life in the Southern Black Belt in the 1901 essay, "The Negro as He Really Is" (Reading 5). Here the focus was on life in Dougherty County, GA. Compared to the earlier study on rural life in Tennessee, this study, while highly descriptive, utilized more statistical data to document the social conditions faced by the African American community. This study also included a pictorial essay of everyday life in rural Dougherty County and the city of Albany. The pictures were taken by A. Radclyffe Dugmore.[3] Du Bois utilized the first few pages of this essay to form the introductory remarks for "Of the Black Belt" in *The Souls of Black Folk.* Much of the remainder of "The Negro as He Really Is" was included in *The Souls of Black Folk* essay, "Of the Quest of the Golden Fleece."

During his early sociological period, Du Bois conducted eight social studies on the quality of African American life in the Southern Black Belt. These studies, which are highlighted in Figure I.2, addressed such important social issues as the availability of schooling, employment, income, land ownership, housing, marital status, debt, and the crop-lien system. These empirically grounded studies were based on varying combinations of quantitative and qualitative data. For instance census data, survey data, and ethnographic description (methodological triangulation) provided the foundation for the 1898 Farmville, VA study.

The 1899 Black Belt sketches of six different geographic areas were based on survey data and observations. The actual data for these sketches had been collected by Atlanta University students, former students who were working in the area, and/or persons who had long-term ties to the area. Student involvement in data collection was one of the distinctive features of the sociology program at Atlanta University headed by Du Bois (Du Bois 1903c; 1904). According to Du Bois, the suppressed Lowndes County, AL study was based on the largest survey he ever conducted. The study was based on a survey of approximately twenty-five thousand African Americans, but the completed manuscript was never published because it dealt with such controversial issues as African American disfranchisement and land ownership (Du Bois [1968] 2007).

"The Negro as He Really Is" is one of two essays that Du Bois provided on African American quality of life in Dougherty Country. The second essay, "Testimony of Prof. W.E. Burghardt Du Bois" was published by the Industrial Commission on Education in 1900–02. In "The Negro as He Really Is" Du Bois pointed out that debt was the most important factor impacting African American quality of life in the Southern Black Belt. The crop-lien system was identified also as an abusive social structure which created and maintained a debt-based relationship between the agricultural worker, who was often African American, and the land owner, who was often white. In this relationship the monies available to pay for the worker's rent or mortgage and other expenses depended on the value and amount of the cotton crop harvested. A poor harvest and/or a low crop value often left an agricultural worker with significant debts.

In 1890 the vast majority (83.8 percent) of Dougherty County's population was African American, and 88 percent of the African American men, women and children were farmers. In addition to high debt levels and poverty, Dougherty County's African American community also experienced crowded housing conditions and limited income opportunities. These limited income opportunities were linked to a delay in marriage and the continued migration from the rural areas to towns. For Du Bois this was the picture of African American life which emerged when one conducted a prolonged, careful, empirically based study of the region. This was not the picture that would be offered by the "car-window sociologist" making a brief stop during the holiday season.

Du Bois (1900–02) provided even more detailed quality of life statistical data on Dougherty County in the Industrial Commission Report. Based on a survey of 6,093 African Americans comprising 764 families conducted in the summer of 1898, Du Bois discovered that 27.2 percent of the African American population was under age ten, and 96 percent of the African American population over age ten was working. The middle and upper class comprised 8.5 percent of the survey population, while the laboring class and the poor comprised 83 percent and 8.5 percent of the survey population respectively. Only 7.5 percent of the families owned land, and three-fourths (73 percent) of the families

Figure I.2. Sociological Studies of the Southern Black Belt by Du Bois: 1898–1908

---

1. "The Negroes of Farmville, Virginia." *Bulletin of the Department of Labor* 3 (1898b): 1-38.

2. "The Negro in the Black Belt: Some Social Sketches." *Bulletin of the Department of Labor* 4 (1899c): 401-17.[a]

3. "Testimony of Prof. W.E. Burghardt Du Bois." *Report of the Industrial Commission on Education*, Volume 15 (1900-02): 159-75.[b]

4. "The Negro as He Really Is." *The World's Work* 2 (1901b): 846-66.[c]

5. "The Negro Landholder of Georgia." *Bulletin of the Department of Labor* 6 (1901e): 647-777.

6. "The Negro Farmer." *Negroes in the United States*, Bureau of the Census, *Bulletin* 8 (1904b): 69-98.[d]

7. "Die Negerfrage in den Vereinigten Staaten." *Archiv fur Socialwissenschaft und Socialpolitik* 22 (1906a): 241-90.[e]

8. "The Negro Sharecroppers of Lowndes County, Alabama." This study was conducted by Du Bois and a team of researchers. The final report was written for the Department of Labor during 1906–08, but it was never published.[f]

Notes: [a] This study is Reading 15 in *The Sociological Souls of Black Folk*.

  [b] Both the third and the fourth studies listed here address African American quality of life in Dougherty County, GA.

  [c] This study is Reading 5 in *The Sociological Souls of Black Folk*.

  [d] The statistical tables for this study were provided by W.C. Hunt and W.F. Willcox. Both workers were affiliated with the Census Bureau. Hunt was a chief statistician and Hunt was a special agent. See Aptheker's editorial comments in Du Bois (1980b).

  [e] This article was recently translated into English by Joseph Fracchia and published as "The Negro Question in the United States." The newly translated article appeared in *The new centennial review* 6 (2006): 241-90.

  [f] For a more detailed discussion of this suppressed work see Du Bois ([1968] 2007), Grossman (1974), and Lewis (2010). The title provided is not the exact title of the study.

---

lived in one to two room cabins. Given Du Bois' findings here and in his other social studies of the Southern Black Belt, it is not all that surprising that almost one hundred years later Wimberley and Morris (1997) documented that the Southern Black Belt continued to be characterized by poverty, unemployment (limited income), and lower levels of educational attainment.

The debate between W.E.B. Du Bois and Booker T. Washington over the path which would best promote African American social and economic advancement is well-known. Washington favored industrial education and capital formation. Voting rights would come later. Du Bois, on the other hand, supported the development of a leadership class, stressed the importance of obtaining a liberal arts education, encouraged land and property ownership, and argued that voting privileges were a basic right. One witnesses the early stages of this debate in Du Bois' July 1901 review of Washington's autobiography, *Up from Slavery* ([1901] 2003). This review, "The Evolution of Negro Leadership" (Reading 6) was published in *The Dial*.

For Du Bois *Up from Slavery* documented Washington's rise to a position of leadership within the African American community. Du Bois then went on to outline three social responses to domination that imprisoned groups have made throughout history. These responses are revolt and revenge, assimilation, and self-development. Referencing the "Atlanta Compromise," Du Bois portrayed Washington as one who promoted racial and cultural assimilation. Washington's focus on industrial education, commercialism, prosperity, and social constraint is presented as being more palatable to the white South and North. Although Washington's work should be recognized and did command respect, Du Bois noted that Washington did not have the total allegiance of the African American community. A new wave of leadership in the self-development tradition of Allen and Douglas was emerging in the work of Dunbar, the Grimkes, and with Du Bois. The key platform of this new leadership group was liberal arts education, the acceptance of African American self-assertion and ambition, and equal voting rights.

Between July 1901, when the original book review of Washington's autobiography appeared, and the April 1903 publication of *The Souls of Black Folk*, the contrast between Du Bois' and Washington's approach to African American progress intensified. The originally published review of Washington's work was significantly expanded and re-titled "Of Mr. Booker T. Washington and Others." In these pages Du Bois further elaborated on his differences with Washington. He argued more forcefully that Washington was essentially asking African Americans to sacrifice political power, civil rights, and higher education. These actions would impede rather than enhance progress. For Du Bois, Washington's program promoted "industrial slavery" and "civic death."

At the same time that Du Bois' review of Washington's autobiography was published (July 1901), "The Relation of the Negroes to the Whites in the South" (Reading 7) was published in the *Annals of the American Academy of Political and Social Sciences*. Earlier in *The Philadelphia Negro* ([1899b] 1996), Du Bois argued that racial prejudice was primarily a function of the legacy of slavery and ignorance. Following a similar train of thought, Du Bois began the 1901 article on race relations by framing race relations within a social problems context. This is quite interesting since Du Bois is rarely discussed in the mainstream social problems literature. Reflecting the impact of James and Schmoller on his thought and his awareness of white supremacist ideologies, Du Bois advocated that the issue of racial contact was to be grounded in the search for truth rather than opinion.

In this essay Du Bois identified six different arenas for racial contact and interaction within the South. The arenas outlined the structured nature of racial inequality in the South. The six structurally defined contact arenas were: 1) residential proximity, 2) economic associations, 3) suffrage and the political domain, 4) public opinion, 5) everyday life social interaction, and 6) religious and humanitarian activities. In the South the color line (Jim Crow segregation) significantly limited racial contact. The lack of educational opportunities and the abusive crop-lien system limited African American participation in certain economic arenas. Political relations were hampered by disfranchisement. To remedy this situation Du Bois argued that voting rights would have to be obtained and an African American leadership class would need to come forward. Perhaps Du Bois was providing his readers with an early glimpse of his understanding of the role of "the talented tenth." Industrial exploitation of African American workers and the African American community's growing distrust of the criminal justice system did little to improve public opinion. Du Bois argued that chain-gangs were essentially schools of crime. The color line also restricted social interaction among African Americans and whites. Intellectual, social, and cultural mingling among the races was minimal. Addressing the issue of benevolence, Du Bois maintained that racial cooperation and cooperation among the classes was needed more than basic acts of charity.

Du Bois concluded the essay on race relations with a call for racial cooperation to prevail over racial segregation. Social conditions and prejudice were intertwined. To effectively address racial inequality African Americans and whites would need to be willing to cooperate and work together in unity. Du Bois appeared to be been keenly aware that the solution to this problem lay in replacing an environment based on racial competition with one grounded in racial cooperation. Here Du Bois appears to be anticipating the primary thesis of Allport's "contact hypothesis." In *The Nature of Prejudice*, Allport ([1954] 1979) argued that contact is a two-edged sword. Contact could stimulate or diminish prejudice. The critical issue is the environment in which the contact occurred. For example, when racial groups share unequal status within a competitive environment, increased contact among the races would stimulate racial prejudice. On the other hand, when racial groups share more equal status within a more cooperative environment, increased racial contact should suppress prejudice. As noted earlier, Du Bois by 1901 was aware of the positive impact that social equality and cooperation could have on prejudice.

Du Bois was keenly aware that the industrial transformation of the South had a significant impact on "the Negro problems." In the 1902 essay, "Of the Training of Black Men" (Reading 8), Du Bois maintained that higher education would play a critical role in preparing African Americans to meet the changing everyday life conditions brought about by this industrial transformation. This essay was originally published in *The Atlantic Monthly* and was the last of four publications from this source to be included in *The Souls of Black Folk*. Except for the opening quote and the few bars of a sorrow song placed at the beginning of the essay, this essay was later reprinted virtually unchanged.

In this essay Du Bois argued that industrial schools and common schools were not fully equipped to meet the changing knowledge and cultural demands that were being brought about by the industrialization of the South. Colleges and universities would play a key role in meeting these changing demands, and African Americans would need greater access to higher education. Addressing the primary function of the Black College, Du Bois advocated that these schools would maintain high educational standards, promote social uplift among African Americans, develop men of high character, and cooperate with the larger society to bring about solutions to racial problems. Atlanta University was an example of an institution seeking to meet these needs.

Three years after the publication of this essay, Du Bois prepared a brief account of the history and mission of Atlanta University that was included in a 1905 book, *From Servitude to Service: Being the Old South Lectures on the History and Work of Southern Institutions for the Education of the Negro*. The work was edited by Robert Ogden. Atlanta University at this time included a common school (grades one to eight), a high school, and a college. The college's purpose was to assist in the development of African American intellectual talent and leadership and to supply qualified African American teachers. Du Bois estimated that, for the 1903–04 academic year, the four-year college enrolled fifty students and the two-year teacher's college enrolled twenty-five students. The college curriculum included coursework in ancient languages, science and math, English and modern foreign languages, as well as history, sociology, philosophy, and pedagogy.

In "Of the Training of Black Men" Du Bois also cited occupational data drawn from the 1900 Atlanta University Conference report, *The College-Bred Negro*. Based on a survey of African American college graduates, the study concluded that graduates could be classified as engaging in the following occupations:

- 53 percent teachers
- 17 percent clergy
- 17 percent professions
- 6 percent merchants, farmers, and artisans
- 4 percent government civil service

These five occupational categories included 97 percent of the known graduates. The primacy of teachers was noted, and it would be these teachers who would play a key role in bringing about African American social uplift. The conference report was published by the Atlanta University Press and also addressed such topics as the Black College, the college curriculum, the number of African American college graduates, the education of women, the family, the occupations of college graduates, the political and group leadership activity of college graduates, property ownership, and the future of the Black College.

Du Bois was hired as a professor of Atlanta University in 1897. While he was there he would offer instruction in sociology, economics, and history as well as direct the activities of the Atlanta Sociological Laboratory and coordinate the annual Atlanta University Conference for the Study of the Negro Problems. He was also responsible for editing the final conference report. From 1898–1913, Du Bois edited twelve conference reports and co-edited another four reports with Augustus Dill. Dill remained as an instructor in sociology after Du Bois left Atlanta University in July of 1910 to assume the editorship of *The Crisis*, the official publication of the NAACP. A listing of the conference reports edited or co-edited by Du Bois is provided in Figure I.3. Four of the conference studies were devoted to education, and two studies addressed social betterment and the African American artisan respectively. Single conference studies dealt with African American business, the Negro Church, crime, health, economic cooperation, the Black family, and African American morals and manners. A select bibliography of works addressing African American life was provided in 1905.

It is fitting that the final essay to be included in the reconstructed *The Sociological Souls of Black Folk* addressed education. The type of education needed to promote the social uplift of the African American community was one of the major points of contention between Du Bois and Washington. For Du Bois, a liberal arts education was the key to African American social mobility. Du Bois (1902, 296) summarized his view of the role of the Black College in this endeavor in the following manner:

> We ought not to forget that despite the pressure of poverty, and despite the active discouragement and even ridicule of friends, the demand for higher training steadily increases among Negro youth: there were, in the years from 1875 to 1880, twenty-two Negro graduates from Northern colleges; from 1885 to 1895 there were forty-three, and from 1895 to 1900, nearly 100 graduates. From Southern Negro colleges there were, in the same three periods, 143, 413, and over 500 graduates. Here, then, is the plain thirst for training; by refusing to give this Talented Tenth the key to knowledge can any sane man imagine that they will lightly lay aside their yearning and contentedly become hewers of wood and drawers of water?

A critical aspect of the training of Black men involved the training of a leadership class. For Du Bois, college educated African Americans, the "Talented Tenth," would be among the first to assume this role.

Contextual Sociological Essays by Du Bois: 1897–1900

Figure I.3. Atlanta University Conference Reports Edited or Co-edited by Du Bois: 1898-1913

Year[a]	Conference Report Title
1898	*Some Efforts of American Negroes for Their Own Betterment*
1899	*The Negro in Business*
1900	*The College-Bred Negro*
1901	*The Negro Common School*
1902	*The Negro Artisan*
1903	*The Negro Church*
1904	*Some Notes on Negro Crime Particularly in Georgia*
1905	*A Select Bibliography of the American Negro*
1906	*The Health and Physique of the Negro American*
1907	*Economic Co-operation among Negro Americans*
1908	*The Negro American Family*
1909	*Efforts for Social Betterment among Negro Americans*
1910	*The College-Bred Negro American*[b]
1911	*The Common School and the Negro American*[b]
1912	*The Negro American Artisan*[b]
1913	*Morals and Manners among Negro Americans*[b]

Note: [a] The year refers to the year the conference was held. Each publication was published in Atlanta by The Atlanta University Press.
[b] This conference report was co-edited by Augustus Dill.

The eight previously published essays just discussed form the kernel of *The Sociological Souls of Black Folk*. Looking back at the chronological sequence of topics addressed in these essays, one discovers that Du Bois: began with a discussion of racial identity (Reading 1), then provided an ethnographic description of educational inequality in the South (Reading 2), focused on the function of the Black Church as an integrative mechanism and a source of social reform in the African American community (Reading 3), provided a detailed discussion of racial inequality as the problem of the twentieth century (Reading 4), addressed quality of life in the Southern Black Belt (Reading 5), discussed his clash with Booker T. Washington over the appropriate mechanisms to enhance African

American mobility (Reading 6), discussed the "Negro problems" as an outcome of poor race relations (Reading 7), and finally argued how liberal arts education would aid in the development of a leadership class within the African American community (Reading 8).

As one looks at the progression of these topics, one is able to see how Du Bois was contextualizing his sociological approach to the empirical study of the "Negro Problems." Four themes emerge in these eight essays originally published between 1897 and 1902. These themes are:

- Racial identity and race relations.
- Education as a source of inequality and social mobility.
- The Black Church as an agent of stability and change.
- Inequality in the Southern Black Belt.

To further enhance the reader's understanding of how Du Bois approached these sociological issues, eight additional sociological essays published during essentially the same time period (1897–1900) are included in this volume on *The Sociological Souls of Black Folk* and are now discussed briefly. These eight contextual sociological essays are arranged according to five major themes and are displayed in Figure I.4. The original publication information is included also with each essay. The five major themes are specific "Negro Problems," race relations, liberal arts education, the Black Church, and the Southern Black Belt. Attention now shifts to a brief discussion of the sociological themes presented in each contextual essay.

Three essays are included under the first topic. The specific "Negro problems" addressed are: the African American business man, crime, and African American quality of life in the state of Georgia and in the United States. "The Results of the Investigation" (Reading 9) is an excerpt from the editorial summary Du Bois provided for the 1899 Atlanta University Conference report entitled, *The Negro in Business*. The excerpt addresses the scope of the study, the survey instrument, and the discussion of different business classes.

This annual conference focusing on the African American business man was held at a very critical time in Du Bois' life. Conference participants assembled on May 30–31, 1899. Du Bois had just experienced the death of his first child, Burghardt, from nasopharyngeal diphtheria on May 24, 1899. Du Bois had just returned from his son's funeral, which was held in Great Barrington, MA. The night before his son's death Du Bois went searching for a doctor who would treat his son but was unsuccessful. There were only a few African American doctors in Atlanta and medical care tended to be dispensed along the color line (D. Lewis 2010). Four years later, Du Bois discusses the death of his son and his son's release from a life within the veil in "Of the Passing of the First-Born," one of the new essays in *The Souls of Black Folk*.

The Negro in Business (1899d) conference report was comprised of three main parts: 1) a summary of the results of the investigation by Du Bois, 2) a brief discussion of the proceedings of the conference as well as a formal state-

Figure I.4. Contextual Sociological Essays by Du Bois: 1897–1900

Specific "Negro Problems"

Reading 9.   "The Negro in Business: The Results of the Investigation"
Pp. 4-15 in *The Negro in Business*, edited by W.E.B. Du Bois. Atlanta University Press, 1899d.

Reading 10.   "The Negro and Crime"
Independent 51 (May 18, 1899e): 1355-57.

Reading 11.   "The American Negro in Paris"
The American Monthly Review of Reviews 22.5 (November 1900d): 575-77.

Race Relations

Reading 12.   "The Conservation of the Races"
American Negro Academy, Occasional Papers, No. 2. Washington, DC: American Negro Academy, 1897c.

Liberal Arts Education

Reading 13.   "Careers Open to College-Bred Negroes"
Two Addresses Delivered by Alumni of Fisk University in Connection with the Anniversary Exercises of the Alma Mata, June, 1898. Nashville, TN: Fisk University, 1898c.

The Black Church

Reading 14.   "The Problem of Amusement"
The Southern Workman 27 (September 1897b): 181-84.

The Southern Black Belt

Reading 15.   "The Negro in the Black Belt: Some Social Sketches"
Bulletin of the Department of Labor 4 (1899c): 401-17.

Reading 16.   "The Georgia Negro Exhibit: A Social Study" (1900c)
See 1900 Paris Exhibition, Exhibit of American Negroes.
http://129.171.53.1/ep/Paris/html/charts_1.html.[a]

Note: [a] The Paris Exposition was held from April 15 – November 12, 1900 (*Exposition Universelle*, 2011). For a more comprehensive discussion of Du Bois' involvement with the 1900 Paris Exhibition see Smith (2004).

ment of the conference resolutions, and 3) a collection of papers submitted to the conference and an address from Allan Candler, the governor of Georgia. The papers submitted focused on such topics as the meaning of business, African American merchants, the work of an African American foundry, African American business men in Columbia, SC, African American businesses in Atlanta, GA, and finally a discussion of Black newspapers. The last paper was provided by Du Bois. The conference's resolutions stressed the need for African Americans to enter into business ventures and maintained that colleges could provide the best training for persons desiring a business career. The African American community was asked to support Black business ventures, and African American business owners were reminded that their customers should be treated with respect. Young persons were encouraged to save money so that they would have the capital needed to start businesses. This correlation between savings and capital was later echoed by Max Weber in his classic study, *The Protestant Ethic and the Spirit of Capitalism* ([1904–05] 2009). As a final action, the conference encouraged the development of "Negro Business Men's Leagues" at the local level. In 1900 Booker T. Washington established the *National Negro Business League* in Boston. Following this national meeting, participants were encouraged to start business leagues at the state and local level (Washington [1901] 2003). On this point Du Bois and Washington were in agreement. Each encouraged the development of African American entrepreneurship.

Returning to the editorial summary of "The Results of the Investigation" (Reading 9), Du Bois stated that the study of African American business men was based on a survey of 1,903 business men representing thirty different states. The survey was essentially a convenience sample drawn from persons known within the African American community. The survey instrument was designed to gather information on the business location, the type of business, the number of years in business, and the dollar amount of the capital invested in the business. In an attempt to limit interpreter bias, Du Bois was the sole interpreter of the survey data. African American business men were identified by state of residence and type of business. Georgia, Texas, Alabama, Tennessee, and Virginia each were home to over one hundred business men, and the business men in these states comprised 44.2 percent of the total sample. The most popular business ventures were grocers, general merchandise dealers, and barbers with over $500 or more invested in the venture.[4] Collectively, 39.9 percent of all African American business men were engaged in these three business ventures.

Based on the survey responses, African American business men were grouped into eight different business classes. These classes were: house servant, field hand, plantation mechanic, traders, capitalists, manufactures, co-operative efforts, and amusements. The house servant class was a derivative of the slaves who had lived in the Plantation house. This group had received educational training and represented the first group of African Americans to experience some degree of economic independence following slavery. This group currently included barbers, restaurant owners, and caterers. The field hand class included persons who owned land and farms. This group included cotton-gin owners and lumber-mill owners. African American builders and contractors were included in the plantation mechanic class, and grocers and general merchants comprised the trader class. Bankers and real-estate dealers were included in the capitalist class, and the makers of shirts, carpets, and rubber goods comprised the manufacturing class. The co-operative efforts class included persons who provided vital services to the entire community like undertakers and druggists. Saloon and pool-room owners were part of the amusement class.

While Du Bois did not provide a specific table on business men by business class, the following table (Table I.1) has been reconstructed by the editor based on the data Du Bois provided in his discussion of each class. The two largest business classes were the trader class (39.5 percent) and the house servant class (26.3 percent). Collectively, these two classes included 65.8 percent of the African American business men included in the survey who could be classified in one of the eight different business classes. Unfortunately, the occupation of 146 African American business men could not be determined. This group represented 7.7 percent of the total sample.

In the discussion of each business man class, Du Bois provided data on the amount of capital invested in the various business enterprises included in that business class. For example, within the house servant class, 75.9 percent of barbers invested $500 to $2,500 in their business venture. Unfortunately, the data are a little "muddy" as Du Bois did not appear to employ mutually exclusive income categories in his breakdown of capital invested. Also, some of the income categories were combined. For example, forty-seven drug store owners and fifty-four saloon owners had invested $1,000 or more in their business enterprises. Capital invested amounts were provided for 51.5 percent of the business men participating in the survey. Although Du Bois did not provide a summary table of African American business capital invested for all business classes by the amount invested, these data are presented in Table I.2. This table has been created by the editor and is based on the capital invested data Du Bois provided for each African American business man class.

Six capital investment ranges are presented and an additional capital investment category is provided to account for overlapping ranges. This creates some "noise" in the data. Furthermore, Du Bois indicated that the capital data were prone to error. Thus, the data summarized in Table I.2 provide at best a rough estimate of the capital invested by the African American business men included in the survey. It appears that almost half (48.7 percent) of the business men had invested $100 to $1,000 in their business enterprise, and only 0.8 percent of the business men had made capital investments of $10,000 or more. According to Du Bois five of the eight persons included in this last category were contractors, and one of the business men in the field hand class had invested $50,000 or more in his business venture. The overlapping capital invested category included 18.0 percent of the African American business men who provided data on capital invested in their business.

The second contextual article included in the section on specific "Negro problems" addresses crime. The linking of crime to poverty and social disorgan-

Table I.1. Descriptive Data for African American Business Men by Business Man Class, 1899

African American Business Man Class[a]	African American Business Men	
	Number	Percentage
House Servant	462	26.3
Field-Hand	61	3.5
Plantation Mechanic	176	10.0
Traders	695	39.5
Capitalists	67	3.8
Manufacturers	9	0.5
Co-operative Efforts	189	10.7
Efforts for Amusement	101	5.7
Total	1,760	100.0

Note: [a] While 1,906 African American business men provided a response to the survey addressing their business activities, 146 responses could not be included in any of the business class categories devised. The percentages in this table have been provided by the editor and are based on the frequencies cited by Du Bois. The percentages in this table are based on 1,760 valid cases.

Source: Du Bois, *The Negro in Business* (1899d).

ization are major tenets of the "Chicago School" illustrated in the work of Merton (1938) and Shaw and McKay (1942). Yet, as early as 1899, Du Bois linked crime to structural factors. This is specifically seen in the 1899 essay, "The Negro and Crime" (Reading 10). One of the structural factors identified was the legacy of slavery. Slavery by definition is an example of structured inequality. The legacy of slavery is a contributing structural factor that appears in Du Bois' studies on "the Negro problems" (Du Bois 1898a; 1911b), the Black Church (Du Bois [1903b] 2003), African American crime (Du Bois 1904a), the African American family (Du Bois 1908), and African American morals and manners (Du Bois and Dill [1914] 2010).

In "The Negro and Crime," Du Bois maintained that a criminal class emerged within the African American community following emancipation. Slavery had destroyed the African American family, African American labor was controlled, and African American women had been sexually exploited by plantation owners. Once the slaves were emancipated, they were essentially set free without being provided with the financial opportunities needed to support themselves. The legacy of slavery and emancipation were contextual factors undergirding the persistence of racial inequality in American society. As American society prepared to enter the twentieth century, Du Bois maintained that the

Table I.2. African American Business Capital Invested for All Business Man Classes, 1899[a]

Capital Invested[b] (Dollar Amount)	African American Business Men	
	Number	Percentage
$100 - $500[c]	197	20.1
$500 - $1,000	281	28.6
$1,000 - $2,500	180	18.3
$2,500 - $5,000	94	9.6
$5,000 - $10,000	30	3.1
$10,000 - $50,000	7	0.7
$50,000 and over	1	0.1
Overlapping Categories[d]	177	18.0
Unknown	14	1.4
Total	981	99.0

Notes: [a] The African American business man classes include house servant, field hand, plantation mechanic, traders, capitalists, manufactures, co-operative efforts, and amusements.

[b] These amount categories overlap, but they are the categories Du Bois provided in his discussions of the capital invested in the various different business man classes.

[c] This category includes 174 grocers and general merchants with businesses started with investment capital in the "under $500" range.

[d] The overlapping categories range has been created by the editor. Included in this group are: twenty-four barbers with capital amounts of $500 or more invested in their business; forty-seven drug store owners and fifty-four saloon owners with capital amounts of $1,000 or more invested in their business enterprises; and twenty-three undertakers, fifteen grocers, and fourteen other merchants with capital amounts of $5,000 or more invested in their business ventures.

Source: Du Bois, *The Negro in Business* (1899d).

problems associated with the convict-lease system, the double standard of justice administered by the Southern courts, mob violence, and segregation ("the color line") were additional factors that contributed to the emergence of a criminal class within the African American community. Du Bois also argued that the removing of the lynch-law would lead to reductions in crime. Here Du Bois and Ida B. Wells-Barnett shared a similar cause. Finally, while acknowledging the emergence of a criminal class within the African American community, Du Bois was quick to comment that most African Americans were law-abiding. Homes were being maintained and property was being acquired.

Throughout his early sociological period (1897–1914), Du Bois continued to write about crime and social disorganization. Several of these writings are presented in Figure I.5. Glancing over the publication dates for these writings, one notes that Du Bois' writing on crime clearly preceded the work of noted "Chicago School" sociologists like Park, McKenzie, and Burgess (1925), Sutherland and Cressey ([1934] 1992), Merton (1938), and Shaw and McKay (1942) on social disorganization, urbanization, and deviance. Contrary to what Odum (1951) noted in his history of the development of sociology in the United States, Du Bois is one of the pioneering figures in the development of the sociology of deviance. This point is specifically noted in the work of Gabbidon (2007; 2001) and in a recent sociology thesis (Melvin 2010).

The 1900 Paris Exhibition presented Du Bois with an opportunity to present some of his empirical findings concerning African American quality of life in the United States and the state of Georgia to an international audience. In "The American Negro at Paris" (Reading 11), published in the November 1900 issue of *The American Monthly Review of Reviews*, Du Bois provided a general summary of four different aspects of the African American experience that were presented in the "exhibit of American Negroes." Included in the exhibit were materials documenting the history of African Americans in the United States, a series of statistical charts and graphs portraying the current social conditions of African Americans in the United States and the state of Georgia, studies conducted at leading Black educational institutions like Fisk University, Atlanta University, and Howard University as well as Tuskegee Institute and Hampton Institute, and finally samples of literary works by African American authors. The exhibit of literary works included 1400 works and 150 periodicals. The exhibit also included over 500 photographs of African Americans and three volumes containing the Black Codes of Georgia.

Du Bois' major contribution to the exhibit was his study, "The Georgia Negro: A Social Study." This study is included in *The Sociological Souls of Black Folk* as Reading 16. This work is discussed in more detail later, but in "The American Negro at Paris," Du Bois provided some of the highlights from the statistical data. He documents the growth of the African American population from 1750 (220,000 persons) to 1890 (7,500,000 persons). He also noted that nationally, 20 percent of African Americans were home owners, and 60 percent of African American children were enrolled in school. Shifting the focus to African American quality of life in the state of Georgia, Du Bois noted that 62 percent of African Americans were employed in agriculture and that African Americans currently owned over one million acres of land. In summarizing the entire exhibit, Du Bois argued that the exhibit was about African Americans and was created by African Americans. It was a work of self-reflection that documented progress and presented plausible prospects for the future.

One of Du Bois' earliest sociological writings addressed race relations. "The Conservation of Races" (Reading 12) was published in 1897 by the American Negro Academy as part of its "Occasional Papers" series. This essay was the second essay published in the series. The American Negro Academy was

Figure I.5. Early Sociological Studies on Crime by Du Bois: 1899–1914

---

1. "The Negro and Crime." *Independent* 51 (1899e): 1355-57.[a]

2. "The Negro Criminal," in *The Philadelphia Negro: A Social Study* ([1899b] 1996).[b]

3. "The Spawn of Slavery: The Convict Lease System in the South." *Missionary Review of the World* 24 (1901f): 737-45.[c]

4. *Some Notes on Negro Crime Particularly in Georgia* (1904a).[d]

5. "Vardaman." *The Voice of the Negro* 3 (1906b): 189-194.[e]

6. "Sound Morals," in *Morals and Manners among Negro Americans* ([1914] 2010).[f]

Notes: [a] This essay is Reading 10 in *The Sociological Souls of Black Folk*.

   [b] Chapter 13 of this book-length study is devoted to crime among African Americans.

   [c] A revised version of this essay appears in the 1904 Atlanta University Conference study on crime.

   [d] The is one of the Atlanta Conference studies directed and edited by Du Bois. Max Weber, the noted German sociologist, attended this conference during his 1904 visit to the United States (Gabbidon 1999). While he was a doctoral student at the University of Berlin, Du Bois ([1968] 2007) attended lectures by Weber.

   [e] James Vardaman, who was governor of Mississippi at the time this essay was written, claimed that the correlation between African American crime and education was positive. He also claimed that African American crime was increasing. Du Bois disputed both of these claims in this essay.

   [f] "Sound Morals" is the title of Section 5 of this Atlanta University Conference report co-edited by Du Bois and Augustus Dill. National-level data on crime by race for 1890 and 1904 are presented and discussed in this section. Causes of crime among younger African Americans are stated, and solutions for African American crime are offered. Some of the causes associated with crime among younger African Americans identified by Du Bois and Dill included racial inequality, bad home environment, poverty, and the demand for convict labor. Some of the solutions for African American crime offered include reforming the criminal justice system, better wages and housing, more educational opportunities, and the acquisition of voting rights.

founded by Alexander Crummell in Washington, D.C. in 1897. The society was the first national learned society for African Americans working in the sciences, literature, and the arts. Du Bois was one of the organization's founding members. The goals of the organization included encouraging scholarship, strengthening African American leadership, and combating white supremacist ideologies (American Negro Academy, 2010). Given the goals and objectives of the organization, it is not surprising that Du Bois devoted one of his earliest socio-logical studies to the topic of race.

In his history of sociology in the United States, Odum (1951) lists the ma-jority of Du Bois' works in a section on the sociology of race. However, it is Robert Park of the "Chicago School" who is generally credited with the devel-opment of the sociological studies of race, and Du Bois' work on the sociology of race has been described as "the path not taken" (Morris 2007). In "The Con-servation of Races," Du Bois asked the question as to the real meaning of race. Du Bois extended his concept of race beyond mere differences in an individual's or group's physical differences. The concept of race must also account for dee-per spiritual and psychical differences. It is within this context, that the reader encounters one of Du Bois' earliest expressions of double consciousness.[5] Here Du Bois ([1897a] 1996, 821) asks, "What, after all, am I? Am I an American or am I a Negro? Can I be both? Or is it my duty to cease to be a Negro as soon as possible and be an American?" Du Bois questioned the merit and validity of racial and cultural assimilation. Turning to the issue of racial prejudice, Du Bois maintained that prejudice is grounded in the friction that exists between two groups. However, if racial groups share significant agreement on such issues as laws, language, religion, and economic opportunities, the racial groups should be able to coexist. Here again Du Bois appears to have foreshadowed some of the major tenets of Allport's ([1954] 1979) contact hypothesis.

Du Bois concluded the essay by addressing the goals, objectives, beliefs, and the work of the American Negro Academy. In this conclusion he also for-mulated seven points which he offered as the *"Academy Creed."* First, challeng-ing white supremacist ideologies, Du Bois maintained that African Americans have much to contribute to human civilization. Second, it is important for Afri-can Americans to recognize the distinctiveness of their racial identity in the larger society. Racial accommodation trumps racial assimilation. Third, Du Bois argued that based on shared political, economic, and religious interests, African Americans and whites could coexist. Fourth, a society grounded in racial in-equality is to be transformed into one based on racial equality. Here Du Bois advocated for the creation of a "color-blind society" rather than one that contin-ued to be defined by "the color line." Fifth, African Americans must also take responsibility for their own social uplift. Strength of character is a key to success in this endeavor. Du Bois argued that racial inequality must be addressed by examining the interaction of structural and cultural factors that undergird in-equality. A similar position has been advocated recently by Wilson (2009) in his examination of the social and economic challenges faced by African Americans residing in inner city environments.[6] Sixth, whites must also be willing to accept African Americans as equals. To solve the race problem, whites and African Americans must be willing to cooperate. Finally, strong manhood and pure wo-manhood were identified as the ideals of the African American community. Leadership, social change, and progress are grounded in these core values.

Throughout his early sociological period, Du Bois infused his empirical so-ciological research with a call for social activism. This is seen in his work with the American Negro Academy, the Niagara Movement, and the NAACP. However, between 1906 and 1910, one begins to witness a shift in Du Bois' approach to "the Negro problems." Rather than focusing primarily on "what is," as Schmoller had taught, Du Bois places more emphasis on social action and "what ought to be." Empirical sociology starts to give way to public sociology. The emphasis on social action is seen in the statement of the principles guiding the work of the Niagara Movement which was incorporated in 1906. These principles included the right to free speech for all, African American voting rights, the abolition of the color line (i.e., the racial caste system), the acknowledgement of the human brotherhood of all people, the promotion of racial equality, a recognition of the dignity of work, and the development of strong leadership within the African American community (Du Bois [1968] 2007). Reviewing these principles and the tenets espoused in the *Academy Creed*, one witnesses the continuity in and the ongoing development of Du Bois' thought with respect to social uplift and social action.

Higher education is generally perceived to have a positive impact on social mobility provided persons have access to high quality educational opportunities (Haveman and Smeeding 2006). Du Bois ([1903c] 2003) argued that a college education played a critical role in promoting African American social mobility and in the development of a leadership class known as the "Talented Tenth." As noted earlier, the type of education received was one of the major points of debate between Du Bois and Washington. In "Careers Open to College-Bred Negroes" (Reading 13), a 1898 commencement address offered to Fisk University graduates, Du Bois commented on the importance and value of a college education.

In this address Du Bois asked the Fisk graduates to consider the practical meaning of their liberal arts education. Commencement marked an important rite of passage from an environment characterized by "study and thought" to the world of "deeds and life" within a society characterized by a racial caste system. To be successful in this world, the graduate would need to understand and implement three "universal laws for making a living." These laws were work, sacrifice, and service to humanity. Du Bois valued hard work, and he exhibited a strong work ethic throughout his life (D. Lewis 2010). This focus on hard work and dedication is also evident in a series of prayers he wrote and offered to Atlanta University students between January 1909 and May 1910 (Du Bois 1980). For Du Bois sacrifice meant delayed gratification. Here Du Bois referenced what was known within the African American community as "the economic ethic of the Black Church" (Lincoln and Mamiya 1990). The core values of this ethic underscored the value of getting an education, securing a job, taking care of one's family, and saving for a rainy day. By graduating from Fisk, these young adults had begun to implement this ethic. In addressing service, Du Bois encouraged the graduates to continue to develop and share their gifts and abilities in ways that would eventually reach beyond the African American community and benefit all humanity. By offering their services to all people, Du Bois was essentially asking these young adults to be willing to break through the barriers set by the racial caste system.[7]

Looking at the careers that were available to college graduates, Du Bois encouraged these graduates to consider becoming farm owners, general merchants, industrial leaders, physicians, lawyers, teachers, Christian ministers who would serve as catalysts for social and moral reform, scientists, and artists. Reflecting on his experiences in life following his own graduation from Fisk ten years earlier, Du Bois ([1898c] 1996, 840) offered the graduating class some sobering, realistic advice.

> It is now ten years since I stood amid these walls of my commencement morning, ten years full of toil and happiness and sorrow, and the full delight of hard work. And as I look back on that youthful gleam, and see the vision splendid, the trailing clouds of glory that lighted then the wide way of life, I am ever glad that I stepped into the world guided of strong faith in its promises, and inspired by no sordid aims. And from that world I come back to welcome you, my brothers and my sisters. I cannot promise you happiness always, but I can promise you divine discontent with the imperfect. I cannot promise you success —'tis not in mortals to command success.

These graduates were being encouraged to face their fear and pursue their dreams. In other words, they were being asked to muster the courage to live their life and not settle for a world marked by the color line. Rather than being tolerated, society's imperfections should be met with "divine discontent." Du Bois concluded his address by stressing that these young people take pride in their racial heritage, act as ladies and gentlemen, and remember that they are Fisk graduates.

As noted earlier Du Bois wrote extensively about the role of the Black Church in the African American experience. "The Problem of Amusement" (Reading 14), originally published in *The Southern Workman* in 1897 represents his first sociological study of the Black Church. It is here rather than in *The Philadelphia Negro* ([1899] 1996) that Du Bois first identified the Black Church as the center of social, economic, and religious life. Within the African American community, the Black Church was viewed as a social organization designed to meet important societal needs. These needs included: social interaction and support, amusements, information dispersion, a venue for cultural expression, a social gathering place, and a gateway into the community. Here Du Bois offered one of the earliest functional analyses of a religious group as this essay preceded Durkheim's *The Elementary Forms of Religious Life* ([1912] 1995) by fifteen years.

Du Bois ([1899b] 1996; [1903a] 2007; [1903b] 2003; and Du Bois and Dill [1914] 2010) believed the Black Church could play a major role in promoting social reform and strengthening morals, but he could be critical of the church's lack of strong leadership and degree of community involvement. In fact, the offering of amusements, opportunities for social interaction and recreation, represented an important need of young people that the church could meet but was failing to do so effectively. Since the African American community was experiencing the beginning stages of the "great migration" from the rural South to the urban North, and the Southern rural Black Church was also being impacted by the migration from the rural South to small towns and cities in the South (Du Bois [1899b] 1996; [1898b] 2009), young people were in search of acceptable recreational and social venues. By not providing these opportunities, the Black Church risked losing the younger generation.

Clergy roles were also addressed in this essay. Preacher, pastor, teacher, and administrator are all important roles assumed by the clergy. However, while preaching may be the preferred role, clergy often find their time consumed by administrative duties (Johnstone 2007). Du Bois noted that rather than being a strong moral and spiritual leader, the minister functioned more as a social organizer and business manager. As he concluded this essay, Du Bois argued that it was time for other organizations to share in meeting the needs traditionally addressed by the Black Church. The school and the family were two social institutions identified to assist in the meeting of these needs. In *Morals and Manners among Negro Americans* ([1914] 2010), the sequel to *The Negro Church* ([1903b] 2003), Du Bois and Dill praised women's organizations for their work in promoting social uplift and the strengthening of character. Echoing statements first made by Du Bois in 1897, Du Bois and Dill ([1914] 2010, 7) reminded Black Church leaders that, while the church was making some progress in the area of social ministry, the church's survival depended upon "adopt[ing] a new attitude towards rational amusements and sound moral habits."

The last two essays included in *The Sociological Souls of Black Folk* address African American quality of life in the Southern Black Belt. The first of the two essays, "The Negro in the Black Belt: Some Social Sketches" (Reading 15), was originally published in 1899 in the *Bulletin of the Department of Labor*. The study is essentially a summary report of six small area studies. Five of the six studies address Georgia locales. The six small area studies included a country district (DeKalb County, GA), a small village (Lithonia, GA), two county seats (Covington, GA and Marion, AL), a large town (Marietta, GA), and a city (Athens, GA). Except for the Marion, AL study, each study was based on an area that was in close proximity to Atlanta.

While Du Bois composed the final report for this study, the data were either collected by former Atlanta University students or persons who had long-term ties to the area being studied. For example, Aletha Howard provided the data for the DeKalb County and Lithonia studies. Miss J.G. Childs supplied the data for the Marion, AL study; W.A. Rogers collected the data for the Marietta, GA study, and Miss C.E. Brydie provided the information on Athens, GA. Rogers and Brydie were members of the Atlanta University senior class when the study was conducted, and Howard and Childs were graduates of Atlanta University. In addition to this study, Du Bois included data collected by undergraduate students in several of the Atlanta University Conference final reports, namely *The Negro Church* ([1903b] 2003); *The Negro American Family* (1908); and *Morals and Manners among Negro Americans* [1914] 2010).[8]

The undergraduate program in sociology at Atlanta University included a year-long study of economics during the junior year, and a year-long study of sociology during the senior year. Some of the sociology courses offered during Du Bois' first tenure at Atlanta University included: Social Reforms, Sociological Laboratory, General Sociology, and Social Conditions of the Negro. An economics course, Wealth, Work, and Wages was offered also (MacLean and Williams 2005). Students were encouraged to engage in library research utilizing primary sources and to engage in fieldwork studies. Students were also introduced to basic statistical analysis and were taught to work with census data (Du Bois 1904c). Since Du Bois actively involved students in his research activities and the work of the Atlanta Sociological Laboratory, Du Bois can be recognized as an early pioneer of service learning.

Data were collected from rural and urban areas within the Southern Black Belt in order to provide a more comprehensive sketch of African American quality of life within the region. The data obtained from the rural areas were utilized to portray the poverty experienced in these areas. However, the data collected from the urban areas were obtained primarily from higher class African American families. The urban data are thus based on a convenience sample and are not statistically representative of the area. Du Bois' decision to focus on higher class families was intentional. By collecting data from this particular group, Du Bois was trying to provide empirical documentation of the social and economic gains African Americans had made since emancipation. This position was also expressed in another 1899 sociological study, *The Philadelphia Negro*. In describing the African American community comprising Philadelphia's Seventh Ward, Du Bois ([1899b] 1996, 316) maintained:

> In many respects it is right and proper to judge a people by its best classes rather than by its worst classes or middle ranks. The highest class of any group represents its possibilities rather than its exceptions, as is so often assumed in regard to the Negro. The colored people are seldom judged by their best classes, and often the very existence of classes among them is ignored.

The sketches of the six Black Belt regions were based on field observations and survey data. Here again one witnesses Du Bois' use of methodological triangulation to provide a richer, more comprehensive description of African American quality of life. Here one sees that sociological studies based on the integration of qualitative and quantitative data are not new to the field. The quantitative data for the Black Belt sketches are based on information obtained from 920 African Americans residing in 195 African American families. Data on average family size are presented in Table I.3. This table has been created by the editor and is based on data gleaned from each sketch. The average family size for all the families included in the study is 4.72 persons. As expected, average family size for the rural areas (DeKalb County, GA and Lithonia, GA) is higher. These large family size figures for the rural areas could reflect the presence of extended family members. However, the exact composition of these families cannot be determined from these data. Average family size could also include non-family members and lodgers. Du Bois ([1899b] 1996; 1908) acknowledged this measurement issue in other sociological studies addressing the family. Saari (2010) addressed this issue in a recent evaluation of early sociological studies of the African American family by Du Bois and E. Franklin Frazier. Additional statistical data were obtained for the six areas. Sometimes these data were summarized in tables, and at other times these data were discussed in summary narratives. The additional data collected included such variables as sex, age group, family income, monthly rent, marital status, home ownership, and number of rooms per house. The Lithonia, GA sketch also included a table providing detailed social and economic data for six African American families. The information collected addressed family size, number of rooms in the house, number of wage earners in the family, occupation of the wage earner, the average weekly wage, the number of weeks employed, the yearly wages of the wage earner, and the family's yearly earnings. The type of statistical data collected for this study closely resembled the type of data collected for the Farmville, VA study (Du Bois [1898b] 2009) and the Philadelphia study (Du Bois [1899a] 1996). These two studies represent detailed, statistically based social studies of a rural and an urban area respectively conducted and published during the same time period.

Table I.3. Average African American Family Size for Six Black Belt Areas, 1899

Location	Families Surveyed Number	Persons Surveyed Number	Average Number of Persons Per Family
DeKalb County, GA	11	131	11.91
Lithonia, GA	16	101	6.31
Covington, GA	50	188	3.76
Marion, AL	33	175	5.30
Marietta, GA	40	162	4.05
Athens, GA	45	163	3.62
Total	195	920	4.72

Source: Du Bois, "The Negro in the Black Belt," 1899c.

African American quality of life varied in the six areas included in the Black Belt sketches study. In the DeKalb County, GA sketch, African American families were described as being impoverished and coming from the lower social class. Families grew what they ate, and the schools were in operation for only three months of the year. Many of the African Americans included in the Lithonia, GA sketch were employed in one of the three rock quarries. Here the school term also lasted only three month, and nine of the sixteen families included in the sketch earned less than $300 annually.

Turning to the more urban areas, quality of life in Covington, GA, the county seat, appeared to be better. The school term was nine months, the number of rooms in the home was slightly larger, and over half (54.0 percent) of the families included in the sketch earned $300 to $750 annually. However, Du Bois did not directly address cost of living differences in the more urban areas, and one must also remember that the sketches for the more urban areas are based on data provided by higher status families. While data were obtained from African Americans from the higher social classes for the Marion, AL sketch, Du Bois noted that three distinct social classes were present within Marion's African American community. African American children in Marion were served by four schools, and twenty-eight of the thirty-three families (84.8 percent) surveyed owned their own home. Home ownership was lower among the African American families selected for the Marietta, GA sketch. Only twenty-six of the forty families (65.0 percent) selected owned their home. Many of the African Americans included in this sketch were employed as laborers and earned 75 to 80 cents daily. According to Du Bois, African Americans residing in Athens, GA could be stratified by four social classes. African American children were served by four schools, and thirty-nine of the forty-five African American families (86.7 percent) included in the sketch owned their home. The African American community was also served by eight Black Churches. Aware of the nonrepresentative nature of the sample, Du Bois concluded this study by reminding readers that few generalizations could be drawn from these small area sketches. He went on to maintain that more education, better jobs, property ownership, marriage, and less crime appeared to be the identifying features of the higher status African American families included in these sketches.

"The Georgia Negro: A Social Study" (Reading 16) is the last of the contextual sociological studies included in *The Sociological Souls of Black Folk*. This reading is actually not a reading. As noted earlier in the discussion of Reading 11, "The Georgia Negro: A Social Study" is actually a collection of sixty-two different tables, charts, maps, and graphs depicting the quality of African American life in the United States and the state of Georgia that Du Bois (1900c) prepared for the 1900 Paris Exhibition. Du Bois was awarded a Gold Medal for this exhibit (Calloway 1900; Du Bois 1900d).

While some of the data included in the photocopy of the exhibit that the editor accessed are no longer legible,[9] for this reading the editor has provided the reader with a reconstructed version of the exhibit. The title page and all sixty-two pages of the exhibit are identified, and where possible the tables that were part of the exhibit are presented. In instances where some of the data were presented in another format, the material has been reconstructed in tabular form. In cases where the data could not be reproduced, the editor has provided a summary of the information contained on that page of the exhibit. All table and page entry numbers have been supplied by the editor.

On the opening page of the exhibit Du Bois states in capital letters, "The Problem of the 20th century is the problem of the color-line." This represents the second time Du Bois was known to have utilized this well-known phrase in print form. Georgia was selected as one of the particular foci of the exhibit because at that time more African Americans resided in Georgia than in any other state. Data on the quality of life of African Americans residing in Georgia were presented in the next thirty-five pages of the exhibit. The statistical data in this section provided information on the African American population[10] with respect to total population, migration, age distribution, marital status, race amalgamation, number of teachers in Georgia public schools, value of property owned, occupation of males aged ten and over, and income and expenditures for one hundred African American families residing in Atlanta, GA. In the next twenty-six pages, quality of life data for all African Americans residing in the United States were presented.[11] The statistical data in this section provided information about African Americans with respect to total population, occupation, illiteracy, city and rural population, marital status, race amalgamation, pauperism, mortality, number of business men, land ownership, property value, crime, and religion.

Conclusion

The Souls of Black Folk is often read by college students in an English literature class, an African American studies class, or a history class. The work is generally seen as a literary work, a chronicle of the history of the African American experience in the South, and a work of interest to ethnomusicologists. It is less likely to be assigned in a sociology class, which is ironic since Du Bois intended it to be a sociological study of "the Negro problems." By highlighting the sociological nature of the eight previously published essays and adding eight additional contextual articles to this "Sociological Souls of Black Folk" project, researchers, students, and general readers interested in Du Bois' work are now able to gain a deeper appreciation for and understanding of the sociological foundation of what eventually became *The Souls of Black Folk*.

As readers work their way through *The Sociological Souls of Black Folk*, they encounter Du Bois' utilization of quantitative and qualitative sociological research methods. Census data, survey data, ethnographic data, and participant observation findings are all accessed to provide an empirical base for the studies presented. The core concepts of sociology:— culture, socialization, social structure, social interaction, deviance, and stratification—are all addressed in these essays. Du Bois focused on key social institutions like religion, and presented his discussion of racial inequality within a social conflict perspective. Prejudice, discrimination, racism, assimilation, accommodation, social change, crime and social control, social class, and occupational and educational inequality are all addressed. These are topics that any student taking an introductory course in sociology or social problems will encounter and recognize.

Du Bois was a pioneering sociological figure in such areas as the sociology of religion, crime and deviance, the family, urban and rural studies, demography, research methods, public sociology, and service learning. In addition to confirming Du Bois' role as a founding figure of American sociology, hopefully *The Sociological Souls of Black Folk* will pave the way for his *The Souls of Black Folk* to be recognized as a classic sociological study in the early development of mainstream American sociology.

Notes

1.   As a child and a youth in Great Barrington, Massachusetts, Du Bois attended a Congregationalist Church. Perhaps it was here that he was first introduced to the "Thirty-Nine Articles of Religion." Adopted by the Church of England in 1563, the articles were not adopted in the United States until 1801 when they were acknowledged by the Protestant Episcopal Church. The first article is "Of Faith in the Holy Spirit" (The Thirty-Nine Articles 2010; Articles of Religion 2007).

2.   Mead and Du Bois each studied under William James while at Harvard. Mead was at Harvard from 1887–88 earning a master's degree while Du Bois was enrolled at Harvard from 1888–91. During this time he earned a second bachelor's degree and a master's degree. Mead and Du Bois each engaged in doctoral studies in Germany. It appears that the concept of the "significant other," which is a hallmark of the symbolic interactionist perspective, may be traced back to the philosophy and psychology of William James.

3.   Since the pictorial essay was not created by Du Bois, it is not included in *The Sociological Souls of Black Folk*. The pictorial essay and the statistical table were also dropped from *The Souls of Black Folk*.

4.   In this particular survey, $500 was set as the capital threshold for a business venture (Du Bois 1899d). However, as is later seen in Table 1.2, 197 African American business men with $100-$500 capital invested in their business enterprise were identified as a capital invested category and included in the figure for the total number of business men with capital invested in business activities. Consequently, these data at best provide only a rough estimate of the number of business men with capital invested in "officially recognized" business activities.

5.   Similar issues are also addressed in another 1897 essay, "Strivings of the Negro People." This essay is Reading 1 in *The Sociological Souls of Black Folk*.

6.   By introducing culture into the discussion of inequality, neither Du Bois nor Wilson is framing their argument within a "blaming the victim" perspective. This is not a culture of poverty argument. Rather, culture is portrayed as an adaptation to prevailing social structures which have been created by and are being maintained by the larger society. To fully understand the nature of inequality, the interaction of structural and cultural dimensions of inequality must be explored. See O. Lewis (1986) for an example of the culture of poverty perspective.

7.   In talking about offering services to one's community and then extending those services to all humanity, Du Bois appears to be describing what Portes (1987) later terms

the development of economic enclaves. According to Portes residential discrimination may restrict a racial or ethnic group to a particular area. That group will then develop services for the immediate community. Over time these services may be offered to persons residing outside the community. The Fisk graduates were well aware of the color line. Du Bois was asking these young people to develop their services and to extend them beyond the African American community so as to benefit all humanity.

8.   The early sociological contributions of less well-known members of the Atlanta Sociological Laboratory have been addressed recently by Earl Wright (2009). While noting some of the work of Atlanta University students, Wright specifically addresses the research activities of Monroe Work and Lucy Laney.

9.   Persons wishing to view and study the photocopies of the original exhibit are directed to the following web site: http://129.171.53.1/ep/Paris/html/charts_1. html. The title of the site is "Paris 1900 World's Fair (*Exposition Universelle*) The Georgia Negro Exhibit."

10.   In the exhibit Du Bois employed the term Negro instead of African American. Throughout the reconstructed exhibit, Negro is employed in all page titles where Du Bois utilized the term.

11.   The titles for the pages included in the part of the exhibit dealing with data for all African Americans residing in the United States were provided in English and French. The titles also included the caption, "Done by Atlanta University."

Part 1:
The Sociological Souls of Black Folk

Reading 1

Strivings of the Negro People[1]

Between me and the other world there is ever an unasked question: unasked by some through feelings of delicacy; by others through the difficulty of rightly framing it. All, nevertheless, flutter round it. They approach me in a half-hesitant sort of way, eye me curiously or compassionately, and then, instead of saying directly, "How does it feel to be a problem?" They say, "I know an excellent colored man in my town;" or, "I fought at Mechanicsville;" or, "Do not these Southern outrages make your blood boil?" At these I smile, or am interested, or reduce the boiling to a simmer, as the occasion may require. To the real question, "How does it feel to be a problem?" I answer seldom a word.

And yet, being a problem is a strange experience,—peculiar even for one who has never been anything else, save perhaps in babyhood and in Europe. It is in the early days of rollicking boyhood that the revelation first bursts upon one, all in a day, as it were. I remember well when the shadow swept across me. I was a little thing, away up in the hills of New England, where the dark Housatonic winds between Hoosac and Taghanic to the sea. In a wee wooden schoolhouse, something put it into the boys' and girls' heads to buy gorgeous visiting-cards—ten cents a package—and exchange. The exchange was merry, till one girl, a tall newcomer, refused my card,—refused it peremptorily, with a glance. Then it dawned upon me with a certain suddenness that I was different from the others; or like, mayhap, in heart and life and longing, but shut out from their world by a vast veil. I had thereafter no desire to tear down that veil, to creep through; I held all beyond it in common contempt, and lived above it in a region of blue sky and great wandering shadows. That sky was bluest when I could beat my mates at examination-time, or beat them at a foot-race, or even beat their stringy heads. Alas, with the years all this fine contempt began to fade; for the words I longed for, and all their dazzling opportunities, were theirs, not mine. But they should not keep these prizes, I said; some, all, I would wrest from them. Just how I would do it I could never decide: by reading law, by healing the sick, by telling the wonderful tales that swam in my head,—some way. With other black boys the strife was not so fiercely sunny: their youth shrunk into tasteless sycophancy, or into silent hatred of the pale world about them mocking distrust of everything white; or wasted itself in a bitter cry, Why did God make

3

me an outcast and a stranger in mine own house? The "shades of the prison-house" closed round about us all: walls strait and stubborn to the whitest, but relentlessly narrow, tall, and unscalable to sons of night who must plod darkly on in resignation, or beat unavailing palms against the stone, or steadily, half hopelessly, watch the streak of blue above.

After the Egyptian and Indian, the Greek and Roman, the Teuton and Mongolian, the Negro is a sort of seventh son, born with a veil, and gifted with second-sight in this American world,—a world which yields him no true self-consciousness, but only lets him see himself through the revelation of the other world. It is a peculiar sensation, this double-consciousness, this sense of always looking at one's self through the eyes of others, of measuring one's soul by the tape of a world that looks on in amused contempt and pity. One ever feels his two-ness,—an American, a Negro; two souls, two thoughts, two unreconciled strivings; two warring ideals in one dark body, whose dogged strength alone keeps it from being torn asunder. The history of the American Negro is the history of this strife,—this longing to attain self-conscious manhood, to merge his double self into a better and truer self. In this merging he wishes neither of the older selves to be lost. He would not Africanize America, for America has too much to teach the world and Africa; he does not wish to bleach his Negro soul in a flood of white Americanism, for he believes—foolishly, perhaps, but fervently —that Negro blood has yet a message for the world. He simply wishes to make it possible for a man to be both a Negro and an American, without being cursed and spit upon by his fellows, without losing the opportunity of self-development.

This, then, is the end of his striving: to be a co-worker in the kingdom of culture, to escape both death and isolation, to husband and use his best powers. These powers of body and mind have in the past been so wasted and dispersed as to lose all effectiveness, and to seem like absence of all power, like weakness. The double-aimed struggle of the black artisan—on the one hand to escape white contempt for a nation of mere hewers of wood and drawers of water, and on the other hand to plough and nail and dig for a poverty-stricken horde, could only result in making him a poor craftsman, for he had but half a heart in either cause. By the poverty and ignorance of his people, the Negro minister or doctor was tempted toward quackery and demagogy, and by the criticism of the other world toward an elaborate preparation that over-fitted him for his lowly tasks. The would-be black savant was confronted by the paradox that the knowledge his people needed was a twice-told tale to his white neighbors, while the know-ledge which would teach the white world was Greek to his own flesh and blood. The innate love of harmony and beauty that set the ruder souls of his people a-dancing, a-singing and a-laughing raised but confusion and doubt in the soul of the black artist; for the beauty revealed to him was the soul-beauty of a race which his larger audience despised, and he could not articulate the message of another people.This waste of double aims, this seeking to satisfy two unreconciled ideals, has wrought sad havoc with the courage and faith and deeds of eight thousand thousand people, has sent them often wooing false gods and invoking false means of salvation, and at times has even seemed destined to make them ashamed of themselves. In the days of bondage they thought to see in one divine event the end of all doubt and disappointment; eighteenth-century Rousseauism never worshiped freedom with half the unquestioning faith that the American Negro did for two centuries. To him slavery was, indeed, the sum of all villainies, the cause of all sorrow, the root of all prejudice; emancipation was the key to a promised land of sweeter beauty than ever stretched before the eyes of wearied Israelites. In his songs and exhortations swelled one refrain; liberty; in his tears and curses the god he implored had freedom in his right hand. At last it came,—suddenly, fearfully, like a dream. With one wild carnival of blood and passion came the message in his own plaintive cadences:—

"Shout, O children! Shout, you're free!
For God has bought your liberty!"

Years have passed away since then,—ten, twenty, thirty. Thirty years of national life, thirty years of renewal and development, and yet the swarthy ghost of Banquo sits in its old place at the national feast. In vain does the nation cry to this our vastest problem,—

"Take any shape but that, and my firm nerves
Shall never tremble!"

The freedman has not yet found in freedom his promised land. Whatever of lesser good may have come in these years of change, the shadow of a deep disappointment rests upon the Negro people,—a disappointment all the more bitter because the unattained ideal was unbounded save by the simple ignorance of a lowly folk.

The first decade was merely a prolongation of the vain search for freedom, the boon that seemed ever barely to elude their grasp,—like a tantalizing will-o'-the-wisp, maddening and misleading the headless host. The holocaust of war, the terrors of the Ku Klux Klan, the lies of carpet-baggers, the disorganization of industry, and the contradictory advice of friends and foes left the bewildered serf with no new watchword beyond the old cry for freedom. As the decade closed, however, he began to grasp a new idea. The ideal of liberty demanded for its attainment powerful means, and these the Fifteenth Amendment gave him. The ballot, which before he had looked upon as a visible sign of freedom, he now regarded as the chief means of gaining and perfecting the liberty with which war had partially endowed him. And why not? Had not votes made war and emancipated millions? Had not votes enfranchised the freedmen? Was anything impossible to a power that had done all this? A million black men started with renewed zeal to vote themselves into the kingdom. The decade fled away,—a decade containing, to the freedman's mind, nothing but suppressed votes, stuffed ballot-boxes, and election outrages that nullified his vaunted right of suffrage. And yet that decade from 1875 to 1885 held another powerful movement, the rise of another ideal to guide the unguided, another pillar of fire by night after a clouded day. It was the ideal of "book-learning;" the curiosity, born of compulsory ignorance, to know and test the power of the cabalistic letters of the white man, the longing to know. Mission and night schools began in the smoke of battle, ran the gauntlet of reconstruction, and at last developed into permanent foundations. Here at last seemed to have been discovered the mountain path to Canaan; longer than the highway of emancipation and law, steep and rugged, but straight, leading to heights high enough to overlook life.

Up the new path the advance guard toiled, slowly, heavily, doggedly; only those who have watched and guided the faltering feet, the misty minds, the dull understandings, of the dark pupils of these schools know how faithfully, how piteously, this people strove to learn. It was weary work. The cold statistician wrote down the inches of progress here and there, noted also where here and there a foot had slipped or someone had fallen. To the tired climbers, the horizon was ever dark, the mists were often cold, the Canaan was always dim and far away. If, however, the vistas disclosed as yet no goal, no resting-place, little but flattery and criticism, the journey at least gave leisure for reflection and self-examination; it changed the child of emancipation to the youth with dawning self-consciousness, self-realization, self-respect. In those somber forests of his striving his own soul rose before him, and he saw himself,—darkly as through a veil; and yet he saw in himself some faint revelation of his power, of his mission. He began to have a dim feeling that, to attain his place in the world, he must be himself, and not another. For the first time he sought to analyze the burden he bore upon his back, that dead-weight of social degradation partially masked behind a half-named Negro problem. He felt his poverty; without a cent, without a home, without land, tools, or savings, he had entered into competition with rich, landed, skilled neighbors. To be a poor man is hard, but to be a poor race in a land of dollars is the very bottom of hardships. He felt the weight of his ignorance,—not simply of letters, but of life, of business, of the humanities; the accumulated sloth and shirking and awkwardness of decades and centuries shackled his hands and feet. Nor was his burden all poverty and ignorance. The red stain of bastardy, which two centuries of systematic legal defilement of Negro women had stamped upon his race, meant not only the loss of ancient African chastity, but also the hereditary weight of a mass of filth from white whoremongers and adulterers, threatening almost the obliteration of the Negro home.

A people thus handicapped ought not to be asked to race with the world, but rather allowed to give all its time and thought to its own social problems. But alas! while sociologists gleefully count his bastards and his prostitutes, the very soul of the toiling, sweating black man is darkened by the shadow of a vast despair. Men call the shadow prejudice, and learnedly explain it as the natural defense of culture against barbarism, learning against ignorance, purity against crime, the "higher" against the "lower" races. To which the Negro cries Amen! and swears that to so much of this strange prejudice as is founded on just homage to civilization, culture, righteousness, and progress, he humbly bows and meekly does obeisance. But before that nameless prejudice that leaps beyond all this he stands helpless, dismayed, and well-nigh speechless; before that personal disrespect and mockery, the ridicule and systematic humiliation, the distortion of fact and wanton license of fancy, the cynical ignoring of the better and the boisterous welcoming of the worse, the all-pervading desire to inculcate disdain for everything black, from Toussaint to the devil,—before this there rises a sickening despair that would disarm and discourage any nation save that black host to whom "discouragement" is an unwritten word.

They press on, they still nurse the dogged hope,—not a hope of nauseating patronage, not a hope of reception into charmed social circles of stock-jobbers, pork-packers, and earl-hunters, but the hope of a higher synthesis of civilization and humanity, a true progress, with which the chorus "Peace, good will to men,"

"May make one music as before, But vaster."

Thus the second decade of the American Negro's freedom was a period of conflict, of inspiration and doubt, of faith and vain questioning, of *Sturm und Drang*.[2] The ideals of physical freedom, political power, of school training, as separate all-sufficient panaceas for social ills, become in the third decade dim and overcast. They were the vain dreams of a credulous race-childhood; not wrong, but incomplete and over-simple. The training of the schools we need today more than ever,—the training of deft hands, quick eyes and ears, and above all the broader, deeper, higher culture of gifted minds. The power of the ballot we need in sheer self-defense, and as a guarantee of good faith. We may misuse it, but we can scarce do worse in this respect than our whilom masters. Freedom, too, the long-sought, we still seek,—the freedom of life and limb, the freedom to work and think. Work, culture, liberty,—all these we need, not singly but together, for today these ideals among the Negro people are gradually coalescing, and finding a higher meaning in the unifying ideal of race;—the ideal of fostering the traits and talents of the Negro, not in opposition to, but in conformity with, the greater ideals of the American republic, in order that some day on American soil two world-races may give each to each those characteristics both so sadly lack. Already we come not altogether empty-handed: there is today no true American music but the wild sweet melodies of the Negro slave; the American fairy tales are Indian and African; we are the sole oasis of simple faith and reverence in a dusty desert of dollars and smartness. Will America be poorer if she replaces her brutal dyspeptic blundering with lighthearted but determined Negro humility; or her coarse and cruel wit with loving jovial good humor; or her Annie Rooney and Steal Away?

Merely a stern concrete test of the underlying principles of the great republic is the Negro Problem, and the spiritual striving of the freedmen's sons is the travail of souls whose burden is almost beyond the measure of their strength, but who bear it in the name of an historic race, in the name of this the land of their fathers' fathers, and in the name of human opportunity.

Notes

1. *Editor's Note:* This reading was originally published in the *Atlantic Monthly*, 80 (1897): 194-198. It appeared in the August issue and was later republished with minor modifications as "Of Our Spiritual Strivings" in *The Souls of Black Folk* (1903). This essay was also the lead essay in *The Souls of Black Folk.*

2. *Editor's note:* This German phrase is loosely translated as "turmoil and stress."

Reading 2

A Negro Schoolmaster in the New South[1]

Once upon a time, I taught school in the hills of Tennessee, where the broad dark vale of the Mississippi begins to role and crumple to greet the Alleghenies. I was a Fisk student then, and all Fisk men think that Tennessee—beyond the Veil—is theirs alone, and in vacation time they sally forth in lusty bands to meet the county school commissioners. Young and happy, I too went, and I shall not soon forget that summer, ten years ago.

First, there was a teachers' Institute at the county-seat; and there distinguished guests of the superintendent taught the teachers fractions and spelling and other mysteries,—white teachers in the morning, Negroes at night. A picnic now and then, and a supper, and the rough world was softened by laughter and song. I remember how—But I wander.

There came a day when all the teachers left the Institute, and began the hunt for schools. I learn from hearsay (for my mother was mortally afraid of firearms) that the hunting of ducks and bears and men is wonderfully interesting, but I am sure that the man who has never hunted a country school has something to learn of the pleasures of the chase. I see now the white, hot roads lazily rise and fall and wind before me under burning July sun; I feel the deep weariness of heart and limb, as ten, eight, six miles stretch relentlessly ahead; I feel my heart sink heavily as I hear again and again, "Got a teacher? Yes." So I walked on and on, —horses were too expensive,—until I had wandered beyond railways, stage lines, to a land of "varmints" and rattlesnakes, where the coming a stranger was an event, and men lived and died in the shadow of one blue hill.

Sprinkled over hill and dale lay cabins and farmhouses, out from the world by the forests and the rolling hills toward the east. There I found at last a little school. Josie told me of it; she was a thin, homely girl of twenty, with a dark brown face and thick, hard hair. I had crossed stream at Watertown, and rested under the great willows; then I had gone to the little cabin in the lot where Josie was resting on her way to town. The gaunt farmer made me welcome, and Josie, hearing my errand, told me anxiously that they wanted a school over the hill; that but once since the war had a teacher been there; that she herself longed to

9

learn,—and thus she ran on, talking fast and loud, with much earnestness and energy.

Next morning I crossed the tall round hill, lingered to look at blue and yellow mountains stretching toward the Carolinas; then I plunged into the wood, and came out at Josie's home. It was a dull frame cottage with four rooms, perched just below the brow of the hill, amid peach trees. The father was a quiet, simple soul, calmly ignorant, with no touch of vulgarity. The mother was different,—strong, bustling, and energetic, with a quick, restless tongue and an ambition to live "like folks." There was a crowd of children. Two boys had gone away. There remained two growing girls; a shy midget of eight; John, tall, awkward, and eighteen; Jim, younger, quicker, and better looking; and two babies of indefinite age. Then there was Josie herself. She seemed to be the center of the family: always busy at service or at home, or berry-picking; a little nervous and inclined to scold, like her mother, yet faithful, too, like her father. She had about her a certain fineness, the shadow of an unconscious moral heroism that would willingly give all of life to make life broader, deeper, and fuller for her and hers. I saw much of this family afterward, and grew to love them for their honest efforts to be decent and comfortable, and for their knowledge of their own ignorance. There was with them no affectation. The mother would scold the father for being so "easy;" Josie would roundly rate the boys for carelessness; and all knew that it was a hard thing to dig a living out of a rocky side hill.

I secured the school. I remember the day I rode horseback out to the commissioner's house, with a pleasant young white fellow, who wanted the white school. The road ran down the bed of a stream; the sun laughed and the water jingled, and we rode on. "Come in," said the commissioner,—"come in. Have a seat. Yes, that certificate will do. Stay for dinner. What do you want a month?" Oh, I thought, this is lucky; but even then fell the awful shadow of the Veil, for they ate first, then I—alone.

The schoolhouse was a log hut, where Colonel Wheeler used to shelter his corn. It sat in a lot behind a rail fence and thorn bushes, near the sweetest of springs. There was an entrance where a door was, and within, a massive rickety fireplace; great chinks between the logs served as windows. Furniture was scarce. A pale blackboard crouched in the corner. My desk was made of three boards, reinforced at critical points, and my chair, borrowed from the landlady, had to be returned every night. Seats for the children,—these puzzled me much. I was haunted by a New England vision of neat little desks and chairs, but, alas, the reality was rough plank benches without backs, at times without legs. They had the one virtue of making naps dangerous,—possibly fatal, for the floor was not to be trusted.

It was a hot morning late July when the school opened. I trembled when I heard the patter of little feet down the dusty road, and saw the growing row of dark solemn faces and bright eager eyes facing me. First came Josie and her brothers and sisters. The longing to know, to be a student in the great school at Nashville, hovered like a star above this child woman amid her work and worry, and she studied doggedly. There were the Dowells from their farm over toward

Alexandria: Fanny, with her smooth black face and wondering eyes; Martha, brown and dull; pretty girl wife of a brother, and the younger brood. There were the Burkes, two brown and yellow lads, and a tiny haughty-eyed girl. Fat Reuben's little chubby girl came, with golden face and old gold hair, faithful and solemn. 'Thenie was on hand early,—a jolly, ugly, good-hearted girl, who slyly dipped snuff and looked after her little bow-legged brother. When her mother could spare her, 'Tildy came,—a midnight beauty, with starry eyes and tapering limbs; and her brother, correspondingly homely. And then the big boys: the hulking Lawrences; the lazy Neills, unfathered sons of mother and daughter; Hickman, with a stoop in his shoulders; and the rest.

There they sat, nearly thirty of them, on the rough benches, their faces shading from a pale cream to a deep brown, the little feet bare and swinging, the eyes full of expectation, with here and there a twinkle of mischief, and the hands grasping Webster's blue-back spelling-book. I loved my school, and the fine faith the children had in the wisdom of their teacher was truly marvelous. We read and spelled together, wrote a little, picked flowers, sang, and listened to stories of the world beyond the hill. At times the school would dwindle away, and I would start out. I would visit Mun Eddings, who lived in two very dirty rooms, and ask why little Lugene, whose flaming face seemed ever ablaze with the dark red hair uncombed, was absent all last week, or why I missed so often the inimitable rags of Mack and Ed. Then the father, who worked Colonel Wheeler's farm on shares, would tell me how the crops needed the boys; and the thin, slovenly mother, whose face was pretty when washed, assured me that Lugene must mind the baby. "But we'll start them again next week." When the Lawrences stopped, I knew that the doubts of the old folks about book-learning had conquered again, and so, toiling up the hill, and getting as far into the cabin as possible, I put *Cicero pro Archia Poeta*[2] into the simplest English with local applications, and usually convinced them—for a week or so.

On Friday nights I often went home with some of the children; sometimes to Doc Burke's farm. He was a great, loud, thin Black, ever working, and trying to buy the seventy-five acres of hill and dale where he lived; but people said that he would surely fail, and the "white folks would get it all." His wife was a magnificent Amazon, with saffron face and shining hair, uncorseted and barefooted, were strong and beautiful. They lived in a one-and-a-half-room cabin in the hollow of the farm, near the spring. The front room was full of great fat white beds, scrupulously neat; and there were bad chromos on the walls, and a tired center-table. In the tiny back kitchen I was often invited to "take out and help" myself to fried chicken and wheat biscuit, "meat" and corn pone, string beans and berries. At first I used to be a little alarmed at the approach of bedtime in the one lone bedroom, but embarrassment was deftly avoided. First, all the children nodded and slept, and were stowed away in one great pile of goose feathers; the mother and the father discreetly slipped away to the kitchen while I went to bed; then, blowing out the dim light, they retired in the dark. In the morning all were up and away before I thought of awaking. Across the road, where fat Reuben lived, they all went outdoors while the teacher retired, because they did not boast the luxury of a kitchen.

I liked to stay with the Dowells, for they had four rooms and plenty good country fare. Uncle Bird had a small, rough farm, all woods and hills, miles from the big road; but he was full of tales,—he preached now and then,—and with his children, berries, horses, and wheat he was happy and prosperous. Often, to keep the peace, I must go where life was less lovely; for instance, 'Tildy's mother was incorrigibly dirty, Reuben's larder was limited seriously, and herds of untamed bedbugs wandered over the Eddingses' beds. Best of all I loved to go to Josie's, and sit on the porch, eating peaches, while the mother bustled and talked: how Josie had bought the sewing-machine; how Josie worked at service in the winter, but that four dollars a month was "mighty little" wages; how Josie longed to go away to school, but that it "looked like" they never could get far enough ahead to let her; how the crops failed and the well was yet unfinished; and, finally, how "mean" some of the white folks were.

For two summers I lived in this little world; it was dull and humdrum. The girls looked at the hill in wistful longing, and the boys fretted, and haunted Alexandria. Alexandria was "town,"—a straggling, lazy village of houses, churches, and shops, and an aristocracy of Toms, Dicks, and Captains. Cuddled on the hill to the north was the village of the colored folks, who lived in three or four room unpainted cottages, some neat and homelike, and some dirty. The dwellings were scattered rather aimlessly, but they centered about the twin temples of the hamlet, the Methodist and the Hard-Shell Baptist[3] churches. These, in turn, leaned gingerly on a sad-colored schoolhouse. Hither my little world wended its crooked way on Sunday to meet other worlds, and make the weekly sacrifice with frenzied priest at the altar of the "old-time religion." Then the soft melody and mighty cadences of Negro song fluttered and thundered.

I have called my tiny community a world, and so its isolation made it; and yet there was among us but a half-awakened common consciousness, sprung from common grief, at burial, birth, or wedding; from a common hardship poverty, poor land, and low wages; and, above all, from the sight of the Veil that hung between us and Opportunity. All this caused us to think some thoughts together; but these, when ripe for speech, were spoken in various languages. Those whose eyes thirty and more years before had seen "the glory of the coming of the Lord" saw in every present hindrance or help a dark fatalism bound to bring all things right in His own good time. The mass of those to whom slavery was a dim recollection of childhood found the world a puzzling thing: it asked little of them, and they answered with little, and yet it ridiculed their offering. Such a paradox they could not understand, and therefore sank into listless indifference, or shiftlessness, or reckless bravado. There were, however, some such as Josie, Jim, and Ben,—they to whom War, Hell, and Slavery were but childhood tales, whose young appetites had been whetted to an edge by school and story and half-awakened thought. Ill could they be content, born without and beyond the World. And their weak wings beat against their barriers,—barriers of caste, of youth, of life; at last, in dangerous moments, against everything that opposed even a whim.

The ten years that follow youth, the years when first the realization comes that life is leading somewhere,—these were years that passed after I left my little school. When they were past, I came by chance once more to walls of Fisk University, to the halls of the chapel of melody. As I lingered there in the joy and pain of meeting old school friends, there swept over me a sudden longing to pass again beyond the blue hill, and to see the homes and the school of other days, and to learn how life had gone with my school-children; and I went.

Josie was dead, and the gray-haired mother said simply, "We've had a heap of trouble since you've been away." I had feared for Jim. With a cultured parentage and a social caste to uphold him, he might have made a venturesome merchant or a West Point cadet. But here he was, angry with life and reckless; and when Farmer Durham charged him with stealing wheat, the old man had to ride last to escape the stones which the furious fool hurled after him. They told Jim to run away; but he would not run, and the constable came that afternoon. It grieved Josie, and great awkward John walked nine miles every day to see his little brother through the bars of Lebanon jail. At last the two came back together in the dark night. The mother cooked supper, and Josie emptied her purse, and the boys stole away. Josie grew thin and silent, yet worked the more. The hill became steep for the quiet old father, and with the boys away there was little to do in the valley. Josie helped them sell the old farm, and they moved nearer town. Brother Dennis, the carpenter, built a new house with six rooms; Josie toiled a year in Nashville, and brought back ninety dollars to furnish the house and change it to a home.

When the spring came, and the birds twittered, and the stream ran proud and full, little sister Lizzie, bold and thoughtless, flushed with the passion of youth, bestowed herself on the tempter, and brought home a nameless child. Josie shivered, and worked on, with the vision of schooldays all fled, with a face wan and tired,—worked until, on a summer's day, someone married another; then Josie crept to her mother like a hurt child, and slept—and sleeps.

I paused to scent the breeze as I entered the valley. The Lawrences have gone; father and son forever, and the other son lazily digs in the earth to live. A new young widow rents out their cabin to fat Reuben. Reuben is a Baptist preacher now, but I fear as lazy as ever, though his cabin has three rooms; and little Ella has grown into a bouncing woman, and is plowing corn on the hot hillside. There are babies a plenty, and one half-witted girl. Across the valley is a house I did not know before, and there I found, rocking one baby and expecting another, one of my schoolgirls, a daughter of Uncle Bird Dowell. She looked somewhat worried with her new duties, but soon bristled into pride over her neat cabin, and the tale of her thrifty husband, the horse and cow, and the farm they were planning to buy.

My log schoolhouse was gone. In its place stood Progress, and Progress, I understand, is necessarily ugly. The crazy foundation stones still marked the former site of my poor little cabin, and not far away, on six weary boulders, perched a jaunty board house, perhaps twenty by thirty feet, with three windows and a door that locked. Some of the window glass was broken, and part of an old iron stove lay mournfully under the house. I peeped through the window half reverently, and found things that were more familiar. The blackboard had grown by about two feet, and the seats were without backs. The county owns the lot now, I hear, and every year there is a session of school. As I sat by the spring and looked on the Old and the New I felt glad, very glad, and yet—

After two long drinks I started on. There was the great double log house on the corner. I remembered the broken, blighted family that used to live there. The strong, hard face of the mother, with its wilderness of hair, rose before me. She had driven her husband away, and while I taught school a strange man lived there, big and jovial, and people talked. I felt sure that Ben and 'Tildy would come to naught from such a home. But this is an odd world; for Ben is a busy farmer in Smith County, "doing well, too," they say, and he had cared for little 'Tildy until last spring, when a lover married her. A hard life the lad had led, toiling for meat, and laughed at because he was homely and crooked. There was Sam Carlon, an impudent old skinflint, who had definite notions about niggers, and hired Ben a summer and would not pay him. Then the hungry boy gathered his sacks together, and in broad daylight went into Carlon's corn; and when the hard-fisted farmer set upon him, the angry boy flew at him like a beast. Doc Burke saved a murder and a lynching that day.

The story reminded me again of the Burkes, and an impatience seized me to know who won in the battle, Doc or the seventy-five acres. For it is a hard thing to make a farm out of nothing, even in fifteen years. So I hurried on, thinking of the Burkes. They used to have a certain magnificent barbarism about them that I liked. They were never vulgar, never immoral, but rather rough and primitive, with an unconventionality that spent itself in loud guffaws, slaps on the back, and naps in the corner. I hurried by the cottage of the misborn Neill boys. It was empty, and they were grown into fat, lazy farm hands. I saw the home of the Hickmans, but Albert, with his stooping shoulders, had passed from the world. Then I came to the Burkes' gate and peered through; the enclosure looked rough and untrimmed, and yet there were the same fences around the old farm save to the left, where lay twenty-five other acres. And lo! The cabin in the hollow had climbed the hill and swollen to a half-finished six-room cottage.

The Burkes held a hundred acres, but they were still in debt. Indeed, the gaunt father who toiled night and day would scarcely be happy out of debt, being so used to it. Some day he must stop, for his massive frame is showing decline. The mother wore shoes, but the lion like physique of other days was broken. The children had grown up. Rob, image of his father, was loud and rough with laughter. Birdie, my school baby of six, had grown to a picture of maiden beauty, tall and tawny. "Edgar is gone," said the mother, with head half bowed, —"gone to work in Nashville; he and his father couldn't agree."

Little Doc, the boy born since the time of my school, took me horseback down the creek next morning toward Farmer Dowell's. The road and the stream were battling for mastery, and the stream had the better of it. We splashed and waded, and the merry boy, perched behind me, chattered and laughed. He showed me where Simon Thompson had bought a bit of ground and a home; but his daughter Lana, a plump, brown, slow girl, was not there. She had married a man and a farm twenty miles away. We wound on down the stream till we came to a gate that I did not recognize, but the boy insisted that it was "Uncle Bird's." The farm was fat with the growing crop. In that little valley was a strange stillness as I rode up; for death and marriage had stolen youth, and left age and childhood there. We sat and talked that night, after the chores were done. Uncle Bird was grayer, and his eyes did not see so well, but he was still jovial. We talked of the acres bought,—one hundred and twenty-five,—of the new chamber added, of Martha's marrying. Then we talked of death: Fanny and Fred were gone; a shadow hung over the other daughter, and when it lifted she was to go to Nashville to school. At last we spoke of the neighbors, and as night fell Uncle Bird told me how, on a night like that, 'Thenie came wandering back to her home over yonder, to escape the blows of her husband. And next morning she died in the home that her little bow-legged brother, working and saving, had bought for their widowed mother.

My journey was done, and behind me lay hill and dale, and Life and Death. How shall man measure Progress there where the dark-faced Josie lies? How many heartfuls or sorrow shall balance a bushel of wheat? How hard a thing is life to the lowly, and yet how human and real! And all this life and love and strife and failure, —is it the twilight of nightfall or the flush of some faint-dawning day?

Thus sadly musing, I rode to Nashville in the Jim Crow car.

Notes

1.   *Editor's note*: This reading was also originally published in *The Atlantic Monthly*, 83 (1899): 99-105. It appeared in the January issue and was later republished with minor modifications as "Of the Meaning of Progress" in *The Souls of Black Folk* (1903). This essay was the second of four *The Atlantic Monthly* essays to be republished in *The Souls of Black Folk*.

2.   *Editor's note*: This is the title given to a Latin speech that Cicero offered in support of Archias' Roman citizenship. Archias was a Greek poet who had been living in Rome for some time. The poet was believed to have been involved in some type of political controversy. See *"Pro Archia* Poeta." http://en.wikipedia.org/wiki/Pro_Archia_Poeta.

3.   *Editor's note*: Hard-Shell Baptist is another name for Primitive Baptist. This religious group is known for its conservative beliefs. The use of musical instruments in worship services is opposed, and the group does not support such activities as Sunday School, missionary work, and the employment of paid ministerial staff (McKee 2011).

Reading 3

The Religion of the American Negro[1]

It was out in the country, far from home, far from my foster home, on a dark Sunday night. The road wandered from our rambling log house up the stony bed of a creek, past wheat and corn, until we could hear dimly across the fields a rhythmic cadence of song,—soft, thrilling, powerful, that swelled and died sorrowfully in our ears. I was a country school teacher then, fresh from the East, and had never seen a southern Negro revival. To be sure, we in Berkshire were not perhaps as stiff and formal as they in Suffolk of olden time; yet we were very quiet and subdued, and I know not what would have happened those clear Sabbath mornings had someone punctuated the sermon with a wild scream, or interrupted the long prayer with a loud Amen! And so most striking to me, as I approached the village and the little plain church perched aloft, was the air of intense excitement that possessed that mass of black folk. A sort of suppressed terror hung in the air and seemed to seize us—a pythian madness, a demoniac possession, that lent terrible reality to song and word. The black and massive form of the preacher swayed and quivered as the words crowded to his lips and flew at us in singular eloquence. The people moaned and fluttered, and then the gaunt-cheeked brown woman beside me suddenly leaped straight into the air and shrieked like a lost soul, while round about came wail and groan and outcry, and a scene of human passion such as I had never conceived before.

Those who have not thus witnessed the frenzy of a Negro revival in the untouched backwoods of the South can but dimly realize the religious feeling of the slave; as described, such scenes appear grotesque and funny, but as seen they are awful. Three things characterized this religion of the slave—the Preacher, the Music and the Frenzy. The Preacher is the most unique personality developed by the Negro on American soil. A leader, a politician, an orator, a "boss," an intriguer, an idealist—all these he is, and ever, too, the center of a group of men, now twenty, now a thousand in number. The combination of a certain adroitness with deep-seated earnestness, of tact with consummate ability, gave him his preeminence, and helps him maintain it. The type, of course, varies according to time and place, from the West Indies in the sixteenth century to New England in the nineteenth, and from the Mississippi bottoms to cities like New Orleans or New York.

The Music of Negro religion is that plaintive rhythmic melody with its touching minor cadences, which, despite caricature and defilement, still remains the most original and beautiful expression of human life and longing yet born on American soil. Sprung from the African forests, where its counterpart can still be heard, it was adapted, changed and intensified by the tragic soul-life of the slave, until, under the stress of law and whip, it became the one true expression of a people's sorrow, despair and hope.

Finally the Frenzy or "Shouting," when the Spirit of the Lord passed by, and, seizing the devotee, made him mad with supernatural joy, was the last essential of Negro religion and the one more devoutly believed in than all the rest. It varied in expression from the silent rapt countenance or the low murmur and moan to the mad abandon of physical fervor—the stamping, shrieking and shouting, the rushing to and fro and wild waving of arms, the weeping and laughing, the vision and the trance. All this is nothing new in the world, but old as religion, as Delphi and Endor. And so firm a hold did it have on the Negro that many generations firmly believed that without this visible manifestation of the god, there could be no true communion with the Invisible.

These were the characteristics of Negro religious life as developed up to the time of Emancipation. Since under the peculiar circumstances of the black man's environment, they were the one expression of his higher life, they are of deep interest to the student of his development, both socially and psychologically. Numerous are the attractive lines of inquiry that here group themselves. What did slavery mean to the African savage? What was his attitude toward the World and Life? What seemed to him good and evil—God and Devil? Whither went his longings and strivings, and wherefore were his heart-burnings and disappointments? Answers to such questions can come only from a study of Negro religion as a development, through its gradual changes from the heathenism of the Gold Coast to the institutional Negro church of Chicago.

Moreover, the religious growth of millions of men, even though they be slaves, cannot be without potent influence upon their contemporaries. The Methodists and Baptists of America owe much of their condition to the silent but potent influence of their millions of Negro converts. Especially is this noticeable in the South, where theology and religious philosophy are on this account a full half century behind the North, and where the religion of the poor whites is a plain copy of Negro thought and methods. The mass of "Gospel" hymns which has swept through American churches and well-nigh ruined our sense of song, consists largely of debased imitations of Negro melodies made by ears that caught the jingle but not the music, the body but not the soul, of the Jubilee songs. It is thus clear that the study of Negro religion is not only a vital part of the history of the Negro in America, but no uninteresting part of American history.

The Negro church of today is the social centre of Negro life in the United States, and the most characteristic expression of African character. Take a typical church in a small Virginian town: it is the "First Baptist"—a roomy brick edifice seating five hundred or more persons, tastefully finished in Georgia pine, with a carpet, a small organ and stained-glass windows. Underneath is a large assembly room with benches. This building is the central club-house of a community of a thousand or more Negroes. Various organizations meet here—the church proper, the Sunday-school, two or three insurance societies, women's societies, secret societies and mass meetings of various kinds. Entertainments, suppers and lectures are held beside the five or six regular weekly religious services. Considerable sums of money are collected and expended here, employment is found for the idle, strangers are introduced, news is disseminated and charity distributed. At the same time this social, intellectual and economic center is a religious center of great power. Depravity, Sin, Redemption, Heaven, Hell and Damnation are preached twice a Sunday with much fervor, and revivals take place every year after the crops are laid by; and few indeed of the community have the hardihood to withstand conversion. Back of this more formal religion, the Church stands as a real conserver of morals, a strengthener of family life, and the final authority on what is Good and Right.

Thus one can see in the Negro church today, reproduced in microcosm, all that great world from which the Negro is cut off by color prejudice and social condition. In the great city churches the same tendency is noticeable and in many respects emphasized. A great church like the Bethel of Philadelphia has 1,104 members, an edifice seating 1,500 persons and valued at $100,000, an annual budget of $5,000 and a government consisting of a pastor with several assisting local preachers, an executive and legislative board, financial boards and tax collectors; general church meetings for making laws; subdivided groups led by class leaders, a company of militia, and twenty-four auxiliary societies. The activity of such a church is immense and far-reaching, and the bishops who preside over these organizations throughout the land are among the most powerful Negro rulers in the world.

Such churches are really governments of men, and consequently a little investigation reveals the curious fact that, in the South, at least, practically every American Negro is a church member. Some, to be sure, are not regularly enrolled, and a few do not habitually attend services; but, practically, a proscribed people must have a social center, and that center for this people is the Negro church. The census of 1890 showed nearly 24,000 Negro churches in the country, with a total enrolled membership of over two and a half million, or ten actual church members to every twenty-eight persons, and in some Southern States one in every two persons. Besides these there is the large number who, while not enrolled as members, attend and take part in many of the activities of the church. There is an organized Negro church for every sixty black families in the nation, and in some States for every forty families, owning, on an average, $1,000 worth of property each, or nearly $26,000,000 in all.

Such, then, is the large development of the Negro church since Emancipation. The question now is, "What have been the successive steps of this social history, and what are the present tendencies?" First, we must realize that no such institution as the Negro church could rear itself without definite historical foundations. These foundations we can find if we remember that the social history of the Negro did not start in America. He was brought from a definite social environment—the polygamous clan life under the headship of the chief and the potent influence of the priest. His religion was nature-worship, with profound belief in invisible surrounding influences, good and bad, and his worship was through incantation and sacrifice. The first rude change in this life was the slave ship and the West Indian sugar-fields. The plantation organization replaced the clan and tribe, and the white master replaced the chief with far greater and more despotic powers. Forced and long-continued toil became the rule of life, the old ties of blood relationship and kinship disappeared, and instead of the family appeared a new polygamy and polyandry, which, in some cases, almost reached promiscuity. It was a terrific social revolution, and yet some traces were retained of the former group life, and the chief remaining institution was the Priest or Medicine-man. He early appeared on the plantation and found his function as the healer of the sick, the interpreter of the Unknown, the comforter of the sorrowing, the supernatural avenger of wrong, and the one who rudely but picturesquely expressed the longing, disappointment and resentment of a stolen and oppressed people. Thus, as bard, physician, judge and priest, within the narrow limits allowed by the slave system, rose the Negro preacher, and under him the first Afro-American institution, the Negro church. This church was not at first by any means Christian nor definitely organized; rather it was an adaptation and mingling of heathen rites among the members of each plantation, and roughly designated as Voodooism. Association with the masters, missionary effort and motives of expediency gave these rites an early veneer of Christianity, and after the lapse of many generations the Negro church became Christian.

Two characteristic things must be noticed in regard to this church. First, it became almost entirely Baptist and Methodist in faith; secondly, as a social institution it antedated by many decades the monogamic[2] Negro home. From the very circumstances of its beginning, the church was confined to the plantation, and consisted primarily of a series of disconnected units; although, later on, some freedom of movement was allowed, still this geographical limitation was always important and was one cause of the spread of the decentralized and democratic Baptist faith among the slaves. At the same time, the visible rite of baptism appealed strongly to their mystic temperament. Today the Baptist Church is still largest in membership among Negroes, and has a million and a half communicants. Next in popularity came the churches organized in connection with the white neighboring churches, chiefly Baptist and Methodist, with a few Episcopalian and others. The Methodists still form the second greatest denomination, with nearly a million members. The faith of these two leading denominations was more suited to the slave church from the prominence they gave to religious feeling and fervor. The Negro membership in other denominations has always been small and relatively unimportant, although the Episcopalians and Presbyterians are gaining among the more intelligent classes today, and the Catholic Church is making headway in certain sections. After emancipation, and still earlier in the North, the Negro churches largely severed such affiliations as they had had with the white churches, either by choice or by compulsion. The Baptist churches became independent, but the Methodists were compelled early to unite for purposes of episcopal government.[3] This gave rise to the great African Methodist Church, the greatest Negro organization in the world, to the Zion Church and the Colored Methodist, and to the black conferences and churches in this and other denominations.

The second fact noted, namely, that the Negro church antedates the Negro home, leads to an explanation of much that is paradoxical in this communistic institution and in the morals of its members. But especially it leads us to regard this institution as peculiarly the expression of the inner ethical life of a people in a sense seldom true elsewhere. Let us turn then from the outer physical development of the church to the more important inner ethical life of the people who compose it. The Negro has already been pointed out many times as a religious animal—a being of that deep emotional nature which turns instinctively toward the supernatural. Endowed with a rich tropical imagination and a keen, delicate appreciation of Nature, the transplanted African lived in a world animate with gods and devils, elves and witches; full of strange influences—of Good to be implored, of Evil to be propitiated. Slavery, then, was to him the dark triumph of Evil over him. All the hateful powers of the Under-world were striving against him, and a spirit of revolt and revenge filled his heart. He called up all the resources of heathenism to aid,—exorcism and witchcraft, the mysterious Obi worship with its barbarous rites, spells and blood-sacrifice even, now and then, of human victims. Weird midnight orgies and mystic conjurations were invoked, the witch-woman and the voodoo-priest became the center of Negro group life, and that vein of vague superstition which characterizes the unlettered Negro even today was deepened and strengthened.

In spite, however, of such success as that of the fierce Maroons, the Danish blacks and others, the spirit of revolt gradually died away under the untiring energy and superior strength of the slave masters. By the middle of the eighteenth century the black slave had sunk, with hushed murmurs, to his place at the bottom of a new economic system, and was unconsciously ripe for a new philosophy of life. Nothing suited his condition then better than the doctrines of passive submission embodied in the newly learned Christianity. Slave masters early realized this, and cheerfully aided religious propaganda within certain bounds. The long system of repression and degradation of the Negro tended to emphasize the elements in his character which made him a valuable chattel: courtesy became humility, moral strength degenerated into submission, and the exquisite native appreciation of the beautiful became an infinite capacity for dumb suffering. The Negro, losing the joy of this world, eagerly seized upon the offered conceptions of the next; the avenging Spirit of the Lord enjoining patience in this world, under sorrow and tribulation until the Great Day when He should lead His dark children home,—this became his comforting dream. His Preacher repeated the prophecy, and his bards sang:

> Children, we all shall be free
> When the Lord shall appear!

This deep religious fatalism, painted so beautifully in Uncle Tom, came soon to breed, as all fatalistic faiths will, the sensualist side by side with the martyr. Under the lax moral life of the plantation, where marriage was a farce, laziness a virtue, and property a theft, a religion of resignation and submission degenerated easily, in less strenuous minds, into a philosophy of indulgence and crime. Many of the worst characteristics of the Negro masses of today had their seed in this period of the slave's ethical growth. Here it was that the Home was ruined under the very shadow of the Church, white and black; here habits of shiftlessness took root, and sullen hopelessness replaced hopeful strife.

With the beginning of the abolition movement and the gradual growth of a class of free Negroes came a change. We often neglect the influence of the freedman before the war, because of the paucity of his numbers and the small weight he had in the history of the nation. But we must not forget that his chief influence was internal—was exerted on the black world, and that there he was the ethical and social leader. Huddled as he was in a few centers like Philadelphia, New York and New Orleans, his chief characteristic was intense earnestness and deep feeling on the slavery question. Freedom became to him a real thing and not a dream. His religion became darker and more intense, and into his ethics crept a note of revenge, into his songs a day of reckoning close at hand. The "Coming of the Lord" swept this side of Death, and came to be a thing to be hoped for in this day. Through fugitive slaves and irrepressible discussion this desire for freedom seized the black millions still in bondage, and became their one ideal of life. The black bards caught new notes, and sometimes even dared to sing:

> Before I'll be a slave
> I'll be buried in my grave,
> And go home to my Jesus
> And be saved.

For fifty years Negro religion thus transformed itself and identified itself with the dream of Abolition until that which was a radical fad in the White North and an anarchistic plot in the White South had become a religion to the Black world. Thus, when Emancipation finally came, it seemed to the freedman a literal Coming of the Lord. His fervid imagination was stirred, as never before, by the tramp of armies, the blood and dust of battle and the wail and whirl of

social upheaval. He stood dumb and motionless before the whirlwind—what had
he to do with it? Was it not the Lord's doing and marvelous in his eyes? Joyed
and bewildered with what came, he stood awaiting new wonders till the inevitable Age of Reaction swept over the nation and brought the crisis of today.

It is difficult to explain clearly the present critical stage of Negro religion.
First, we must remember that living as the blacks do in close contact with a great
modern nation and sharing, although imperfectly, the soul-life of that nation,
they must necessarily be affected more or less directly by all the religious and
ethical forces that are today moving the United States. These questions and
movements are, however, overshadowed and dwarfed by the all-important question (to them) of their civil, political and economic status. They must perpetually
discuss the "Negro Problem—live, move, and have their being in it, and inter-
pret all else in its light or darkness. With this come, too, peculiar problems of
their inner life, —of the status of women, the maintenance of Home, the training
of children, the accumulation of wealth and the prevention of crime. All this
must mean a time of intense ethical ferment, of religious heart-searching and
intellectual unrest. From the double life every American Negro must live, as a
Negro and as an American, as swept on by the current of the nineteenth while
yet struggling in the eddies of the fifteenth century,—from this must arise a
painful self-consciousness, an almost morbid sense of personality and a moral
hesitancy which is fatal to self-confidence. The worlds within and without the
Veil of Color are changing, and changing rapidly, but not at the same rate, not in
the same way; and this must produce a peculiar wrenching of the soul, a peculiar
sense of doubt and bewilderment. Such a double life, with double thoughts,
double duties and double social classes, must give rise to double words and
double ideals, and tempt the mind to pretense or to revolt, to hypocrisy or to
radicalism.

In some such doubtful words and phrases can one perhaps most clearly picture the peculiar ethical paradox that faces the Negro of today and is tingeing
and changing his religious life. Feeling that his rights and his dearest ideals are
being trampled upon, that the public conscience is even more deaf to his righ-
teous appeal, and that all the reactionary forces of prejudice, greed and revenge
are daily gaining new strength and fresh allies, the Negro faces no enviable dilemma. Conscious of his impotence, and pessimistic, he often becomes bitter
and vindictive, and his religion, instead of a worship, is a complaint and a curse,
a wail rather than a hope, a sneer rather than a faith. On the other hand, another
type of mind, shrewder and keener and more tortuous too, sees in the very
strength of the anti-Negro movement its patent weaknesses, and with Jesuitical[4]
casuistry is deterred by no ethical considerations in the endeavor to turn this
weakness to the black man's strength. Thus we have two great and hardly recon-
cilable streams of thought and ethical strivings; the danger of the one lies in
anarchy, that of the other in hypocrisy. The one type of Negro stands almost
ready to curse God and die, and the other is too often found a traitor to right and
a coward before force; the one is wedded to ideals remote, whimsical, perhaps

impossible of realization; the other forgets that life is more than meat and the body more than raiment. But, after all, is not all this simply the writhing of the age translated into black? The triumph of the Lie which today, with its false culture, faces the hideousness of the anarchist assassin?

Today the two groups of Negroes, the one in the North, the other in the South, represent these divergent ethical tendencies, the first tending toward radicalism, the other toward hypocritical compromise. It is no idle regret with which the white South mourns the loss of the old-time Negro—the frank, honest, simple old servant who stood for the earlier religious age of submission and humility. With all his laziness and lack of many elements of true manhood he was at least open-hearted, faithful and sincere. Today he is gone, but who is to blame for his going? Is it not those very persons who mourn for him? Is it not the tendency born of Reconstruction and Reaction to found a society on lawlessness and deception, to tamper with the moral fiber of a naturally honest and straightforward people until the whites threaten to become ungovernable tyrants and the blacks criminals and hypocrites? Deception is the natural defense of the weak against the strong, and the South used it for many years against its conquerors; today it must be prepared to see its black proletariat turn that same two-edged weapon against itself. And how natural this is! The death of Nat Turner and John Brown proved long since to the Negro the present hopelessness of physical defense. Political defense is becoming less and less available, and economic defense is still only partially effective. But there is a patent defense at hand,—the defense of deception and flattery, of cajoling and lying. It is the same defense which the Jews of the Middle Age used and which left its stamp on their character for centuries. Today the young Negro of the South who would succeed cannot be frank and outspoken, honest and self-assertive; but rather he is daily tempted to be silent and wary, politic and sly; he must flatter and be pleasant, endure petty insults with a smile, shut his eyes to wrong; in too many cases he sees positive personal advantage in deception and lying. His real thoughts, his real aspirations must be guarded in whispers; he must not criticize, he must not complain. Patience, humility and adroitness must, in these growing black youth, replace impulse, manliness and courage. With this sacrifice there is an economic opening, and perhaps peace and some prosperity. Without this there is riot, migration or crime. Nor is this situation peculiar to the southern United States—is it not rather the only method by which undeveloped races have gained the right to share modern culture? The price of culture is a Lie.

On the other hand, in the North the tendency is to emphasize the radicalism of the Negro. Driven from his birthright in the South by a situation at which every fiber of his more outspoken and assertive nature revolts, he finds himself in a land where he can scarcely earn a decent living amid the harsh competition and the color discrimination. At the same time, through schools and periodicals, discussions and lectures, he is intellectually quickened and awakened. The soul, long pent up and dwarfed, suddenly expanded in new-found freedom. What wonder that every tendency is to excess,—radical complaint, radical remedies, bitter denunciation or angry silence. Some sink, some rise. The criminal and the sensualist leave the church for the gambling hell and the bawdy-house, and fill the slums of Chicago and Baltimore; the better classes segregate themselves from the group-life of both white and black, and form an aristocracy, cultured but pessimistic, whose bitter criticism stings while it points out no way of escape. They despise the submission and subservience[5] of the Southern Negroes, but offer no other means by which a poor and oppressed minority can exist side by side with its masters. Feeling deeply and keenly the tendencies and opportunities of the age in which they live, their souls are bitter at the fate which drops the Veil between, and the very fact that this bitterness is natural and justifiable only serves to intensify it and make it more maddening.

Between the two extreme types of ethical attitude which I have thus sought to make clear, wavers the mass of the millions of Negroes North and South; and their religious life and activity partake of this social conflict within their ranks. Their churches are differentiating; now into groups of cold, fashionable devotees, in no way distinguishable from similar white groups save in color of skin; now into large social and business institutions catering to the desire for information and amusement of their members, warily avoiding unpleasant questions both within and without the black world and preaching in effect if not in word: *Dum vivimus, vivamus.*[6]

But, back of this, still brood silently the deep religious feeling of the real Negro heart, the stirring, unguided might of powerful human souls who have lost the guiding star of the past and are seeking in the great night a new religious ideal. Some day the Awakening will come, when the pent-up vigor of ten million souls shall sweep irresistibly toward the Goal, out of the Valley of the Shadow of Death, where all that makes life worth living—Liberty, Justice and Right —is marked "For White People Only."

Notes

1. *Editor's note*: This reading was also originally published in *New World* 9 (1900): 99-105. It appeared in the December issue and was later republished with minor modifications as "Of the Faith of the Fathers" in *The Souls of Black Folk* (1903). This essay was Du Bois' second sociological study of the Black Church.

2. *Editor's note*: The term, monogamic, may be equated with "monogamous."

3. *Editor's note*: The three types of church government are episcopal, presbyterian, and congregational. Episcopal government is hierarchical. Power flows through the organization in a top-down manner and lies with the priests or religious leaders. The presbyterian form of church government is based on the principle of shared governance. Clergy and a council of representative laity make decisions collectively. Each member has an equal vote with the congregational form of church government. Religious leaders and lay members have an equal vote within the decision-making process.

4. *Editor's note*: Du Bois employed the word, "Jesuitic," at this point in the text.

5.   *Editor's note*: "Subservience" is used to replace "subserviency" in the original text.

6.   *Editor's note*: This is a Latin phrase which may be translated, "while we live, let us live." See *"Dum vivimus vivamus."* http://www.merriamwebster.com/dictionary/dum20%vivamus20%vivamus. Du Bois was often critical of the Black Church's lack of involvement in addressing community needs. He believed that the Black Church could be an important agent of social uplift (Wortham 2010a, 2005; Du Bois and Dill [1914] 2010).

Reading 4

The Freedman's Bureau[1]

The problem of the twentieth century is the problem of the color line; the relation of the darker to the lighter races of men in Asia and Africa, in America and the islands of the sea. It was a phase of this problem that caused the Civil War; and however much they who marched south and north in 1861 may have fixed on the technical points of union and local autonomy as a shibboleth, all nevertheless knew, as we know, that the question of Negro slavery was the deeper cause of the conflict. Curious it was, too, how this deeper question ever forced itself to the surface, despite effort and disclaimer. No sooner had Northern armies touched Southern soil than this old question, newly guised, sprang from the earth,—What shall be done with slaves? Peremptory military commands, this way and that, could not answer the query; the Emancipation Proclamation seemed but to broaden and intensify the difficulties; and so at last there arose in the South a government of men caned the Freedmen's Bureau, which lasted, legally, from 1865 to 1872, but in a sense from 1861 to 1876, and which sought to settle the Negro problems in the United States of America.

It is the aim of this essay to study the Freedmen's Bureau,—the occasion of its rise, the character of its work, and its final success and failure,—not only as a part of American history, but above all as one of the most singular and interesting of the attempts made by a great nation to grapple with vast problems of race and social condition.

No sooner had the armies, east and west, penetrated Virginia and Tennessee than fugitive slaves appeared within their lines. They came at night, when the flickering camp fires of the blue hosts shone like vast unsteady stars along the black horizon: old men, and thin, with gray and tufted hair; women with frightened eyes, dragging whimpering, hungry children; men and girls, stalwart and gaunt,—a horde of starving vagabonds, homeless, helpless, and pitiable in their dark distress. Two methods of treating these newcomers seemed equally logical to opposite sorts of minds. Said some, "We have nothing to do with slaves." "Hereafter," commanded Halleck, "no slaves should be allowed to come into your lines at all; if any come without your knowledge, when owners call for them, deliver them." But others said, "We take grain and fowl; why not slaves?" Whereupon Fremont, as early as August, 1861, declared the slaves of Missouri rebels free. Such radical action was quickly countermanded, but at the same time

27

the opposite policy could not be enforced; some of the black refugees declared themselves freemen, others showed their masters had deserted them, and still others were captured with forts and plantations. Evidently, too, slaves were a source of strength to the Confederacy, and were being used as laborers and producers. "They constitute a military resource," wrote the Secretary of War, late in 1861; "and being such, that they should not be turned over to the enemy is too plain to discuss." So the tone of the army chiefs changed, Congress forbade the rendition of fugitives, and Butler's "contrabands" were welcomed as military laborers. This complicated rather than solved the problem; for now the scattering fugitives became a steady stream, which flowed faster as the armies marched.

Then the long-headed man, with care-chiseled face, who sat in the White House, saw the inevitable, and emancipated the slaves of rebels on New Year's, 1863. A month later Congress called earnestly for the Negro soldiers whom the act of July, 1862, had half grudgingly allowed to enlist. Thus the barriers were leveled, and the deed was done. The stream of fugitives swelled to a flood, and anxious officers kept inquiring: "What must be done with slaves arriving almost daily? Am I to find food and shelter for women and children?"

It was a Pierce of Boston who pointed out the way, and thus became in a sense the founder of the Freedmen's Bureau. Being specially detailed from the ranks to care for the freedmen at Fortress Monroe, he afterward founded the celebrated Port Royal experiment and started the Freedmen's Aid Societies. Thus, under the timid Treasury officials and bold army officers, Pierce's plan widened and developed. At first, the able-bodied men were enlisted as soldiers or hired as laborers, the women and children were herded into central camps under guard, and "superintendents of contrabands" multiplied here and there. Centers of massed freedmen arose at Fortress Monroe, VA., Washington, D.C., Beaufort and Port Royal, SC, New Orleans, LA., Vicksburg and Corinth, MS, Columbus, KY, Cairo, IL., and elsewhere, and the army chaplains found here new and fruitful fields.

Then came the Freedmen's Aid Societies, born of the touching appeals for relief and help from these centers of distress. There was the American Missionary Association, sprung from the Amistad, and now full grown for work, the various church organizations, the National Freedmen's Relief Association, the American Freedmen's Union, the Western Freedmen's Aid Commission,—in all fifty or more active organizations, which sent clothes, money, schoolbooks, and teachers southward. All they did was needed, for the destitution of the freedmen was often reported as "too appalling for belief," and the situation was growing daily worse rather than better.

And daily, too, it seemed more plain that this was no ordinary matter of temporary relief, but a national crisis; for here loomed a labor problem of vast dimensions. Masses of Negroes stood idle, or, if they worked spasmodically, were never sure of pay; and if perchance they received pay, squandered the new thing thoughtlessly. In these and in other ways were camp life and the new liberty demoralizing the freedmen. The broader economic organization thus clearly demanded sprang up here and there as accident and local conditions determined.

Here again Pierce's Port Royal plan of leased plantations and guided workmen pointed out the rough way. In Washington, the military governor, at the urgent appeal of the superintendent, opened confiscated estates to the cultivation of the fugitives, and there in the shadow of the dome gathered black farm villages. General Dix gave over estates to the freedmen of Fortress Monroe, and so on through the South. The government and the benevolent societies furnished the means of cultivation, and the Negro turned again slowly to work. The systems of control, thus started, rapidly grew, here and there, into strange little governments, like that of General Banks in Louisiana, with its 90,000 black subjects, its 50,000 guided laborers, and its annual budget of $100,000 and more. It made out 4,000 pay rolls, registered all freedmen, inquired into grievances and redressed them, laid and collected taxes, and established a system of public schools. So too Colonel Eaton, the superintendent of Tennessee and Arkansas, ruled over 100,000, leased and cultivated 7,000 acres of cotton land, and furnished food for 10,000 paupers. In South Carolina was General Saxton, with his deep interest in black folk. He succeeded Pierce and the Treasury officials, and sold forfeited estates, leased abandoned plantations, encouraged schools, and received from Sherman, after the terribly picturesque march to the sea, thousands of the wretched camp followers.

Three characteristic things one might have seen in Sherman's raid through Georgia, which threw the new situation in deep and shadowy relief: the Conqueror, the Conquered, and the Negro. Some see all significance in the grim front of the destroyer, and some in the bitter sufferers of the lost cause. But to me neither soldier nor fugitive speaks with so deep a meaning as that dark and human cloud that clung like remorse on the rear of those swift columns, swelling at times to half their size, almost engulfing and choking them. In vain were they ordered back, in vain were bridges hewn from beneath their feet; on they trudged and writhed and surged, until they rolled into Savannah, a starved and naked horde of tens of thousands. There too came the characteristic military remedy: "The islands from Charleston south, the abandoned rice fields along the rivers for thirty miles back from the sea, and the country bordering the St. John's River, Florida, are reserved and set apart for the settlement of Negroes now made free by act of war!" So read the celebrated field order.

All these experiments, orders, and systems were bound to attract and perplex the government and the nation. Directly after the Emancipation Proclamation, Representative Eliot had introduced a bill creating a Bureau of Emancipation, but it was never reported. The following June, a committee of inquiry, appointed by the Secretary of War, reported in favor of a temporary bureau for the "improvement, protection, and employment of refugee freedmen," on much the same lines as were afterward followed. Petitions came in to President Lincoln from distinguished citizens and organizations, strongly urging a comprehensive and unified plan of dealing with the freedmen, under a bureau which should be "charged with the study of plans and execution of measures for easily guiding, and in every way judiciously and humanely aiding, the passage of our emancipated and yet to be emancipated blacks from the old condition of forced labor to their new state of voluntary industry."

Some half-hearted steps were early taken by the government to put both freedmen and abandoned estates under the supervision of the Treasury officials. Laws of 1863 and 1864 directed them to take charge of and lease abandoned lands for periods not exceeding twelve months, and to "provide in such leases or otherwise for the employment and general welfare" of the freedmen. Most of the army officers looked upon this as a welcome relief from perplexing "Negro affairs;" but the Treasury hesitated and blundered, and although it leased large quantities of land and employed many Negroes, especially along the Mississippi, yet it left the virtual control of the laborers and their relations to their neighbors in the hands of the army.

In March, 1864, Congress at last turned its attention to the subject, and the House passed a bill, by a majority of two, establishing a Bureau for Freedmen in the War Department. Senator Sumner, who had charge of the bill in the Senate, argued that freedmen and abandoned lands ought to be under the same department, and reported a substitute for the House bill, attaching the Bureau to the Treasury Department. This bill passed, but too late for action in the House. The debates wandered over the whole policy of the administration and the general question of slavery, without touching very closely the specific merits of the measure in hand.

Meantime the election took place, and the administration, returning from the country with a vote of renewed confidence, addressed itself to the matter more seriously. A conference between the houses agreed upon a carefully drawn measure which contained the chief provisions of Charles Sumner's bill, but made the proposed organization a department independent of both the War and Treasury officials. The bill was conservative, giving the new department "general superintendence of all freedmen." It was to "establish regulations" for them, protect them, lease them lands, adjust their wages, and appear in civil and military courts as their "next friend." There were many limitations attached to the powers thus granted, and the organization was made permanent. Nevertheless, the Senate defeated the bill, and a new conference committee was appointed. This committee reported a new bill, February 28, which was whirled through just as the session closed, and which became the act of 1865 establishing in the War Department a "Bureau of Refugees, Freedmen, and Abandoned Lands."

This last compromise was a hasty bit of legislation, vague and uncertain in outline. A Bureau was created, "to continue during the present War of Rebellion, and for one year thereafter," to which was given "the supervision and management of all abandoned lands, and the control of all subjects relating to refugees and freedmen," under "such rules and regulations as may be presented by the head of the Bureau and approved by the President." A commissioner, appointed by the President and Senate, was to control the Bureau, with an office force not exceeding ten clerks. The President might also appoint assistant commissioners in the seceded states, and to all these offices military officials might be detailed at regular pay. The Secretary of War could issue rations, clothing, and fuel to the destitute, and all abandoned property was placed in the hands of the Bureau for eventual lease and sale to ex-slaves in forty-acre parcels.

Thus did the United States government definitely assume charge of the emancipated Negro as the ward of the nation. It was a tremendous undertaking. Here, at a stroke of the pen, was erected a government of millions of men,—and not ordinary men, either, but black men emasculated by a peculiarly complete system of slavery, centuries old; and now, suddenly, violently, they come into a new birthright, at a time of war and passion, in the midst of the stricken, embittered population of their former masters. Any man might well have hesitated to assume charge of such a work, with vast responsibilities, indefinite powers, and limited resources. Probably no one but a soldier would have answered such a call promptly; and indeed no one but a soldier could be called, for Congress had appropriated no money for salaries and expenses.

Less than a month after the weary emancipator passed to his rest, his successor assigned Major General Oliver O. Howard to duty as commissioner of the new Bureau. He was a Maine man, then only thirty-five years of age. He had marched with Sherman to the sea, had fought well at Gettysburg, and had but a year before been assigned to the command of the Department of Tennessee. An honest and sincere man, with rather too much faith in human nature, little aptitude for systematic business and intricate detail, he was nevertheless conservative, hard-working, and, above all, acquainted at first-hand with much of the work before him. And of that work it has been truly said, "No approximately correct history of civilization can ever be written which does not throw out in bold relief, as one of the great landmarks of political and social progress, the organization and administration of the Freedmen's Bureau."

On May 12, 1865, Howard was appointed, and he assumed the duties of his office promptly on the 15th, and began examining the field of work. A curious mess he looked upon: little despotisms, communistic experiments, slavery, peonage, business speculations, organized charity, unorganized almsgiving,—all reeling on under the guise of helping the freedman, and all enshrined in the smoke and blood of war and the cursing and silence of angry men. On May 19 the new government—for a government it really was—issued its constitution; commissioners were to be appointed in each of the seceded states, who were to take charge of "all subjects relating to refugees and freedmen," and all relief and rations were to be given by their consent alone. The Bureau invited continued cooperation with benevolent societies, and declared, "It will be the object of all commissioners to introduce practicable systems of compensated labor," and to establish schools. Forthwith nine assistant commissioners were appointed. They were to hasten to their fields of work; seek gradually to close relief establishments, and make the destitute self-supporting; act as courts of law where there were no courts, or where Negroes were not recognized in them as free; establish the institution of marriage among ex-slaves, and keep records; see that freedmen were free to choose their employers, and help in making fair contracts for them; and finally, the circular said, "Simple good faith, for which we hope on all hands for those concerned in the passing away of slavery, will especially relieve the assistant commissioners in the discharge of their duties toward the freedmen, as well as promote the general welfare."

No sooner was the work thus started, and the general system and local organization in some measure begun, than two grave difficulties appeared which changed largely the theory and outcome of Bureau work. First, there were the abandoned lands of the South. It had long been the more or less definitely expressed theory of the North that all the chief problems of emancipation might be settled by establishing the slaves on the forfeited lands of their masters,—a sort of poetic justice, said some. But this poetry done into solemn prose meant either wholesale confiscation of private property in the South, or vast appropriations. Now Congress had not appropriated a cent, and no sooner did the proclamations of general amnesty appear than the 800,000 acres of abandoned lands in the hands of the Freedmen's Bureau melted quickly away. The second difficulty lay in perfecting the local organization of the Bureau throughout the wide field of work. Making a new machine and sending out officials of duly ascertained fitness for a great work of social reform is no child's task; but this task was even harder, for a new central organization had to be fitted on a heterogeneous and confused but already existing system of relief and control of ex-slaves; and the agents available for this work must be sought for in an army still busy with war operations,—men in the very nature of the case ill fitted for delicate social work, —or among the questionable camp followers of an invading host. Thus, after a year's work, vigorously as it was pushed, the problem looked even more difficult to grasp and solve than at the beginning. Nevertheless, three things that year's work did, well worth the doing: it relieved a vast amount of physical suffering; it transported 7,000 fugitives from congested centers back to the farm; and, best of all, it inaugurated the crusade of the New England schoolma'am.

The annals of this Ninth Crusade are yet to be written, the tale of a mission that seemed to our age far more quixotic than the quest of St. Louis seemed to his. Behind the mists of ruin and rapine waved the calico dresses of women who dared, and after the hoarse mouthings of the field guns rang the rhythm of the alphabet. Rich and poor they were, serious and curious. Bereaved now of a father, now of a brother, now of more than these, they came seeking a life work in planting New England schoolhouses among the white and black of the South. They did their work well. In that first year they taught 100,000 souls, and more.

Evidently, Congress must soon legislate again on the hastily organized Bureau, which had so quickly grown into wide significance and vast possibilities. An institution such as that was well-nigh as difficult to end as to begin. Early in 1866 Congress took up the matter, when Senator Trumbull, of Illinois, introduced a bill to extend the Bureau and enlarge its powers. This measure received, at the hands of Congress, far more thorough discussion and attention than its predecessor. The war cloud had thinned enough to allow a clearer conception of the work of emancipation. The champions of the bill argued that the strengthening of the Freedmen's Bureau was still a military necessity; that it was needed for the proper carrying out of the Thirteenth Amendment, and was a work of sheer justice to the ex-slave, at a trifling cost to the government. The opponents of the measure declared that the war was over, and the necessity for war measures past; that the Bureau, by reason of its extraordinary powers, was clearly unconstitutional in time of peace, and was destined to irritate the South and pauperize the freedmen, at a final cost of possibly hundreds of millions. Two of these arguments were unanswered, and indeed unanswerable: the one that the extraordinary powers of the Bureau threatened the civil rights of all citizens; and the other that the government must have power to do what manifestly must be done, and that present abandonment of the freedmen meant their practical reenslavement. The bill which finally passed enlarged and made permanent the Freedmen's Bureau. It was promptly vetoed by President Johnson, as "unconstitutional," "unnecessary," and "extrajudicial," and failed of passage over the veto. Meantime, however, the breach between Congress and the President began to broaden, and a modified form of the lost bill was finally passed over the President's second veto, July 16.

The act of 1866 gave the Freedmen's Bureau its final form,—the form by which it will be known to posterity and judged of men. It extended the existence of the Bureau to July, 1868; it authorized additional assistant commissioners, the retention of army officers mustered out of regular service, the sale of certain forfeited lands to freedmen on nominal terms, the sale of Confederate public property for Negro schools, and a wider field of judicial interpretation and cognizance. The government of the unreconstructed South was thus put very largely in the hands of the Freedmen's Bureau, especially as in many cases the departmental military commander was now made also assistant commissioner. It was thus that the Freedmen's Bureau became a full-fledged government of men. It made laws, executed them and interpreted them; it laid and collected taxes, defined and punished crime, maintained and used military force, and dictated such measures as it thought necessary and proper for the accomplishment of its varied ends. Naturally, all these powers were not exercised continuously nor to their fullest extent; and yet, as General Howard has said, "scarcely any subject that has to be legislated upon in civil society failed, at one time or another, to demand the action or this singular Bureau."

To understand and criticize intelligently so vast a work, one must not forget an instant the drift of things in the later sixties: Lee had surrendered, Lincoln was dead, and Johnson and Congress were at loggerheads; the Thirteenth Amendment was adopted, the Fourteenth pending, and the Fifteenth declared in force in 1870. Guerrilla raiding, the ever present flickering after-flame of war, was spending its force against the Negroes, and all the Southern land was awakening as from some wild dream to poverty and social revolution. In a time of perfect calm, amid willing neighbors and streaming wealth, the social uplifting of 4,000,000 slaves to an assured and self-sustaining place in the body politic and economic would have been an herculean task; but when to the inherent difficulties of so delicate and nice a social operation were added the spite and hate of conflict, the Hell of War; when suspicion and cruelty were rife, and gaunt

Hunger wept beside Bereavement,—in such a case, the work of any instrument of social regeneration was in large part foredoomed to failure. The very name of the Bureau stood for a thing in the South which for two centuries and better men had refused even to argue,—that life amid free Negroes was simply unthinkable, the maddest of experiments. The agents which the Bureau could command varied all the way from unselfish philanthropists to narrow-minded busybodies and thieves; and even though it be true that the average was far better than the worst, it was the one fly that helped to spoil the ointment. Then, amid all this crouched the freed slave, bewildered between friend and foe. He had emerged from slavery: not the worst slavery in the world, not a slavery that made all life unbearable,—rather, a slavery that had here and there much of kindliness, fidelity, and happiness,—but withal slavery, which, so far as human aspiration and desert were concerned, classed the black man and the ox together. And the Negro knew full well that, whatever their deeper convictions may have been, Southern men had fought with desperate energy to perpetuate this slavery, under which the black masses, with half-articulate thought, had writhed and shivered. They welcomed freedom with a cry. They fled to the friends that had freed them. They shrank from the master who still strove for their chains. So the cleft between the white and black South grew. Idle to say it never should have been; it was as inevitable as its results were pitiable. Curiously incongruous elements were left arrayed against each other: the North, the government, the carpetbagger, and the slave, here; and there, all the South that was white, whether gentleman or vagabond, honest man or rascal, lawless murderer or martyr to duty.

Thus it is doubly difficult to write of this period calmly, so intense was the feeling, so mighty the human passions, that swayed and blinded men. Amid it all two figures ever stand to typify that day to coming men: the one a gray-haired gentleman, whose fathers had quit themselves like men, whose sons lay in nameless graves; who bowed to the evil of slavery because its abolition boded untold ill to all; who stood at last, in the evening of life, a blighted, ruined form, with hate in his eyes. And the other, a form hovering dark and mother-like, her awful face black with the mists of centuries, had aforetime bent in love over her white master's cradle, rocked his sons and daughters to sleep, and closed in death the sunken eyes of his wife to the world; ay, too, had laid herself low to his lust and borne a tawny man child to the world, only to see her dark boy's limbs scattered to the winds by midnight marauders riding after Damned Niggers. These were the saddest sights of that woeful day; and no man clasped the hands of these two passing figures of the present-past; but hating they went to their long home, and hating their children's children live today.

Here, then, was the field of work for the Freedmen's Bureau; and since, with some hesitation, it was continued by the act of 1868 till 1869, let us look upon four years of its work as a whole. There were, in 1868, 900 Bureau officials scattered from Washington to Texas, ruling, directly and indirectly, many millions of men. And the deeds of these rulers fall mainly under seven heads,— the relief of physical suffering, the overseeing of the beginnings of free labor, the buying and selling of land, the establishment of schools, the paying of bounties, the administration of justice, and the financiering of all these activities. Up to June, 1869, over half a million patients had been treated by Bureau physicians and surgeons, and sixty hospitals and asylums had been in operation. In fifty months of work 21,000,000 free rations were distributed at a cost of over $4,000,000, beginning at the rate of 30,000 rations a day in 1865, and discontinuing in 1869. Next came the difficult question of labor. First, 30,000 black men were transported from the refuges and relief stations back to the farms, back to the critical trial of a new way of working. Plain, simple instructions went out from Washington,—the freedom of laborers to choose employers, no fixed rates of wages, no peonage or forced labor. So far so good; but where local agents differed *toto coelo*[2] in capacity and character, where the personnel was continually changing, the outcome was varied. The largest element of success lay in the fact that the majority of the freedmen were willing, often eager, to work. So contracts were written,—50,000 in a single state,—laborers advised, wages guaranteed, and employers supplied. In truth, the organization became a vast labor bureau; not perfect, indeed,—notably defective here and there,—but on the whole, considering the situation, successful beyond the dreams of thoughtful men. The two great obstacles which confronted the officers at every turn were the tyrant and the idler: the slaveholder, who believed slavery was right, and was determined to perpetuate it under another name; and the freedman, who regarded freedom as perpetual rest. These were the Devil and the Deep Sea.

In the work of establishing the Negroes as peasant proprietors the Bureau was severely handicapped, as I have shown. Nevertheless, something was done. Abandoned lands were leased so long as they remained in the hands of the Bureau, and a total revenue of $400,000 derived front black tenants. Some other lands to which the nation had gained title were sold, and public lands were opened for the settlement of the few blacks who had tools and capital. The vision of landowning, however, the righteous and reasonable ambition for forty acres and a mule which filled the freedmen's dreams, was doomed in most cases to disappointment. And those men of marvelous hind-sight, who today are seeking to preach the Negro back to the soil, know well, or ought to know, that it was here, in 1865, that the finest opportunity of binding the black peasant to the soil was lost. Yet, with help and striving, the Negro gained some land, and by 1874, in the one state of Georgia, owned near 350,000 acres.

The greatest success of the Freedmen's Bureau lay in the planting of the free school among Negroes, and the idea of free elementary education among all classes in the South. It not only called the schoolmistresses through the benevolent agencies, and built them schoolhouses, but it helped discover and support such apostles of human development as Edmund Ware, Erastus Cravath, and Samuel Armstrong. State superintendents of education were appointed, and by 1870 150,000 children were in school. The opposition to Negro education was bitter in the South, for the South believed an educated Negro to be a dangerous Negro. And the South was not wholly wrong; for education among all kinds of men always has had, and always will have, an element of danger and revolution, of dissatisfaction and discontent. Nevertheless, men strive to know. It was some inkling of this paradox, even in the unquiet days of the Bureau, that allayed an opposition to human training, which still today lies smoldering, but not flaming. Fisk, Atlanta, Howard, and Hampton were founded in these days, and nearly $6,000,000 was expended in five years for educational work, $750,000 of which came from the freedmen themselves.

Such contributions, together with the buying of land and various other enterprises, showed that the ex-slave was handling some free capital already. The chief initial source of this was labor ill the army, and his pay and bounty as a soldier. Payments to Negro soldiers were at first complicated by the ignorance of the recipients, and the fact that the quotas of colored regiments from Northern states were largely filled by recruits from the South, unknown to their fellow soldiers. Consequently, payments were accompanied by such frauds that Congress, by joint resolution in 1867, put the whole matter in the hands of the Freedmen's Bureau. In two years $6,000,000 was thus distributed to 5,000 claimants, and in the end the sum exceeded $8,000,000. Even in this system fraud was frequent; but still the work put needed capital in the hands of practical paupers, and some, at least, was well spent.

The most perplexing and least successful part of the Bureau's work lay in the exercise of its judicial functions. In a distracted land where slavery had hardly fallen, to keep the strong from wanton abuse of the weak, and the weak from gloating insolently over the half-shorn strength of the strong, was a thankless, hopeless task. The former masters of the land were peremptorily ordered about, seized and imprisoned, and punished over and again, with scant courtesy from army officers. The former slaves were intimidated, beaten, raped, and butchered by angry and revengeful men. Bureau courts tended to become centers simply for punishing whites, while the regular civil courts tended to become solely institutions for perpetuating the slavery of blacks. Almost every law and method ingenuity could devise was employed by the legislatures to reduce the Negroes to serfdom,—to make them the slaves of the state, if not of individual owners; while the Bureau officials too often were found striving to put the "bottom rail on top," and give the freedmen a power and independence which they could not yet use. It is all well enough for us of another generation to wax wise with advice to those who bore the burden in the heat of the day. It is full easy now to see that the man who lost home, fortune, and family at a stroke, and saw his land ruled by "mules and niggers," was really benefited by the passing of slavery. It is not difficult now to say to the young freedman, cheated and cuffed about, who has seen his father's head beaten to a jelly and his own mother namelessly assaulted, that the meek shall inherit the earth. Above all, nothing is more convenient than to heap on the Freedmen's Bureau all the evils of that evil day, and damn it utterly for every mistake and blunder that was made. All this is easy, but it is neither sensible nor just. Someone had blundered, but that was long before Oliver Howard was born; there was criminal aggression and heedless neglect, but without some system of control there would have been far more than there was. Had that control been from within, the Negro would have been re-enslaved, to all intents and purposes. Coming as the control did from without, perfect men and methods would have bettered all things; and even with imperfect agents and questionable methods, the work accomplished was not undeserving of much commendation. The regular Bureau court consisted of one representative of the employer, one of the Negro, and one of the Bureau. If the Bureau could have maintained a perfectly judicial attitude, this arrangement would have been ideal, and must in time have gained confidence; but the nature of its other activities and the character of its personnel prejudiced the Bureau in favor of the black litigants, and led without doubt to much injustice and annoyance. On the other hand, to leave the Negro in the hands of Southern courts was impossible.

What the Freedmen's Bureau cost the nation is difficult to determine accurately. Its methods of bookkeeping were not good, and the whole system of its work and records partook of the hurry and turmoil of the time. General Howard himself disbursed some $15,000,000 during his incumbency; but this includes the bounties paid colored soldiers, which perhaps should not be counted as an expense of the Bureau. In bounties, prize money, and all other expenses, the Bureau disbursed over $20,000,000 before all of its departments were finally closed. To this ought to be added the large expenses of the various departments of Negro affairs before 1865; but these are hardly extricable from war expenditures, nor can we estimate with any accuracy the contributions of benevolent societies during all these years.

Such was the work of the Freedmen's Bureau. To sum it up in brief, we may say: it set going a system of free labor; it established the black peasant proprietor; it secured the recognition of black freemen before courts of law; it founded the free public school in the South. On the other hand, it failed to establish good will between ex-masters and freedmen; to guard its work wholly from paternalistic methods that discouraged self-reliance; to make Negroes landholders in any considerable numbers. Its successes were the result of hard work, supplemented by the aid of philanthropists and the eager striving of black men. Its failures were the result of bad local agents, inherent difficulties of the work, and national neglect. The Freedmen's Bureau expired by limitation in 1869, save its educational and bounty departments. The educational work came to an end in 1872, and General Howard's connection with the Bureau ceased at that time. The work of paying bounties was transferred to the adjutant general's office, where it was continued three or four years longer.

Such an institution, from its wide powers, great responsibilities, large control of moneys, and generally conspicuous position, was naturally open to repeated and bitter attacks. It sustained a searching congressional investigation at the instance of Fernando Wood in 1870. It was, with blunt discourtesy, transferred from Howard's control, in his absence, to the supervision of Secretary of War Belknap in 1872, on the Secretary's recommendation. Finally, in consequence of grave intimations of wrongdoing made by the Secretary and his subordinates, General Howard was court-martialed in 1874. In each of these trials,

and in other attacks, the commissioner of the Freedmen's Bureau was exone-
rated from any willful misdoing, and his work heartily commended. Nevertheless, many unpleasant things were brought to light: the methods of transacting
the business of the Bureau were faulty; several cases of defalcation among officials in the field were proven, and further frauds hinted at; there were some
business transactions which savored of dangerous speculation, if not dishonesty;
and, above all, the smirch of the Freedmen's Bank, which, while legally distinct
from, was morally and practically a part of the Bureau, will ever blacken the
record of this great institution. Not even ten additional years of slavery could
have done as much to throttle the thrift of the freedmen as the mismanagement
and bankruptcy of the savings bank chartered by the nation for their especial aid.
Yet it is but fair to say that the perfect honesty of purpose and unselfish devotion
of General Howard have passed untarnished through the fire of criticism. Not so
with all his subordinates, although in the case of the great majority of these there
were shown bravery and devotion to duty, even though sometimes linked to nar-
rowness and incompetency.

The most bitter attacks on the Freedmen's Bureau were aimed not so much
at its conduct or policy under the law as at the necessity for any such organization at all. Such attacks came naturally from the border states and the South, and
they were summed up by Senator Davis, of Kentucky, when he moved to entitle
the act of 1866 a bill "to promote strife and conflict between the white and black
races ... by a grant of unconstitutional power." The argument was of tremendous strength, but its very strength was its weakness. For, argued the plain common sense of the nation, if it is unconstitutional, unpractical,[3] and futile for the
nation to stand guardian over its helpless wards, then there is left but one alternative: to make those wards their own guardians by arming them with the ballot.
The alternative offered the nation then was not between full and restricted Negro
suffrage; else every sensible man, black and white, would easily have chosen the
latter. It was rather a choice between suffrage and slavery, after endless blood
and gold had flowed to sweep human bondage away. Not a single Southern legislature stood ready to admit a Negro, under any conditions, to the polls; not a
single Southern legislature believed free Negro labor was possible without a
system of restrictions that took all its freedom away; there was scarcely a white
man in the South who did not honestly regard emancipation as a crime, and its
practical nullification as a duty. In such a situation, the granting of the ballot to
the black man was a necessity, the very least a guilty nation could grant a
wronged race. Had the opposition to government guardianship of Negroes been
less bitter, and the attachment to the slave system less strong, the social seer can
well imagine a far better policy: a permanent Freedmen's Bureau, with a national system of Negro schools; a carefully supervised employment and labor office;
a system of impartial protection before the regular courts; and such institutions
for social betterment as savings banks, land and building associations, and social
settlements. All this vast expenditure of money and brains might have formed a
great school of prospective citizenship, and solved in a way we have not yet
solved the most perplexing and persistent of the Negro problems.

That such an institution was unthinkable in 1870 was due in part to certain acts of the Freedmen's Bureau itself. It came to regard its work as merely temporary, and Negro suffrage as a final answer to all present perplexities. The political ambition of many of its agents and protégés led it far afield into questionable activities, until the South, nursing its own deep prejudices, came easily to ignore all the good deeds of the Bureau, and hate its very name with perfect hatred. So the Freedmen's Bureau died, and its child was the Fifteenth Amendment.

The passing of a great human institution before its work is done, like the untimely passing of a single soul, but leaves a legacy of striving for other men. The legacy of the Freedmen's Bureau is the heavy heritage of this generation. Today, when new and vaster problems are destined to strain every fiber of the national mind and soul, would it not be well to count this legacy honestly and carefully? For this much all men know: despite compromise, struggle, war, and struggle, the Negro is not free. In the backwoods of the Gulf states, for miles and miles, he may not leave the plantation of his birth; in well-nigh the whole rural South the black farmers are peons, bound by law and custom to an economic slavery, from which the only escape is death or the penitentiary. In the most cultured sections and cities of the South the Negroes are a segregated servile caste, with restricted rights and privileges. Before the courts, both in law and custom, they stand on a different and peculiar basis. Taxation without representation is the rule of their political life. And the result of all this is, and in nature must have been, lawlessness and crime. That is the large legacy of the Freedmen's Bureau, the work it did not do because it could not.

I have seen a land right merry with the sun; where children sing, and rolling hills lie like passionate[4] women, wanton with harvest. And there in the King's Highway sat and sits a figure, veiled and bowed, by which the traveler's footsteps hasten as they go. On the tainted air broods fear. Three centuries' thought has been the raising and unveiling of that bowed human heart, and now, behold, my fellows, a century new for the duty and the deed. The problem of the twentieth century is the problem of the color line.

Notes

1.   *Editor's note*: This reading was originally published in *The Atlantic Monthly*, 87 (1901): 354-65. It appeared in the March issue and was later republished with minor modifications as "Of the Dawn of Freedom" in *The Souls of Black Folk* (1903). This essay was the third of four *The Atlantic Monthly* essays to be republished in *The Souls of Black Folk*.

2.   *Editor's note*: This is a Latin expression which may be translated "by the whole extent of the heavens." See "*Toto caelo*." http://www.merriam-webster.com/dictionary/toto20%coelo. It appears that Du Bois wanted to recognize that the local agents representing the Freedmen's Bureau differed significantly with respect to ability and character. Some agents were more effective than others.

3. *Editor's note*: Du Bois employed the word, unpracticable, in the original text.
4. *Editor's note*: The editor has replaced "passioned" with "passionate."

Reading 5

The Negro as He Really Is[1]

Out of the North the train thundered, and we woke to see the crimson soil of Georgia stretching away bare and monotonous right and left. Here and there lay straggling unlovely villages; but we did not nod and weary of the scene for this is historic ground. Right across our track De Soto wandered 360 years ago; here lies busy Atlanta, the City of the Poor White, and on to the southwest we passed into the land of Cherokees, the geographical center of the Negro Problems—the center of those 9,000,000 men who are the dark legacy of slavery. Georgia is not only thus in the middle of the black population of America, but in many other respects, this race question has focused itself here. No other state can count as many as 850,000 Negroes in its population, and no other state fought so long and strenuously to gather this host of Africans.

On we rode. The bare red clay and pines of North Georgia began to disappear, and in their place came rich rolling soil, here and there well tilled. Then the land and the people grew darker, cotton fields and dilapidated buildings appeared, and we entered the Black Belt.

Two hundred miles south of Atlanta, two hundred miles west of the Atlantic, and one hundred miles north of the great Gulf, lies Dougherty County. Its largest town, Albany, lies in the heart of the Black Belt, and is today a wide-stretched, placid, Southern town, with a broad street of stores and saloons flanked by rows of homes—whites usually to the north, and blacks to the south. Six days in the week the town looks decidedly too small for itself, and takes frequent and prolonged naps; but on Saturday suddenly the whole country disgorges itself upon this one spot, and a flood of black peasantry passes through the streets, fills the stores, blocks the sidewalks, chokes the thoroughfares, and takes full possession of the town. They are uncouth country folk, good-natured and simple, talkative to a degree, yet far more silent and brooding than the crowds of the Rhine-Pfalz, Naples, or Cracow. They drink a good deal of whiskey, but they do not get very drunk; they talk and laugh loudly at times, but they seldom quarrel or fight. They walk up and down the streets, meet and gossip with friends, stare at the shop-windows, buy coffee, cheap candy and clothes, and at dusk drive home happy.

41

Thus Albany is a real capital—a typical southern country town, the center
of the life of ten thousand souls; their point of contact with the outer world, their
center of news and gossip, their market for buying and selling, borrowing and
lending, their fountain of justice and law.[2]

We seldom study the condition of the Negro today honestly and carefully. It
is so much easier to assume that we know it all. And yet, how little we know of
these millions—of their daily lives and longings, of their homely joys and sor-
rows, of their real shortcomings and the meaning of their crimes.

Dougherty County, Georgia, had, in 1890, ten thousand black folks and two
thousand whites. Its growth in population[3] may thus be pictured:

**Table 5.1. Population of Dougherty County, GA
by Race: 1820-1899[4]**

Year	Race		Totals
	Negroes	Whites	
1820	225	551	776
1830	276	977	1,253
1840	1,779	2,447	4,226
1850	3,769	4,351	8,120
1860	6,088	2,207	8,295
1870	9,424	2,093	11,517
1880	10,670	1,952	12,622
1890	10,231	1,975	12,206
1899	9,000	-----	-----

This is the Cotton Kingdom, the shadow of a dream of lave empire which
for a generation intoxicated a people. Yonder is the heir of its ruins—a black
renter, fighting a failing battle with debt. A feeling of silent depression falls on
one as he gazes on this scarred and stricken land, with its silent mansions, deserted cabins and fallen fences. Here is a land rich in natural resources, yet poor;
for despite the fact that few industries pay better dividends than cotton manufac-
ture; despite the fact that the modern dry-goods store with its mass of cotton-
fabrics represents the high-water mark of retail store-keeping; despite all this,
the truth remains that half the cotton-growers of the South are nearly bankrupt
and the black laborer in the cotton fields is a serf.

The key-note of the Black Belt is debt. Not credit, in the commercial sense
of the term, but debt in the sense of continued inability to make income cover
expense. This is the direct heritage of the South from the wasteful economics of
the slave regime, but it was emphasized and brought to a crisis by the emancipation of the slaves. In 1860 Dougherty County had 6,079 slaves worth probably
$2,500,000; its farms were estimated at $2,995,923. Here was $5,500,000 of
property, the value of which depended largely on the slave system, and on the

speculative demand for land once marvelously rich, but already devitalized by careless and exhaustive culture. The war then meant a financial crash; in place of the $5,500,000 of 1860, there remained in 1870 only farms valued at $1,739,470. With this came increased competition in cotton culture from the rich lands of Texas, a steady fall in the price of cotton followed from about fourteen cents a pound in 1860[5] until it reached four cents in 1893. Such a financial revolution was it that involved the owners of the cotton belt in debt. And if things went ill with the master, how fared it with the man?

The plantations of Dougherty in slavery days were not so imposing and aristocratic as those of Virginia. The Big House was smaller and usually one-storied, and set very near the slave cabins.

The form and disposition of the laborers' cabins throughout the Black Belt, is today, the same as in slavery days. All are sprinkled in little groups over the face of the land centering about some dilapidated Big House where the head tenant or agent lives. There were reported in the county outside the corporate town of Albany 1,424 Negro families in 1899. Out of all these only a single one occupied a house of seven rooms; only fourteen have five rooms or more. The mass live in one and two room homes.

The size and arrangements of a people's homes are a fair index to their condition. All over the face of the land is the one-room cabin; now standing in the shadow of the Big House, now staring at the dusty road, now rising dark and somber amid the green of the cotton fields. It is nearly always old and bare, built of rough boards and neither plastered nor sealed. Light and ventilation are supplied by the single door and the square hole in the wall with its wooden shutter. Within is a fire-place, black and smoky, and usually unsteady with age. A bed or two, a table, a wooden chest and a few chairs make up the furniture, while a stray show-bill or a newspaper decorate the walls.

We have come to associate crowding with homes in cities almost exclusively. Here in Dougherty County, in the open country, is crowding enough. The rooms in these cabins are seldom over twenty or twenty-five feet square, and frequently smaller; yet one family of eleven lives, eats and sleeps in one room, while thirty families of eight or more members live in such one-room dwellings.

To sum up, there are among these Negroes over twenty-five persons for every ten rooms of house accommodation. In the worst tenement abominations of New York and Boston there are in no case over twenty-two persons to each ten rooms, and usually not over ten. Of course, one small, close room in a city, without a yard, is in many respects worse than the larger single country room.

The one decided advantage the Negro has is a place to live outside his home —that is the open fields, where most of his life is spent.

Ninety-four percent of these homes are rented and the question therefore arises, what in the industrial system of the Black Belt is responsible for these wretched tenements? There would seem to be four main causes. First, long custom, born in the time of slavery, has assigned this sort of a home to Negroes, until land owners seldom think of offering better houses. Should white labor be imported here, or the capital here invested be transferred to industries where whites are employed, the owners would not hesitate to erect cozy, decent homes, such as are often found near the new cotton factories. This explains why the substitution of white for black labor is often profitable—the laborer is far better paid and cared for. In the second place, the low standard of living among slaves is naturally inherited among freedmen and their sons; the mass of them do not demand better houses because they do not know what better houses are. Thirdly, the landlords as a class have not yet come to realize that it is a good business investment to raise the standard of living among laborers by slow and judicious methods; that a Negro laborer who demands three rooms and fifty cents a day would give far more efficient work and leave a larger profit than a discouraged toiler herding his family in one room and working for thirty cents. Lastly, among such conditions of life there are few incentives to make the laborer become a better farmer. If he is ambitious, he moves to town or tries other kinds of labor; as a tenant farmer his outlook is almost hopeless, and following it as a makeshift he takes the house that is given him without protest.

That we may see more fully the working out of these social forces, let us turn from the home to the family that lives in it. The Negroes in this country are noticeable both for large and small families; nearly a tenth of all the families are families of one—that is, lone persons living by themselves. Then, too, there is an unusual number of families of ten or more. The average family is not large, however, owing to the system of labor and the size of the homes, which tends to the separation of family groups. Then the large and continuous migration of young people to town brings down the average. So that one finds many families with hosts of babies, and many newly-married young couples, but comparatively few families with half-grown and grown children.

The families of one are interesting. Some of them—about a fifth—are old people. Away down at the edge of the woods will live some old grizzle-haired black man, digging wearily in the earth for his last bread. Or yonder, near some prosperous Negro farmer, will sit alone a swarthy auntie, fat and good-humored, supported half in charity and half by odd jobs.

Probably the size of Negro families is decreasing, and that, too, from postponement of marriage, rather than from immorality or loss of physical stamina. Today in this county only two percent of the boys and sixteen percent of the girls under twenty are married. Most of the young men marry between the ages of twenty-five and thirty-five, and the girls between twenty and thirty—an advanced age for a rural people of low average culture.

The cause of this is without doubt economic stress—the difficulty of earning sufficient to rear a family. The result is the breaking of the marriage tie and sexual looseness.

The number of separated persons is thirty-five per 1,000—a very large number. It would of course be unfair to compare this number with divorce statistics for many of these separated are in reality widowed, were the truth known, and in other cases the separation is not permanent. Nevertheless here lies the seat of greatest moral danger; there is little or no prostitution among these Negroes, and over four-fifths of the families, after house to house investigation, deserve to be classed as decent people with considerable regard for female chastity. The plague-spot in sexual relations is easy marriage and easy separation. This is no sudden development, nor the fruit of emancipation. It is a plain heritage from slavery. In those days Sam, with his master's consent, "took up" with Mary. No ceremony was necessary, and in the busy life of great plantations of the Black Belt, it was usually dispensed with. If now the master needed Sam's work on another plantation or in another part of the same plantation, or if he took a notion to sell the slave, Sam's married life with Mary was usually unceremoniously broken, and then it was clearly to the master's interest to have both of them take new mates. This wide-spread custom of two centuries has not been eradicated in thirty years. Probably seventy-five percent of the marriages now are performed by the pastors. Nevertheless, the evil is still deep seated and only a general raising of the standard of living will finally cure it.

The ignorance of the ex-slaves is far deeper than crude estimates indicate. It is ignorance of the world and its meaning, of modern economic organization, of the function of government, of individual worth and possibility—indeed, of all those things as to which it was for the interest of the slave system to keep the laboring class in profound darkness. Those very things then which a white boy absorbs from his earliest social atmosphere—starts with, so to speak, are the puzzling problems of the black boy's mature years. And this, too, not by reason of dullness but for lack of opportunity.

It is hard for an individual mind to grasp and comprehend the real social condition of a mass of human beings without losing itself in details and forgetting that after all each unit studied is a throbbing soul. Ignorant it may be, and poverty-stricken, black and curious in limb and ways and thought; and yet it loves and hates, it toils and tires, it laughs and weeps its bitter tears, and looks in vague and awful longing at the grim horizon of its life—all this, even as you and I. These black thousands are not lazy; they are improvident and careless, they insist on breaking the monotony of toil with a glimpse at the great town-world on Saturday, they have their loafers and ne'er-do-wells, but the great mass of them work continuously and faithfully for a return and under circumstances that would call forth equal voluntary effort from few, if any, other modern laboring class. Over 88 percent of them, men, women and children, are farmers. The rest are laborers on railroads, in the turpentine forests and elsewhere, teamsters and porters, artisans and servants. There are ten merchants, four teachers, and twenty-one who preach and farm.

Most of the children get their schooling after the "crops are laid by" and very few there are that stay in school after the spring work has commenced.

Child-labor is found here in some of its worst phases, as fostering ignorance and stunting physical development.

Among this people there is no leisure class; 96 percent of them are toiling—no one with leisure to turn the bare and cheerless cabin into a home, no old folks to sit beside the fire and hand down traditions of the past, little of careless, happy childhood and dreaming youth. The dull monotony of daily life is broken only by the Saturday trips to town.

The land is still fertile, despite long abuse. For nine and ten months in succession the crops will come if asked; garden vegetables in April, grain in May, melons in June and July, hay in August, sweet potatoes in September, and cotton from then to Christmas. And yet over two-thirds of the land there is but one crop and that leaves the toilers in debt. Why is this?

The merchant of the Black Belt is a curious institution—part banker, part landlord, part contractor, and part despot. His store which used most frequently to stand at the crossroads and become the center of a weekly village, has now moved to town and thither the Negro tenant follows him. The merchant keeps everything—clothes and shoes, coffee and sugar, pork and meal, canned and dried goods, wagons and plows, seed and fertilizer—and what he has not in stock, he can give you an order for at the store across the way. Here, then, comes the tenant, Sam Scott, after he has contracted with some absent landlord's agent for hiring forty acres of land; he fingers his hat nervously until the merchant finishes his morning chat with Colonel Sanders, when he calls out "Well, Sam, what do you want?" Sam wants him to "furnish" him—i.e., to advance him food and clothing for the year, and perhaps seed and tools, until his crop is raised and sold. If Sam seems a favorable subject, he and the merchant go to a lawyer and Sam executes a chattel mortgage on his mule and wagon in return for seed and a week's rations. As soon as the green cotton leaves appear above the ground another mortgage is given on the "crop." Every Saturday or at longer intervals Sam calls upon the merchant for his "rations;" a family of five usually gets about thirty pounds of fat side-pork and a couple of bushels of corn-meal a month. Beside this, clothing and shoes must be furnished; if Sam or his family is sick there are orders on the druggist and doctor; if the mule wants shoeing, an order on the blacksmith, etc. If Sam is a hard worker and crops promise well, he is often encouraged to buy more—sugar, extra clothes, perhaps a buggy. But he is seldom encouraged to save. When cotton rose to ten cents last fall the shrewd merchants sold a thousand buggies in one season, mostly to black men.

The security offered for such transactions—a crop and chattel mortgage—may at first seem slight. And indeed, the merchants tell many a true tale of shiftlessness and cheating; of cotton picked at night, mules disappearing and tenants absconding. But on the whole the merchant of the Black Belt is the most prosperous man in the section. So skillfully and so closely has he drawn the bonds of the law about the tenant that the black man has often simply to choose between pauperism and crime; he "waives" all homestead exemptions in his contract; he cannot touch his own mortgaged crop, which the laws put almost in the full control of the landowner and of the merchant. When the crop is growing, the merchant watches it like a hawk; as soon as it is ready for market, he takes possession of it, sells it, pays the landowner his rent, subtracts his bill for supplies and if, as sometimes happens, there is anything left he hands it over to the black serf for his Christmas celebration.

The direct result of this system is an all-cotton scheme of agriculture and the continued bankruptcy of the tenant. The currency of the Black Belt is cotton. It is a crop always salable for ready money, not usually subject to great yearly fluctuations in price, and one which the Negroes know how to raise. The landlord therefore demands his rent in cotton, and the merchant will accept mortgages on no other crop. There is no use asking the black tenant then to diversify his crops—he cannot under this system. Moreover, the system is bound to bankrupt the tenant. I remember once meeting a little one-mule wagon on the River road. A young black fellow sat in it driving listlessly, his elbows on his knees. His dark-faced wife sat beside him stolid, silent.

"Hello!" cried my driver—he has a most impudent way of addressing these people, though they seem used to it—"what have you got there?"

"Meat and meal," answered the man, stopping. The meat lay uncovered in the bottom of the wagon, a great thin side of fat pork covered with salt; the meal was in a white bushel bag.

"What did you pay for that meat?"

"Ten cents a pound." It could have been bought for six or seven cents cash.

"And the meal?"

"Two dollars." One dollar and ten cents is the cash price in town. So here was a man paying $5 for goods which he could have bought for $3 cash, and raised for $1 or $1.50.

Yet it is not wholly his fault. The Negro farmer started behind—started in debt. This was not his choosing, but the crime of this happy-go-lucky nation which goes blundering along with its Reconstruction tragedies, its Spanish War interludes and Philippine matinees, just as though God really were dead. Once in debt it is no easy matter for a whole race to emerge.

The other underlying causes of this situation are complicated but discernible. And one of the chief, outside the carelessness of the nation in letting the slave start with nothing, is the wide-spread opinion among the merchants and employers of the Black Belt that only by the slavery of debt can the Negro be kept at work. Behind this honest and widespread opinion, dishonesty and cheating of the ignorant laborers have a good chance to take refuge.[6] And to all this must be added the obvious fact that a slave ancestry and a system of unrequited toil have not improved the efficiency or temper of the mass of black laborers. Nor is this peculiar to Sambo—it has in history been just as true of John and Hans, of Jacques and Pat, of all ground-down peasantries. Such is the situation of the mass of the Negroes in the Black Belt today, and they are thinking about

it. Crime and a cheap, dangerous socialism are the inevitable results of this pon-
dering. I see now that ragged black man sitting on a log, aimlessly whittling a
stick. He mutters to me with the murmur of many ages when he says: "White
man sit down whole year; Nigger work day and night and make crop; Nigger
hardly gits bread and meat; white man sittin' down gits all. It's wrong."

A modern laboring class in most lands would find a remedy for this situation in migration. And so does the Negro, but his movement is restricted in
many ways.

In considerable parts of all the Gulf States, and especially in Mississippi,
Louisiana and Arkansas, the Negroes on the plantations in the back country districts are still held at forced labor practically without wages. Especially is this
true in districts where the farmers are composed of the more ignorant class of
poor whites, and the Negroes are beyond the reach of schools and intercourse
with their advancing fellows. If such a peon should run away, the sheriff, elected
by white suffrage, can usually be depended on to catch the fugitive, return him
and ask no questions. If he escape to another county, a charge of petty thieving,
easily true, can be depended on to secure his return. Even if some unduly offi-
cious person insists upon a trial, neighborly comity will probably make his conviction sure, and then the labor due the county can easily be bought by the master.

Such a system is unusual in the more civilized parts of the South, or near
the large towns and cities; but in those vast stretches of land beyond the tele-
graph and newspaper, the spirit of the Fourteenth Amendment is sadly broken.[7]
This represents the lowest economic depths of the black American peasant, and
in a study of the rise and condition of the Negro freeholder, we must trace his
economic progress from this modern serfdom.

Even in the better ordered country districts of the South the free movement
of agricultural laborers is hindered by the migration agent laws. The Associated
Press informed the world not long since of the arrest of a young white man in
south Georgia who represented the "Atlantic Naval Supplies Company," and
who "was caught in the act of enticing hands from the turpentine farm of Mr.
John Greer." The crime for which this young man was arrested is taxed $500 for
each county in which the employment agent proposes to gather laborers for
work outside the state. Thus the Negroes' ignorance of the labor market outside
his own vicinity is increased rather than diminished by the laws of nearly every
southern state.

Similar to such measures is the unwritten law of the back districts and small
towns of the South, that the character of all Negroes unknown to the mass of the
community must be vouched for by some white man. This is really a revival of
the old Roman idea of the patron under whose protection the new-made freedman was put. In many instances this system has been of great good to the Negro,
and very often, under the protection and guidance of the former master's family
or other white friends, the freedman progressed in wealth and morality. But the

same system has in other cases resulted in the refusal of whole communities to recognize the right of a Negro to change his habitation and to be master of his own fortunes. A black stranger in Baker County, Georgia, for instance is liable to be stopped anywhere on the public highway and made to state his business to the satisfaction of any white interrogator. If he fails to give a suitable answer or seems too independent or "sassy" he may be arrested or summarily driven away.

As a result of such a situation arose, first, the Black Belt and, second, the Migration to Town. The Black Belt was not, as many assumed, a movement towards fields of labor under more genial climatic conditions; it was primarily a huddling together for self-protection; a massing of the black population for mutual defense in order to secure the peace and tranquility necessary to economic advance. This movement took place between emancipation and 1880 and only partially accomplished the desired results. The rush to town since 1880 is the counter movement of men disappointed in the economic opportunities of the Black Belt.

In Dougherty County, Georgia, one can see easily the results of this experiment in huddling for protection. Only ten percent of the adult population was born in the county, and yet the blacks outnumber the whites four or five to one. There is undoubtedly a security to the blacks in their very numbers—a personal freedom from arbitrary treatment, which makes hundreds of laborers cling to Dougherty in spite of low wages and economic distress. But a change is coming, and slowly but surely even here the agricultural laborers are drifting to town and leaving the broad acres behind. Why is this? Why do not the Negroes become landowners and build up the black landed peasantry, which has for a generation and more been the dream of philanthropist and statesman?

This is the question which this paper seeks to answer; it seeks to trace the rise of the black freeholder in one county of Georgia's Black Belt, and his struggle for survival, to picture present conditions and show why migration to town is the Negro's remedy. To the car-window sociologist, to the man who seeks to understand and know the South by devoting the few leisure hours of a holiday trip to unraveling the snarl of centuries—to such men very often the whole trouble with the black field-hand may be summed up by Aunt Ophelia's word: "Shiftless!" And yet they are not lazy, these men; they work hard when they do work, and they work willingly. They have no sordid selfish money-getting ways but rather a fine disdain for mere cash. They'll loaf before your face and work behind your back with good-natured honesty. Their great defect as laborers lies in their lack of incentive to work beyond the mere pleasure of physical exertion. They are careless because they have not found that it pays to be careful; they are improvident because the improvident ones of their acquaintance get on about as well as the provident. Above all they cannot see why they should take unusual pains to make the white man's land better or to take more care of his mule and corn.

On the other hand the white land-owner argues that any attempt to improve these laborers by increased responsibility or higher wages or better homes or land of their own would be sure to result in failure. He shows his Northern visitor the scarred land; the ruined mansions, the worn-out soil and mortgaged acres and says, "This is Negro freedom!"

Now it happens that both master and man have just enough argument on their respective sides to make it difficult for them to understand each other. The Negro dimly personifies in the white man all his ills and misfortunes; if he is poor it is because the white man secures the fruits of his toil; if he is ignorant it is because the white man gives him neither time nor facilities to learn. And, indeed, if any misfortune happens to him, it is because of some hidden machinations of "white folks." On the other hand, the masters and the masters' sons have never been able to see why the Negroes, instead of settling down to be day laborers for bread and clothes, are infected with a silly desire to "rise" in the world, and are sulky, dissatisfied and careless where their fathers were happy and dumb and faithful. "Why! these niggers have an easier time than I do," said a puzzled Albany merchant to his black customer. "Yes," he replied, "and so does yo' hogs."

Looking now at the county black population as a whole, we might attempt to divide it roughly into social classes. Forty-four families, all landowners, from their intelligence, property and home life would correspond to good middle class people anywhere. Seventy-six other families are honest working people of fair intelligence. One hundred and twenty-five families fall distinctly below the line of respectability and should be classed with the lewd, vicious and potentially criminal. This leaves the mass of the population, 1,229 families composed of the poor, the ignorant, the plodding toilers and shiftless workers—honest and well-meaning, with some, but not great, sexual looseness, handicapped by their history and present economic condition.

The class lines are by no means fixed and immutable. A bad harvest may ruin many of the best and increase the numbers of the worst.

The croppers are entirely without capital, even in the limited sense of food or money, to keep them from seed-time to harvest. All they furnish then is labor; the landowner furnishes land, stock, tools, seed and house, and at the end of the year the laborer gets from a third to a half of the crop. Out of his share, however, comes payment and interest for food and clothing advanced him during the year. Thus we have a laborer without capital and without wages, and an employer whose capital is largely his employees' wages. It is an unsatisfactory arrangement both to hirer and hired, and is usually in vogue on poor land with hard-pressed owners.

Above the croppers come the great mass of the black population who work the land on their own responsibility, paying rent in cotton and supported by the crop mortgage system. After the war this system was attractive to the freedmen on account of its larger freedom and its possibilities for making a surplus. But with the carrying out of the crop-lien system, the deterioration of the land and the slavery of debt, the position of the metayers has sunk to a dead level of practically unrewarded toil. Formerly all tenants had some capital, and often considerable, but absentee landlordism, rack-rent and falling cotton, have stripped them well nigh of all, and probably not over half of them in 1898 owned mules. The change from cropper to tenant was accomplished by fixing the rent. If, now, the rent fixed was reasonable, this was an incentive to the tenant to strive. On the other hand, if the rent was too high, or if the land deteriorated, the result was to discourage and check the efforts of the black peasantry. There is no doubt that the latter case is true; thus in Dougherty County every economic advantage of the price of cotton in the market and of the strivings of the tenant, has been taken advantage of by the landlords and merchants, and swallowed up in rent and interest. If cotton rose in price, the rent rose even higher. If cotton fell the rent remained, or followed reluctantly. If a tenant worked hard and raised a large crop, his rent was raised the next year. If that year the crop failed, his corn was confiscated and his mule sold for debt. There were, of course, exceptions to this —cases of personal kindness and forbearance, but in the vast majority of cases the rule was to extract the uttermost farthing from the mass of the black farm laborers.

The result of such rack-rent can only be evil—abuse and neglect of the soil, deterioration in the character of the laborers, and a widespread sense of injustice. On this low plane half the black population of Dougherty County—perhaps more than half the black millions of this land—are today struggling.

A degree above these we may place those laborers who receive money for their work. Some receive a house with perhaps a garden spot, their supplies of food and clothing advanced and certain fixed wages at the end of the year varying from $30 to $60, out of which the supplies must be paid for with interest. About 18 percent of the population belongs to this class of semi-metayers, while 22 percent are laborers paid by the month or year and either "furnished" by their own savings or perhaps more usually by some merchant who takes his chances of payment. Such laborers receive 35 cents to 40 cents a day during the working season. They are usually young unmarried persons, some being women, and when they marry they sink to the class of metayers, or, more seldom, become renters.

The renters for fixed money rentals are the first of the emerging classes and form 4.6 percent of the families. The sole advantage of this small class is their freedom to choose their crops, and the increased responsibility which comes through having money transactions. While some of the renters differ little in condition from the metayers, yet on the whole they are more intelligent and responsible persons and are the ones who eventually become landowners.

Landholding in this county by Negroes has steadily increased. They held nothing in 1870, but in 1880 they had 2,500 acres. By 1890 this had increased to 10,000 acres, and to 15,000 acres in 1898, owned by 81 families. Of the 185

Negro families who at one time or another have held land in this county during the last thirty years, 1 held his land 25 to 30 years; 4 held their land 20–25 years; 12 held their land 15–20 years; 12 held their land 10–15 years; 41 held their land 5–10 years, and 115 held their land 1–5 years. Most of those in the shorter period still hold their land, so that the record is not complete.

If all the black landowners who had ever held land here had kept it or left it in the hands of black men, the Negroes would have owned nearer 30,000 acres than the 15,000 they now hold. And yet these 15,000 acres are a creditable showing—a proof of no little weight of the worth and ability of the Negro people. If they had been given an economic start at emancipation, if they had been in an enlightened and rich community which really desired their best good, then we might perhaps call such a result small or even insignificant. But for a few thousand ignorant field hands in the face of poverty, a falling market, and social stress to save and capitalize $200,000 in a generation has meant a tremendous effort. The rise of a nation, the pressing forward of a social class, means a bitter struggle—a hard and soul-sickening battle with the world such as few of the more favored classes know or appreciate.

Out of the hard economic conditions of this portion of the Black Belt, only six percent of the population has succeeded in emerging into peasant-proprietorship, and these are not all firmly fixed, but grow and shrink in number with the wavering of the cotton market. Fully 94 percent have struggled for land and failed, and half of them sit in hopeless serfdom. For these there is one other avenue of escape toward which they have turned in increasing numbers, namely, migration to town. A glance at the distribution of land among the black owners curiously reveals this fact. In 1898 the holdings were as follows: Under 40 acres, 49 families; 40 to 250 acres, 17 families; 250 to 1,000 acres, 13 families; 1,000 or more acres, 2 families. Now in 1890 there were forty-four holdings, but only nine of these were under forty acres. The great increase of holdings then has come in the buying of small homesteads near town, where their owners really share in the town life. This then is a part of the rush to town. And for every landowner who has thus hurried away from the narrow life and hard conditions of country life how many field hands, how many tenants, how many ruined renters have joined that long procession? Is it not strange compensation? The sin of the country districts is visited on the town, and the social sores of city life today may, here in Dougherty County and perhaps in many places, near and far, look for their final healing without the city walls.

Notes

1. *Editor's Note*: This essay was originally published in *The World's Work*, 2 (1901): 848-866. The sub-title of the essay is "A Definitive Study of One Locality in Georgia Showing the Exact Conditions of Every Negro Family—Their Economic Sta-

tus—Their Ownership of Land—Their Morals— Their Family Life—The Houses They Line In and the Results of the Mortgage System." This essay provided the basis for "Of the Black Belt" and "Of the Quest of the Golden Fleece" in *The Souls of Black Folk* (1903). The statistical table, the map, and the photographic essay which appeared in the original essay were removed when the material was edited for *The Souls of Black Folk*.

    2.   *Editor's Note*: The material from the beginning of the original essay through this sentence formed the introduction to "Of the Black Belt" in *The Souls of Black Folk*. The remainder of "Of the Black Belt" was based on new material. The information beginning with the next paragraph in "The Negro as He Really Is" to the end of the essay became part of "Of the Quest of the Golden Fleece."

    3.   The boundaries of the county have frequently changed. It was a part of Early County first, then of Baker, and finally was laid out as Dougherty in 1853.

    4.   *Editor's Note*: The title for this table has been supplied by the editor.

    5.   Omitting famine prices during the war.

    6.   *Editor's Note*: At this point in the article, Du Bois provided a map portraying the distribution of the Negro population of the United States. The density of the Negro population per state was provided in a black-grey-white shaded format. The legend identified the number of African Americans to every 100,000 whites. The categories identified were: over 100,000; 50,000 to 100,000; 10,000 to 50,000; 1,000 to 10,000; and less than 1,000. Mississippi, Louisiana and South Carolina were identified as states having over 100,000 African Americans for every 100,000 whites. States having 50,000–100,000 African American population to every 100,000 whites included Alabama, Georgia, Florida, North Carolina, and Virginia. Since the article was published in 1901 and since the population data for Dougherty County by race ended with the 1890 data (see Table 5.1), it is assumed that the map was based on 1890 census data. Du Bois did not provide a date or a source for the data.

    7.   *Editor's Note*: The Fourteenth Amendment was ratified on July 9, 1868. This was during the early stages of Reconstruction. The amendment guaranteed citizenship status for African Americans and limited an individual state's power to limit or deny citizenship. This provision was addressed in the first section of the amendment. The complete text is stated below.

All persons born or naturalized in the United States, and subject to the jurisdiction thereof, are citizens of the United States and of the state wherein they reside. No state shall make or enforce any law which shall abridge the privileges or immunities of citizens of the United States; nor shall any state deprive any person of life, liberty, or property, without due process of law; nor deny to any person within its jurisdiction the equal protection of the laws.

See "Fourteenth Amendment to the United States Constitution." http://en.wikipedia.org/wiki/Fourteenth_Amendment_to_the_United_States_Constitution.

Reading 6

The Evolution of Negro Leadership[1,2]

In every generation of our national life, from Phillis Wheatley to Booker Washington, the Negro race in America has succeeded in bringing forth men whom the country, at times spontaneously, at times in spite of itself, has been impelled to honor and respect. Mr. Washington is one of the most striking of these cases, and his autobiography is a partial history of the steps which made him a group leader, and the one man who in the eyes of the nation typifies at present more nearly than all others the work and worth of his nine million fellows.

The way in which groups of human beings are led to choose certain of their number as their spokesmen and leaders is at once the most elementary and the nicest problem of social growth. History is but the record of this group leadership; and yet how infinitely changeful is its type and history! And of all types and kinds, what can be more instructive than the leadership of a group within a group—that curious double movement where real progress may be negative and actual advance be relative retrogression? All this is the social student's inspiration and despair.

When sticks and stones and beasts form the sole environment of a people, their attitude is ever one of determined opposition to, and conquest of, natural forces. But when to earth and brute is added an environment of men and ideas, then the attitude of the imprisoned group may take three main forms: a feeling of revolt and revenge; an attempt to adjust all thought and action to the will of the greater group; or, finally, a determined attempt at self-development, self-realization, in spite of environing discouragements and prejudice. The influence of all three of these attitudes is plainly to be traced in the evolution of race leaders among American negroes. Before 1750 there was but the one motive of revolt and revenge which animated the terrible Maroons and veiled all the Americas in fear of insurrection. But the liberalizing tendencies of the latter half of the eighteenth century brought the first thought of adjustment and assimilation in the crude and earnest songs of Phillis and the martyrdom of Attucks and Salem.

The cotton-gin changed all this, and men then, as the Lyman Abbotts of to-day, found a new meaning in human blackness. A season of hesitation and stress settled on the black world as the hope of emancipation receded. Forten and the free Negroes of the North still hoped for eventual assimilation with the nation;

Allen, the founder of the great African Methodist Church, strove for unbending self-development, and the Southern freedmen followed him; while among the black slaves at the South arose the avenging Nat Turner, fired by the memory of Toussaint the Savior. So far, Negro leadership had been local and spasmodic; but now, about 1840, arose a national leadership—a dynasty not to be broken. Frederick Douglass and the moral revolt against slavery dominated Negro thought and effort until after the war. Then, with the sole weapon of self-defense in perilous times, the ballot, which the nation gave the freedmen, men like Langston and Bruce sought to guide the political fortunes of the blacks, while Payne and Price still clung to the old ideal of self-development.

Then came the reaction. War memories and ideals rapidly passed, and a period of astonishing commercial development and expansion ensued. A time of doubt and hesitation, of storm and stress, overtook the freedmen's sons; and then it was that Booker Washington's leadership began. Mr. Washington came with a clear simple program, at the psychological moment; at a time when the nation was a little ashamed of having bestowed so much sentiment on Negroes and was concentrating its energies on Dollars. The industrial training of Negro youth was not an idea originating with Mr. Washington, nor was the policy of conciliating the white South wholly his. But he first put life, unlimited energy, and perfect faith into this program; he changed it from an article of belief into a whole creed; he broadened it from a by-path into a veritable Way of Life. And the method by which he accomplished this is an interesting study of human life.

Mr. Washington's narrative gives but glimpses of the real struggle which he has had for leadership. First of all, he strove to gain the sympathy and cooperation of the white South, and gained it after that epoch-making sentence spoken at Atlanta: "In all things that are purely social we can be as separate as the fingers, yet one as the hand in all things essential to mutual progress" (p. 221). This conquest of the South is by all odds the most notable thing in Mr. Washington's career. Next to this comes his achievement in gaining place and consideration in the North. Many others less shrewd and tactful would have fallen between these two stools; but as Mr. Washington knew the heart of the South from birth and training, so by singular insight he intuitively grasped the spirit of the age that was dominating the North. He learned so thoroughly the speech and thought of triumphant commercialism and the ideals of material prosperity that he pictures as the height of absurdity a black boy studying a French grammar in the midst of weeds and dirt. One wonders how Socrates or St. Francis of Assissi would receive this!

And yet this very singleness of vision and thorough oneness with his age is a mark of the successful man. It is as though Nature must needs make men a little narrow to give them force. At the same time, Mr. Washington's success, North and South, with his gospel of Work and Money, raised opposition to him from widely divergent sources. The spiritual sons of the Abolitionists were not prepared to acknowledge that the schools founded before Tuskegee, by men of broad ideals and self-sacrificing souls, were wholly failures, or worthy of ridicule. On the other hand, among his own people Mr. Washington found deep suspicion and dislike for a man on such good terms with Southern whites.

Such opposition has only been silenced by Mr. Washington's very evident sincerity of purpose. We forgive much to honest purpose which is accomplishing something. We may not agree with the man at all points, but we admire him and cooperate with him so far as we conscientiously can. It is no ordinary tribute to this man's tact and power, that, steering as he must amid so many diverse interests and opinions, he today commands not simply the applause of those who believe in his theories, but also the respect of those who do not.

Among the Negroes, Mr. Washington is still far from a popular leader. Educated and thoughtful Negroes everywhere are glad to honor him and aid him, but all cannot agree with him. He represents in Negro thought the old attitude of adjustment to environment, emphasizing the economic phase; but the two other strong currents of feeling, descended from the past, still oppose him. One is the thought of a small but not unimportant group, unfortunate in their choice of spokesman, but nevertheless of much weight, who represent the old ideas of revolt and revenge, and see in migration alone an outlet for the Negro people. The second attitude is that of the large and important group represented by Dunbar, Tanner, Chesnut, Miller, and the Grimkes, who, without any single definite program, and with complex aims, seek nevertheless that self-development and self-realization in all lines of human endeavor which they believe will eventually place the Negro beside the other races. While these men respect the Hampton-Tuskegee idea to a degree, they believe it falls far short of a complete program. They believe, therefore, also in the higher education of Fisk and Atlanta Universities; they believe in self-assertion and ambition; and they believe in the right of suffrage for blacks on the same terms with whites.

Such is the complicated world of thought and action in which Mr. Booker Washington has been called of God and man to lead, and in which he has gained so rare a meed of success.[3]

Notes

1. *Up From Slavery. An Autobiography.* By Booker Washington. New York: Doubleday, Page & Co.

2. *Editor's note*: The reading is based on a book review of Washington's autobiography as indicated in the note above. The review was published in 1901 in the July 16th edition of *The Dial* and appeared on pages 53–55. This review appeared in a significantly expanded form as "Of Mr. Booker T. Washington and Others" in *The Souls of Black Folk* (1903).

3. *Editor's note*: At the end of the review, the following citation was provided: W.E. Burghardt Du Bois. Atlanta University, Atlanta, Ga.

Reading 7

The Relation of the Negroes to the Whites in the South[1]

In the discussion of great social problems, it is extremely difficult for those who are themselves actors in the drama to avoid the attitude of partisans and advocates. And yet I take it that the examination of the most serious of the race problems of America is not in the nature of a debate but rather a joint endeavor to seek the truth beneath a mass of assertion and opinion, of passion and distress. And I trust that whatever disagreement may arise between those who view the situation from opposite sides of the color line will be rather in the nature of additional information than of contradiction.

The world-old phenomenon of the contact of diverse races of men is to have new exemplification during the new century. Indeed the characteristic of the age is the contact of European civilization with the world's undeveloped peoples. Whatever we may say of the results of such contact in the past, it certainly forms a chapter in human action not pleasant to look back upon. War, murder, slavery, extermination and debauchery—this has again and again been the result of carrying civilization and the blessed gospel to the isles of the sea and the heathen without the law. Nor does it altogether satisfy the conscience of the modern world to be told complacently that all this has been right and proper, the fated triumph of strength over weakness, of righteousness over evil, of superiors over inferiors. It would certainly be soothing if one could readily believe all this, and yet there are too many ugly facts, for everything to be thus easily explained away. We feel and know that there are many delicate differences in race psychology, numberless changes which our crude social measurements are not yet able to follow minutely, which explain much of history and social development. At the same time, too, we know that these considerations have never adequately explained or excused the triumph of brute force and cunning over weakness and innocence.

It is then the strife of all honorable men of the twentieth century to see that in the future competition of races, the survival of the fittest shall mean the triumph of the good, the beautiful and the true; that we may be able to preserve for future Civilization all that is really fine and noble and strong, and not continue to put a premium on greed and impudence and cruelty. To bring this hope to fruition we are compelled daily to turn more and more to a conscientious study of the phenomena of race contact—to a study frank and fair, and not falsified and colored by our wishes or our fears. And we have here in the South as fine a field for such a study as the world affords: a field to be sure which the average American scientist deems somewhat beneath his dignity, and which the average man who is not a scientist knows all about, but nevertheless a line of study which by reason of the enormous race complications, with which God seems about to punish this nation; must increasingly claim our sober attention, study and thought. We must ask: "What are the actual relations of whites and blacks in the South, and we must be answered not by apology or faultfinding, but by a plain, unvarnished tale."

In the civilized life of today the contact of men and their relations to each other fall in a few main lines of action and communication: there is first the physical proximity of homes and dwelling places, the way in which neighborhoods group themselves, and the contiguity of neighborhoods. Secondly, and in our age chiefly, there are the economic relations—the methods by which individuals cooperate for earning a living, for the mutual satisfaction of wants, for the production of wealth. Next there are the political relations, the cooperation in social control, in group government, in laying and paying the burden of taxation. In the fourth place there are the less tangible but highly important forms of intellectual contact and commerce, the interchange of ideas through conversation and conference, through, periodicals and libraries, and above all the gradual formation for each community of that curious *tertium quid* [2] which we call public opinion. Closely allied with this come the various forms of social contact in everyday life, in travel, in theaters, in house gatherings, in marrying and giving in marriage. Finally, there are the varying forms of religious enterprise, of moral teaching and benevolent endeavor.

These are the principal ways in which men living in the same communities are brought into contact with each other. It is my task this afternoon, therefore, to point out from my point of view how the black race in the South meets and mingles with the whites, in these matters of everyday life.

First as to physical dwelling, it is usually possible, as most of you know, to draw in nearly every Southern community a physical color line on the map, to the one side of which whites dwell and the other Negroes. The winding and intricacy of the geographical color line varies of course in different communities. I know some towns where a straight line drawn through the middle of the main street separates nine-tenths of the whites from nine-tenths of the blacks. In other towns the older settlement of whites has been encircled by a broad band of blacks; in still other cases little settlements or nuclei of blacks have sprung up amid surrounding whites. Usually in cities each street has its distinctive color, and only now and then do the colors meet in close proximity. Even in the country something of this segregation is manifest in the smaller areas, and of course in the larger phenomena of the black belt.

All this segregation by color is largely independent of that natural clustering by social grades common to all communities. A Negro slum may be in dangerous proximity to a white residence quarter, while it is quite common to find a white slum planted in the heart of a respectable Negro district. One thing, however, seldom occurs: the best of the whites and the best of the Negroes almost never live in anything like close proximity. It thus happens that in nearly every Southern town and city, both whites and blacks see commonly the worst of each other. This is a vast change from the situation in the past when through the close contact of master and house-servant in the patriarchal big house, one found the best of both races in close contact and sympathy, while at the same time the squalor and dull round of toil among the field hands was removed from the sight and hearing of the family. One can easily see how a person who saw slavery thus from his father's parlors and sees freedom on the streets of a great city fails to grasp or comprehend the whole of the new picture. On the other hand, the settled belief of the mass of the Negroes that the Southern white people do not have the black man's best interests at heart has been intensified in later years by this continual daily contact of the better class of blacks with the worst representatives of the white race.

Coming now to the economic relations of the races we are on ground made familiar by study, much discussion and no little philanthropic effort. And yet with all this there are many essential elements in the co-operation of Negroes and whites for work and wealth, that are too readily overlooked or not thoroughly understood. The average American can easily conceive of a rich land awaiting development and filled with black laborers. To him the Southern problem is simply that of making efficient workingmen out of this material by giving them the requisite technical skill and the help of invested capital. The problem, however, is by no means as simple as this, from the obvious fact that these workingmen have been trained for centuries as slaves. They exhibit, therefore, all the advantages and defects of such training; they are willing and good-natured, but not self-reliant, provident or careful. If now the economic development of the South is to be pushed to the verge of exploitation, as seems probable, then you have a mass of workingmen thrown into relentless competition with the workingmen of the world but handicapped by a training the very opposite to that of the modern self-reliant democratic laborer. What the black laborer needs is careful personal guidance, group leadership of men with hearts in their bosoms, to train them to foresight, carefulness and honesty. Nor does it require any fine-spun theories of racial differences to prove the necessity of such group training after the brains of the race have been knocked out by two hundred and fifty years of assiduous education in submission, carelessness and stealing. After emancipation it was the plain duty of someone to assume this group leadership and training of the Negro laborer. I will not stop here to inquire *whose* duty it was—whether that of the white ex-master who had profited by unpaid toil, or the Northern philanthropist whose persistence brought the crisis, or of the National Government whose edict freed the bondsmen—I will not stop to ask *whose* duty it was, but I insist it was the duty of *someone* to see that these workingmen were not left alone and unguided without capital, landless, without skill, without economic organization, without even the bald protection of law, order and decency; left in a great land not to settle down to slow and careful internal development, but destined to be thrown almost immediately into relentless, sharp competition with the best of modern workingmen under an economic system where every participant is fighting for himself, and too often utterly regardless of the rights or welfare of his neighbor.

For we must never forget that the economic system of the South today which has succeeded the old regime is not the same system as that of the old industrial North, of England or of France with their trades unions, their restrictive laws, their written and unwritten commercial customs and their long experience. It is rather a copy of that England of the early nineteenth century, before the factory acts, the England that wrung pity from thinkers and fired the wrath of Carlyle. The rod of empire that passed from the hands of Southern gentlemen in 1865, partly by force, partly by their own petulance, has never returned to them. Rather it has passed to those men who have come to take charge of the industrial exploitation of the New South—the sons of poor whites fired with a new thirst for wealth and power, thrifty and avaricious Yankees, shrewd and unscrupulous Jews. Into the hands of these men the Southern laborers, white and black, have fallen, and this to their sorrow. For the laborers as such there is in these new captains of industry neither love nor hate, neither sympathy nor romance—it is a cold question of dollars and dividends. Under such a system all labor is bound to suffer. Even the white laborers are not yet intelligent, thrifty and well trained enough to maintain themselves against the powerful inroads of organized capital. The result among them even, is long hours of toil, low wages, child labor, and lack of protection against usury and cheating. But among the black laborers all this is aggravated, first, by a race prejudice which varies from a doubt and distrust among the best element of whites to a frenzied hatred among the worst; and, secondly, it is aggravated, as I have said before, by the wretched economic heritage of the freedmen from slavery. With this training it is difficult for the freedman to learn to, grasp the opportunities already opened to him, and the new opportunities are seldom given him but go by favor to the whites.

Left by the best elements of the South with little protection or oversight, he has been made in law and custom the victim of the worst and most unscrupulous men in each community. The crop-lien system which is depopulating the fields of the South is not simply the result of shiftlessness on the part of Negroes but is also the result of cunningly devised laws as to mortgages, liens and misdemeanors which can be made by conscienceless men to entrap and snare the unwary until escape is impossible, further toil a farce, and protest a crime. I have seen in the black belt of Georgia an ignorant, honest Negro buy and pay for a farm in installments three separate times, and then in the face of law and decency the enterprising Russian Jew who sold it to him pocketed money and deed and left the black man landless, to labor on his own land at thirty cents a day. I have seen a black farmer fall in debt to a white storekeeper and that storekeeper go to his farm and strip it of every single marketable article—mules, plows, stored crops, tools, furniture, bedding, clocks, looking-glass, and all this without a warrant, without process of law, without a sheriff or officer, in the face of the law for homestead exemptions, and without rendering to a single responsible person any account or reckoning. And such proceedings can happen and will happen in any community where a class of ignorant toilers are placed by custom and race prejudice beyond the pale of sympathy and race brotherhood. So long as the best elements of a community do not feel in duty bound to protect and train and care for the weaker members of their group they leave them to be preyed upon by these swindlers and rascals.

This unfortunate economic situation does not mean the hindrance of all advance in the black south, or the absence of a class of black landlords and mechanics who, in spite of disadvantages, are accumulating property and making good citizens. But it does mean that this class is not nearly so large as a fairer economic system might easily make it, that those who survive in the competition are handicapped so as to accomplish much less than they deserve to, and that above all, the personnel of the successful class is left to chance and accident, and not to any intelligent culling or reasonable methods of selection. As a remedy for this, there is but one possible procedure. We must accept some of the race prejudice in the South as a fact—deplorable in its intensity, unfortunate in results, and dangerous for the future, but nevertheless a hard fact which only time can efface. We cannot hope then in this generation, or for several generations, that the mass of the whites can be brought to assume that close sympathetic and self-sacrificing leadership of the blacks which their present situation so eloquently demands. Such leadership, such social teaching and example, must come from the blacks themselves. For some time men doubted as to whether the Negro could develop such leaders, but today no one seriously disputes the capability of individual Negroes to assimilate the culture and common sense of modern civilization, and to pass it on to some extent, at least, to their fellows. If this be true, then here is the path out of the economic situation, and here is the imperative demand for trained Negro leaders of character and intelligence, men of skill, men of light and leading, college-bred men, black captains of industry and missionaries of culture. Men who thoroughly comprehend and know modern civilization and can take hold of Negro communities and raise and train them by force of precept and example, deep sympathy and the inspiration of common blood and ideals. But if such men are to be effective they must have some power —they must be backed by the best public opinion of these communities, and able to wield for their objects and aims such weapons as the experience of the world has taught are indispensable to human progress.

Of such weapons the greatest, perhaps, in the modern world is the power of the ballot, and this brings me to a consideration of the third form of contact between whites and blacks in the South—political activity.

In the attitude of the American mind toward Negro suffrage, can be traced with singular accuracy the prevalent conceptions of government. In the sixties we were near enough the echoes of the French Revolution to believe pretty thoroughly in universal suffrage. We argued, as we thought then rather logically, that no social class was so good, so true and so disinterested as to be trusted wholly with, the political destiny of their neighbors; that in every state the best arbiters of their own welfare are the persons directly affected, consequently it is only by arming every hand with a ballot—with the right to have a voice in the policy of the state—that the greatest good to the greatest number could be attained. To be sure there were objections to these arguments, but we thought we had answered them tersely and convincingly; if someone complained of the ignorance of voters, we answered: "Educate them." If another complained of their venality we replied: "Disfranchise them or put them in jail." And finally to the men who feared demagogues and the natural perversity of some human beings, we insisted that time and bitter experience would teach the most hardheaded. It was at this time that the question of Negro suffrage in the South was raised. Here were a defenseless people suddenly made free. How were they to be protected from those who did not believe in their freedom and were determined to thwart it? Not by force, said the North; not by government guardianship, said the South; then by the ballot, the sole and legitimate defense of a free people, said the Common Sense of the nation. No one thought at the time that the ex-slaves could use the ballot intelligently or very effectively, but they did think that the possession of so great [a] power, by a great class in the nation would compel their fellows to educate this class to its intelligent use.

Meantime new thoughts came to the nation: the inevitable period of moral retrogression and political trickery that ever follows in the wake of war overtook us. So flagrant became the political scandals that reputable men began to leave politics alone, and politics consequently became disreputable. Men began to pride themselves on having nothing to do with their, own government and to agree tacitly with those who regarded public office as a private perquisite. In this state of mind it became easy to wink at the suppression of the Negro vote in the South, and to advise self-respecting Negroes to leave politics entirely alone. The decent and reputable citizens of the North who neglected their own civic duties grew hilarious over the exaggerated importance with which the Negro regarded the franchise. Thus it easily happened that more and more the better class of Negroes followed the advice from abroad and the pressure from home and took no further interest in politics, leaving to the careless and the venal of their race the exercise of their rights as voters. This black vote which still remained was not trained and educated but further debauched by open and unblushing bribery, or force and fraud, until the Negro voter was thoroughly inoculated with the idea that politics was a method of private gain by disreputable means.

And finally, now, today, when we are awakening to the fact that the perpetuity of republican institutions on this continent depends on the purification of the ballot, the civic training of voters, and the raising of voting to the plane of a solemn duty which a patriotic citizen neglects to his peril and to the peril of his children's children—in this day when we are striving for a renaissance of civic virtue, what are we going to say to the black voter of the South? Are we going to tell him still that politics is a disreputable and useless form of human activity? Are we going to induce the best class of Negroes to take less and less interest in government and give up their right to take such an interest without a protest? I am not saying a word against all legitimate efforts to purge the ballot of ignorance, pauperism and crime. But few have pretended that the present movement for disfranchisement in the South is for such a purpose; it has been plainly and frankly declared in nearly every case that the object of the disfranchising laws is the elimination of the black man from politics.

Now is this a minor matter which has no influence on the main question of the industrial and intellectual development of the Negro? Can we establish a mass of black laborers, artisans and landholders in the South who by law and public opinion have absolutely no voice in shaping the laws under which they live and work? Can the modern organization of industry, assuming as it does free democratic government and the power and ability of the laboring classes to compel respect for their welfare—can this system be carried out in the South when half its laboring force is voiceless in the public councils and powerless in its own defense? Today the black man of the South has almost nothing to say as to how much he shall be taxed, or how those taxes shall be expended; as to who shall execute the laws and how they shall do it; as to who shall make the laws and how they shall be made. It is pitiable that frantic efforts must be made at critical times to get lawmakers in some states even to listen to the respectful presentation of the black side of a current controversy. Daily the Negro is coming more and more to look upon law and justice not as protecting safeguards but as sources of humiliation and oppression. The laws are made by men who as yet have little interest in him; they are executed by men who have absolutely no motive for treating the black people with courtesy or consideration, and finally the accused lawbreaker is tried not by his peers but too often by men who would rather punish ten innocent Negroes than let one guilty one escape.

I should be the last one to deny the patent weaknesses and shortcomings of the Negro people; I should be the last to withhold sympathy from the white South in its efforts to solve its intricate social problems. I freely acknowledge that it is possible and sometimes best that a partially undeveloped people should be ruled by the best of their stronger and better neighbors for their own good, until such time as they can start and fight the world's battles alone. I have already pointed out how sorely in need of such economic and spiritual guidance the emancipated Negro was, and I am quite willing to admit that if the representatives of the best white southern public opinion were the ruling and guiding powers in the South today that the conditions indicated would be fairly well ful-filled. But the point I have insisted upon and now emphasize again is that the best opinion of the South today is not the ruling opinion. That to leave the Negro helpless and without a ballot today is to leave him not to the guidance of the best but rather to the exploitation and debauchment of the worst; that this is no truer of the South than of the North—of the North than of Europe—in any land, in any country under modern free competition, to lay any class of weak and des-pised people, be they white, black or blue, at the political mercy of their strong-er, richer and more resourceful fellows is a temptation which human nature sel-dom has and seldom will withstand.

Moreover the political status of the Negro in the South is closely connected with the question of Negro crime. There can be no doubt that crime among Ne-groes has greatly increased in the last twenty years and that there has appeared in the slums of great cities a distinct criminal class among the blacks. In explain-ing this unfortunate development we must note two things, (1) that the inevitable result of emancipation was to increase crime and criminals, and (2) that the po-lice system of the South was primarily designed to control slaves. As to the first point we must not forget that under a strict slave regime there can scarcely be such a thing as crime. But when these variously constituted human particles are suddenly thrown broadcast on the sea of life, some swim, some sink, and some hang suspended, to be forced up or down by the chance currents of a busy hurry-ing world. So great an economic and social revolution as swept the South in '63 meant a weeding out among the Negroes of the incompetents and vicious—the beginning of a differentiation of social grades. Now a rising group of people are not lifted bodily from the ground like an inert solid mass, but rather stretch up-ward like a living plant with its roots still clinging in the mold. The appearance, therefore, of the Negro criminal was a phenomenon to be awaited, and while it causes anxiety it should not occasion surprise.

Here again the hope for the future depended peculiarly on careful and deli-cate dealing with these criminals. Their offenses at first were those of laziness, carelessness and impulse rather than of malignity or ungoverned viciousness. Such misdemeanors needed discriminating treatment, firm but reformatory, with no hint of injustice and full proof of guilt. For such dealing with criminals, white or black, the South had no machinery, no adequate jails or reformatories and a police system arranged to deal with blacks alone, and which tacitly assumed that every white man was *ipso facto*[3] a member of that police. Thus grew up a double system of justice which erred on the white side by undue leniency and the prac-tical immunity of red-handed criminals, and erred on the black side by undue severity, injustice and lack of discrimination. For, as I have said, the police sys-tem of the South was originally designed to keep track of all Negroes, not simp-ly of criminals, and when the Negroes were freed and the whole South was con-vinced of the impossibility of free Negro labor, the first and almost universal device was to use the courts as a means of re-enslaving the blacks. It was not then a question of crime but rather of color that settled a man's conviction on almost any charge. Thus Negroes came to look upon courts as instruments of injustice and oppression, and upon those convicted in them as martyrs and victims.

When now the real Negro criminal appeared and, instead of petty stealing and vagrancy, we began to have highway robbery, burglary, murder and rape, it had a curious effect on both sides [of] the color line; the Negroes refused to believe the evidence of white witnesses or the fairness of white juries, so that the greatest deterrent to crime, the public opinion of one's own social caste was lost and the criminal still looked upon as crucified rather than hanged. On the other hand the Whites, used to being careless as to the guilt or innocence of accused Negroes, were swept in moments of passion beyond law, reason and decency. Such a situation is bound to increase crime and has increased it. To natural viciousness and vagrancy are being daily added motives of revolt and revenge which stir up all the latent savagery of both races and make peaceful attention to economic development often impossible.

But the chief problem in any community cursed with crime is not the punishment of the criminals but the preventing of the young from being trained to crime. And here again the peculiar conditions of the South have prevented proper precautions. I have seen twelve-year-old boys working in chains on the public streets of Atlanta, directly in front of the schools, in company with old and hardened criminals; and this indiscriminate mingling of men, women and children makes the chain-gangs perfect schools of crime and debauchery. The struggle for reformatories which has gone on in Virginia, Georgia and other states is the one encouraging sign of the awakening of some communities to the suicidal results of this policy.

It is the public schools, however, which can be made outside the homes the greatest means of training decent self-respecting citizens. We have been so hotly engaged recently in discussing trade schools and the higher education that the pitiable plight of the public school system in the South has almost dropped from view. Of every five dollars spent for public education in the State of Georgia, the white schools get four dollars and the Negro one dollar, and even then the white public school system, save in the cities, is bad and cries for reform. If this be true of the whites, what of the blacks? I am becoming more and more convinced as I look upon the system of common school training in the South that the national government must soon step in and aid popular education in some way. Today it has been only by the most strenuous efforts on the part of the thinking men of the South that the Negro's share of the school fund has not been cut down to a pittance in some half dozen states, and that movement not only is not dead but in many communities is gaining strength. What in the name of reason does this nation expect of a people poorly trained and hard pressed in severe economic competition, without political rights and with ludicrously inadequate common school facilities? What can it expect but crime and listlessness, offset here and there by the dogged struggles of the fortunate and more determined who are themselves buoyed by the hope that in due time the country will come to its senses?

I have thus far sought to make clear the physical, economic and political relations of the Negroes and whites in the South as I have conceived them, including for the reasons set forth, crime and education. But after all that has been said on these more tangible matters of human contact there still remains a part essential to a proper description of the South which it is difficult to describe or fix in terms easily understood by strangers. It is, in fine, the atmosphere of the land, the thought and feeling, the thousand and one little actions which go to make up life. In any community or nation it is these little things which are most elusive to the grasp and yet most essential to any clear conception of the group life, taken as a whole. What is thus true of all communities is peculiarly true of the South where, outside of written history and outside of printed law, there has been going on for a generation, as deep a storm and stress of human souls, as intense a ferment of feeling, as intricate a writhing of spirit as ever a people experienced. Within and without the somber veil of color, vast social forces have been at, work, efforts for human betterment, movements toward disintegration and despair, tragedies and comedies in social and economic life, and a swaying and lifting and sinking of human hearts which have made this land a land of mingled sorrow and joy, of change and excitement.

The center of this spiritual turmoil has ever been the millions of black freedmen and their sons, whose destiny is so fatefully bound up with that of the nation. And yet the casual observer visiting the South sees at first little of this. He notes the growing frequency of dark faces as he rides on, but otherwise the days slip lazily on, the sun shines and this little world seems as happy and contented as other worlds he has visited. Indeed, on the question of questions, the Negro problem, he hears so little that there almost seems to be a conspiracy of silence; the morning papers seldom mention it, and then usually in a far-fetched academic way, and indeed almost everyone seems to forget and ignore the darker half of the land, until the astonished visitor is inclined to ask if after all there *is* any problem here. But if he lingers long enough there comes the awakening: perhaps in a sudden whirl of passion which leaves him gasping at its bitter intensity; more likely in a gradually dawning sense of things he had not at first noticed. Slowly but surely his eyes begin to catch the shadows of the color line; here he meets crowds of Negroes and whites; then he is suddenly aware that he cannot discover a single dark face; or again at the close of a day's wandering he may find himself in some strange assembly, where all faces are tinged brown or black, and where he has the vague uncomfortable feeling of the stranger. He realizes at last that silently, resistlessly, the world about flows by him in two great streams. They ripple on in the same sunshine, they approach here and mingle their waters in seeming carelessness, they divide then and flow wide apart. It is done quietly, no mistakes are made, or if one occurs the swift arm of the law and public opinion swings down for a moment, as when the other day a black man and a white woman were arrested for talking together on Whitehall street, in Atlanta.

Now if one notices carefully one will see that between these two worlds, despite much physical contact and daily intermingling, there is almost no community of intellectual life or points of transference where the thoughts and feelings of one race can come with direct contact and sympathy with the thoughts and feelings of the other. Before and directly after the war when all the best of the Negroes were domestic servants in the best of the white families, there were bonds of intimacy, affection, and sometimes blood relationship between the races. They lived in the same home, shared in the family life, attended the same church often and talked and conversed with each other. But the increasing civilization of the Negro since has naturally meant the development of higher classes: there are increasing numbers of ministers, teachers, physicians, merchants, mechanics and independent farmers, who by nature and training are the aristocracy and leaders of the blacks, Between them, however, and the best element of the whites, there is little or no intellectual commerce. They go to separate churches, they live in separate sections, they are strictly separated in all public gatherings, they travel separately, and they are beginning to read different papers and books. To most libraries, lectures, concerts and museums Negroes are either not admitted at all or on terms peculiarly galling to the pride of the very classes who might otherwise be attracted. The daily paper chronicles the doings of the black world from afar with no great regard for accuracy; and so on throughout the category of means for intellectual communication; schools, conferences, efforts for social betterment and the like, it is usually true that the very representatives of the two races who for mutual benefit and the welfare of the land ought to be in complete understanding and sympathy are so far strangers that one side thinks all whites are narrow and prejudiced and the other thinks educated Negroes dangerous and insolent. Moreover, in a land where the tyranny of public opinion and the intolerance of criticism are for obvious historical reasons so strong as in the South, such a situation is extremely difficult to correct. The white man as well as the Negro is bound and tied by the color line and many a scheme of friendliness and philanthropy, of broad-minded sympathy, and generous fellowship between the two has dropped still-born because some busy-body has forced the color question to the front and brought the tremendous force of unwritten law against the innovators.

It is hardly necessary for me to add to this very much in regard to the social contact between the races. Nothing has come to replace that finer sympathy and love between some masters and house servants, which the radical and more uncompromising drawing of the color line in recent years has caused almost completely to disappear. In a world where it means so much to take a man by the hand and sit beside him; to look frankly into his eyes and feel his heart beating with red blood—in a world where a social cigar or a cup of tea together means more than legislative halls and magazine articles and speeches, one can imagine the consequences of the almost utter absence of such social amenities between estranged races, whose separation extends even to parks and street cars.

Here there can be none of that social going down to the people; the opening of heart and hand of the best to the worst, in generous acknowledgment of a common humanity and a common destiny. On the other hand, in matters of simple almsgiving, where there be no question of social contact, and in the succor of the aged and sick, the South, as if stirred by a feeling of its unfortunate limitations, is generous to a fault. The black beggar is never turned away without a good deal more than a crust, and a call for help for the unfortunate meets quick response. I remember, one cold winter, in Atlanta, when I refrained from contributing to a public relief fund lest Negroes should be discriminated against; I afterward inquired of a friend: Were any black people receiving aid?" "Why," said he, "they were *all* black."

And yet this does not touch the kernel of the problem. Human advancement is not a mere question of almsgiving, but rather of sympathy and cooperation among classes who would scorn charity. And here is a land where, in the higher walks of life, in all the higher striving for the good and noble and true, the color line comes to separate natural friends and co-workers, while at the bottom of the social group in the saloon, the gambling hell and the bawdy-house that same line wavers and disappears.

I have sought to paint an average picture of real relations between the races in the South. I have not glossed over matters for policy's sake, for I fear we have already gone too far in that sort of thing. On the other hand, I have sincerely sought to let no unfair exaggerations creep in. I do not doubt but that in some Southern communities conditions are far better than those I have indicated. On the other hand, I am certain that in other communities they are far worse.

Nor does the paradox and danger of this situation fail to interest and perplex the best conscience of the South. Deeply religious and intensely democratic as are the mass of the whites, they feel acutely the false position in which the Negro problems place them. Such an essentially honest-hearted and generous people cannot cite the caste-leveling precepts of Christianity, or believe in equality of opportunity, for all men, without coming to feel more and more with each generation that the present drawing of the color line is a flat contradiction to their beliefs and professions. But just as often as they come to this point the present social condition of the Negro stands as a menace and a portent before even the most open-minded: if there were nothing to charge against the Negro but his blackness or other physical peculiarities, they argue, the problem would be comparatively simple; but what can we say to his ignorance, shiftlessness, poverty and crime: can a self-respecting group hold anything but the least possible fellowship with such persons and survive? And shall we let a mawkish sentiment sweep away the culture of our fathers or the hope of our children? The argument so put is of great strength, but it is not a whit stronger than the argument of thinking Negroes; granted, they reply, that the condition of our masses is bad, there is certainly on the one hand adequate historical cause for this, and unmistakable evidence that no small number have, in spite of tremendous disadvantages, risen to the level of American civilization. And when by proscription and prejudice, these same Negroes are classed with, and treated like the lowest of their people simply *because* they are Negroes, such a policy not only discourages thrift and intelligence among black men, but puts a direct premium on the very things you complain of—inefficiency and crime. Draw lines of crime, of incompetency, of vice as tightly and uncompromisingly as you will, for these things must be proscribed, but a color line not only does not accomplish this purpose, but thwarts it.

In the face of two such arguments, the future of the South depends on the ability of the representatives of these opposing views to see and appreciate, and sympathize with each other's position; for the Negro to realize more deeply than he does at present the need of uplifting the masses of his people, for the white people to realize more vividly than they have yet done the deadening and disastrous effect of a color prejudice that classes Paul Lawrence Dunbar and Sam Hose in the same despised class.

It is not enough for the Negroes to declare that color prejudice is the sole cause of their social condition, nor for the white South to reply that their social condition is the main cause of prejudice. They both act as reciprocal cause and effect and a change in neither *alone* will bring the desired effect. Both must change or neither can improve to any great extent. The Negro cannot stand the present reactionary tendencies and unreasoning drawing of the color line much longer without discouragement and retrogression. And the condition of the Negro is ever, the excuse for further discrimination. Only by a union of intelligence and sympathy across the color line in this critical period of the Republic shall justice and right triumph, and

> "Mind and heart according well,
> Shall make one music as before,
> But vaster."

Notes

1. *Editor's note*: This essay that was originally published in the *Annals of the American Academy of Political and Social Sciences* 18 (1901): 121-140. A slightly revised version of the essay appeared as "Of the Sons of Master and Man," in *The Souls of Black Folk* (1903).

2. *Editor's note*: This is a Latin expression meaning "third thing." See "*Tertium quid.*" http://en.wikipedia.org/wiki/Tertium_quid. Du Bois cited this expression in his discussion of the forming of public opinion and with respect to the possibilities for intellectual interaction between African Americans and Whites. According to the white supremacist ideology of the time, non-whites were often characterized as being between human and animal in nature. Hence, African Americans were placed in a "third" catego-

ry, a category that was "betwixt and between." For examples of white supremacist thought see Carroll (1900) and Dixon (1902). Blum (2007) has provided a comprehensive discussion of Du Bois' response to white supremacist thought.

    3.   *Editor's note*: This Latin phrase may be translated, "by the fact itself." The expression is often utilized to express the cause and effect relationship that may exist between two phenomena. See "*Ipso facto*." http://en.wikipedia.org/wiki/Ipso_facto. Du Bois cited this expression while referring to the double standard of justice which was administered within the Southern court system. African Americans often received harsher sentences, and Whites were viewed as being in control of the courts.

Reading 8

Of the Training of Black Men[1]

From the shimmering swirl of waters where many, many thoughts ago the slave-ship first saw the square tower of Jamestown have flowed down to our day three streams of thinking: one from the larger world here and overseas, saying, the multiplying of human wants in culture lands calls for the worldwide cooperation of men in satisfying them. Hence arises a new human unity, pulling the ends of earth nearer, and all men, black, yellow, and white. The larger humanity strives to feel in this contact of living nations and sleeping hordes a thrill of new life in the world, crying, If the contact of Life and Sleep be Death, shame on such Life. To be sure, behind this thought lurks the afterthought of force and dominion,—the making of brown men to delve when the temptation of beads and red calico cloys.

The second thought streaming from the death-ship and the curving river is the thought of the older South: the sincere and passionate belief that somewhere between men and cattle God created a *tertium quid*,[2] and called it a Negro,—a clownish, simple creature, at times even lovable within its limitations, but straitly foreordained to walk within the Veil. To be sure, behind the thought lurks the afterthought,—some of them with favoring chance might become men, but in sheer self-defense we dare not let them, and build about them walls so high, and hang between them and the light a veil so thick, that they shall not even think of breaking through.

And last of all there trickles down that third and darker thought, the thought of the things themselves, the confused half-conscious mutter of men who are black and whitened, crying Liberty, Freedom, Opportunity—vouchsafe to us, O boastful World, the chance of living men! To be sure, behind the thought lurks the afterthought: suppose, after all, the World is right and we are less than men? Suppose this mad impulse within is all wrong, some mock mirage from the untrue?

So here we stand among thoughts of human unity, even through conquest and slavery; the inferiority of black men, even if forced by fraud; a shriek in the night for the freedom of men who themselves are not yet sure of their right to demand it. This is the tangle of thought and afterthought wherein we are called to solve the problem of training men for life.

Behind all its curiousness, so attractive alike to sage and dilettante, lie its dim dangers, throwing across us shadows at once grotesque and awful. Plain it is to us that what the world seeks through desert and wild we have within our threshold;—a stalwart laboring force, suited to the semi-tropics; if, deaf to the voice of the *Zeitgeist*,[3] we refuse to use and develop these men, we risk poverty and loss. If, on the other hand, seized by the brutal afterthought, we debauch the race thus caught in our talons, selfishly sucking their blood and brains in the future as in the past, what shall save us from national decadence? Only that saner selfishness which, Education teaches men, can find the rights of all in the whirl of work.

Again, we may decry the color prejudice of the South, yet it remains a heavy fact. Such curious kinks of the human mind exist and must be reckoned with soberly. They cannot be laughed away, nor always successfully stormed at, nor easily abolished by act of legislature. And yet they cannot be encouraged by being let alone. They must be recognized as facts, but unpleasant facts; things that stand in the way of civilization and religion and common decency. They can be met in but one way: by the breadth and broadening of human reason, by catholicity of taste and culture. And so, too, the native ambition and aspiration of men, even though they be black, backward, and ungraceful, must not lightly be dealt with. To stimulate wildly weak and untrained minds is to play with mighty fires; to flout their striving idly is to welcome a harvest of brutish crime and shameless lethargy in our very laps. The guiding of thought and the deft coordination of deed is at once the path of honor and humanity.

And so, in this great question of reconciling three vast and partially contradictory streams of thought, the one panacea of Education leaps to the lips of all; such human training as will best use the labor of all men without enslaving or brutalizing; such training as will give us poise to encourage the prejudices that bulwark society, and stamp out those that in sheer barbarity deafen us to the wail of prisoned souls within the Veil, and the mounting fury of shackled men.

But when we have vaguely said Education will set this tangle straight, what have we uttered but a truism? Training for life teaches living; but what training for the profitable living together of black men and white? Two hundred years ago our task would have seemed easier. Then Dr. Johnson blandly assured us that education was needed solely for the embellishments of life, and was useless for ordinary vermin. Today we have climbed to heights where we would open at least the outer courts of knowledge to all, display its treasures to many, and select the few to whom its mystery of Truth is revealed, not wholly by truth or the accidents of the stock market, but at least in part according to deftness and aim, talent and character. This program, however, we are sorely puzzled in carrying out through that part of the land where the blight of slavery fell hardest, and where we are dealing with two backward peoples. To make here in human education that ever necessary combination of the permanent and the contingent—of the ideal and the practical in workable equilibrium—has been there, as it ever must be in every age and place, a matter of infinite experiment and frequent mistakes.

In rough approximation we may point out four varying decades of work in Southern education since the Civil War. From the close of the war until 1876 was the period of uncertain groping and temporary relief. There were army schools, mission schools, and schools of the Freedmen's Bureau in chaotic disarrangement, seeking system and cooperation. Then followed ten years of constructive definite effort toward the building of complete school systems in the South. Normal schools and colleges were founded for the freedmen, and teachers trained there to man the public schools. There was the inevitable tendency of war to underestimate the prejudice of the master and the ignorance of the slave, and all seemed clear sailing out of the wreckage of the storm. Meantime, starting in this decade yet especially developing from 1885 to 1895, began the industrial revolution of the South. The land saw glimpses of a new destiny and the stirring of new ideals. The educational system striving to complete itself saw new obstacles and a field of work ever broader and deeper. The Negro colleges, hurriedly founded, were inadequately equipped, illogically distributed, and of varying efficiency and grade; the normal and high schools were doing little more than common school work, and the common schools were training but a third of the children who ought to be in them, and training these too often poorly. At the same time the white South, by reason of its sudden conversion from the slavery ideal, by so much the more became set and strengthened in its racial prejudice, and crystallized it into harsh law and harsher custom; while the marvelous pushing forward of the poor white daily threatened to take even bread and butter from the mouths of the heavily handicapped sons of the freedmen. In the midst, then, of the larger problem of Negro education sprang up the more practical question of work, the inevitable economic quandary that faces a people in the transition from slavery to freedom, and especially those who make that change amid hate and prejudice, lawlessness, and ruthless competition.

The industrial school springing to notice in this decade, but coming to full recognition in the decade beginning with 1895, was the proffered answer to this combined educational and economic crisis, and an answer of singular wisdom and timeliness. From the very first in nearly all the schools some attention had been given to training in handiwork, but now was this training first raised to a dignity that brought it in direct touch with the South's magnificent industrial development, and given an emphasis which reminded black folk that before the Temple of Knowledge swing the Gates of Toil.

Yet after all they are but gates, and when turning our eyes from the temporary and the contingent in the Negro problem to the broader question of the permanent uplifting and civilization of black men in America, we have a right to inquire, as this enthusiasm for material advancement mounts to its height, if after all the industrial school is the final and sufficient answer in the training of the Negro race; and to ask gently, but in all sincerity, the ever recurring query of the ages, Is not life more than meat, and the body more than raiment? And men ask this today all the more eagerly because of sinister signs in recent educational movements. The tendency is here born of slavery and quickened to renewed life by the crazy imperialism of the day, to regard human beings as among the material resources of a land to be trained with an eye single to future dividends. Race prejudices, which keep brown and black men in their "places," we are coming to regard as useful allies with such a theory, no matter how much they may dull the ambition and sicken the hearts of struggling human beings. And above all, we daily hear that an education that encourages aspiration, that sets the loftiest of ideals and seeks as an end culture and character than bread-winning, is the privilege of white men and the danger and delusion of black.

Especially has criticism been directed against the former educational efforts to aid the Negro. In the four periods I have mentioned, we find first boundless, planless enthusiasm and sacrifice; then the preparation of teachers for a vast public school system; then the launching and expansion of that school system amid increasing difficulties; and finally the training of workmen for the new and growing industries. This development has been sharply ridiculed as a logical anomaly and flat reversal of nature. Soothly we have been told that first industrial and manual training should have taught the Negro to work, then simple schools should have taught him to read and write, and finally, after years, high and normal schools could have completed the system, as intelligence and wealth demanded.

That a system logically so complete was historically impossible, it needs but a little thought to prove. Progress in human affairs is more often a pull than a push, surging forward of the exceptional man, and the lifting of his duller brethren slowly and painfully to his vantage ground. Thus it was no accident that gave birth to universities centuries before the common schools, that made fair Harvard the first flower of our wilderness. So in the South: the mass of the freedmen at the end of the war lacked the intelligence so necessary to modern workingmen. They must first have the common school to teach them to read, write, and cipher. The white teachers who flocked South went to establish such a common school system. They had no idea of founding colleges; they themselves at first would have laughed at the idea. But they faced, as all men since them have faced, that central paradox of the South, the social separation of the races. Then it was the sudden volcanic rupture of nearly all relations between black and white, in work and government and family life. Since then a new adjustment of relations in economic and political affairs has grown up,—an adjustment subtle and difficult to grasp, yet singularly ingenious, which leaves still that frightful chasm at the color line across which men pass at their peril. Thus, then and now, there stand in the South two separate worlds; and separate not simply in the higher realms of social intercourse, but also in church and school, on railway and street car, in hotels and theatres, in streets and city sections, in books and newspapers, in asylums and jails, in hospitals and graveyards. There is still enough of contact for large economic and group cooperation, but the separation is so thorough and deep, that it absolutely precludes for the present between the races anything like that sympathetic and effective group training and leadership of the one by the other, such as the American Negro and all backward peoples must have for effectual progress.

This the missionaries of '68 soon saw; and if effective industrial and trade schools were impractical before the establishment of a common school system, just as certainly no adequate common schools could be founded until there were teachers to teach them. Southern whites would not teach them; Northern whites in sufficient numbers could not be had. If the Negro was to learn, he must teach himself, and the most effective help that could be given him was the establishment of schools to train Negro teachers. This conclusion was slowly but surely reached by every student of the situation until simultaneously, in widely separated regions, without consultation or systematic plan, there arose a series of institutions designed to furnish teachers for the untaught. Above the sneers of critics at the obvious defects of this procedure must ever stand its one crushing rejoinder: in a single generation they put thirty thousand black teachers in the South; they wiped out the illiteracy of the majority of the black people of the land, and they made Tuskegee possible.

Such higher training schools tended naturally to deepen broader development: at first they were common and grammar schools, then some became high schools. And finally, by 1900, some thirty-four had one year or more of studies of college grade. This development was reached with different degrees of speed in different institutions: Hampton is still a high school, while Fisk University started her college in 1871, and Spelman Seminary about 1896. In all cases the aim was identical: to maintain the standards of the lower training by giving teachers and leaders the best practicable training; and above all to furnish the black world with adequate standards of human culture and lofty ideals of life. It was not enough that the teachers of teachers should be trained in technical normal methods; they must also, so far as possible, be broad-minded, cultured men and women, to scatter civilization among a people whose ignorance was not simply of letters, but of life itself.

It can thus be seen that the work of education in the South began with higher institutions of training, which threw off as their foliage common schools, and later industrial schools, and at the same time strove to shoot their roots ever deeper toward college and university training. That this was an inevitable and necessary development, sooner or later, goes without saying; but there has been, and still is, a question in many minds if the natural growth was not forced, and if the higher training was not either overdone or done with cheap and unsound methods. Among white Southerners this feeling is widespread and positive. A prominent Southern journal voiced this in a recent editorial:

> The experiment that has been made to give the colored students classical training has not been satisfactory. Even though many were able to pursue the course, most of them did so in a parrot-like way, learning what was taught, but not seeming to appropriate the truth and import of their instruction, and gra-

duating without sensible aim or valuable occupation for their future. The whole scheme has proved a waste of time, efforts, and the money of the state.

While most far-minded men would recognize this as extreme and over-drawn, still without doubt many are asking, Are there a sufficient number of Negroes ready for college training to warrant the undertaking? Are not too many students prematurely forced into this work? Does it not have the effect of dissa-tisfying the young Negro with his environment? And do these graduates succeed in real life? Such natural questions cannot be evaded, nor on the other hand must a nation naturally skeptical as to Negro ability assume an unfavorable answer without careful inquiry and patient openness to conviction. We must not forget that most Americans answer all queries regarding the Negro a priori, and that the least that human courtesy can do is to listen to evidence.

The advocates of the higher education of the Negro would be the last to de-ny the incompleteness and glaring defects of the present system: too many insti-tutions have attempted to do college work, the work in some cases has not been thoroughly done, and quantity rather than quality has sometimes been sought. But all this can be said of higher education throughout the land: it is the almost inevitable incident of educational growth, and leaves the deeper question of the legitimate demand for the higher training of Negroes untouched. And this latter question can be settled in but one way—by a first-hand study of the facts. If we leave out of view all institutions which have not actually graduated students from a course higher than that of a New England high school, even though they be called colleges; if then we take the thirty-four remaining institutions, we may clear up many misapprehensions by asking searchingly, What kind of institu-tions are they, what do they teach, and what sort of men do they graduate?

And first we may say that this type of college, including Atlanta, Fisk and Howard, Wilberforce and Lincoln, Biddle, Shaw, and the rest, is peculiar, al-most unique. Through the shining trees that whisper before me as I write, I catch glimpses of a boulder of New England granite, covering a grave, which gra-duates of Atlanta University have placed there:

IN GRATEFUL MEMORY OF THEIR FORMER TEACHER AND FRIEND AND OF THE UNSELFISH LIFE HE LIVED, AND THE NOBLE WORK HE WROUGHT; THAT THEY, THEIR CHILDREN, AND THEIR CHILDREN'S CHILDREN MIGHT BE BLESSED.

This was the gift of New England to the freed Negro: not alms, but a friend; not cash, but character. It was not and is not money these seething millions want, but love and sympathy, the pulse of hearts beating with red blood; a gift which today only their own kindred and race can bring to the masses, but which once saintly souls brought to their favored children in the crusade of the sixties, that finest thing in American history, and one of the few things untainted by sordid greed and cheap vainglory. The teachers in these institutions came not to keep the Negroes in their place, but to raise them out of their places where the filth of slavery had wallowed them. The colleges they founded were social settlements; homes where the best of the sons of the freedmen came in close and sympathetic touch with the best traditions of New England. They lived and ate together, studies and worked, hoped and harkened in the dawning light. In actual formal content their curriculum was doubtless old-fashioned, but in educational power it was supreme, for it was the contact of living souls.

From such schools about two thousand Negroes have gone forth with the bachelor's degree. The number in itself is enough to put at rest the argument that too large a proportion of Negroes are receiving higher training. If the ratio to population of all Negro students throughout the land, in both college and secondary training, be counted, Commissioner Harris assures us "it must be increased to five times its present average" to equal the average of the land.

Fifty years ago the ability of Negro students in any appreciable numbers to master a modern college course would have been difficult to prove. Today it is proved by the fact that four hundred Negroes, many of whom have been reported as brilliant students, have received the bachelor's degree from Harvard, Yale, Oberlin, and seventy other leading colleges. Here we have, then, nearly twenty-five hundred Negro graduates, of whom the crucial query must be made. How far did their training fit them for life? It is of course extremely difficult to collect satisfactory data on such a point,—difficult to reach the men, to get trustworthy testimony, and to gauge that testimony by any generally acceptable criterion of success. In 1900, the Conference at Atlanta University undertook to study these graduates, and published the results. First they sought to know what these graduates were doing, and succeeded in getting answers from nearly two thirds of the living. The direct testimony was in almost all cases corroborated by the reports of the colleges where they graduated, so that in the main the reports were worthy of credence. Fifty-three percent of these graduates were teachers, —presidents of institutions, heads of normal schools, principals of city school systems, and the like. Seventeen percent were clergymen; another seventeen percent were in the professions, chiefly as physicians. Over six percent were merchants, farmers, and artisans, and four percent were in the government civil service. Granting even that a considerable proportion of the third unheard from are unsuccessful, this is a record of usefulness. Personally I know many hundreds of these graduates and have corresponded with more than a thousand; through others I have followed carefully the life-work of scores; I have taught some of them and some of the pupils whom they have taught, lived in homes which they have builded, and looked at life through their eyes. Comparing them as a class with my fellow students in New England and in Europe, I cannot hesitate in saying that nowhere have I met men and women with a broader spirit of helpfulness, with deeper devotion to their life-work, or with more consecrated determination to succeed in the face of bitter difficulties than among Negro college-bred men.

They have, to be sure, their proportion of ne'er-do-weels,[4] their pedants and lettered fools, but they have a surprisingly small proportion of them; they have not that culture of manner which we instinctively associate with university men, forgetting that in reality it is the heritage from cultured homes, and that no people a generation removed from slavery can escape a certain unpleasant rawness and *gaucherie*,[5] despite the best of training.

With all their larger vision and deeper sensibility, these men have usually been conservative, careful leaders. They have seldom been agitators, have withstood the temptation to head the mob, and have worked steadily and faithfully in a thousand communities in the South. As teachers they have given the South a commendable system of city schools and large numbers of private normal schools and academies. Colored college-bred men have worked side by side with white college graduates at Hampton; almost from the beginning the backbone of Tuskegee's teaching force has been formed of graduates from Fisk and Atlanta. And today the institute is filled with college graduates, from the energetic wife of the principal down to the teacher of agriculture, including nearly half of the executive council and a majority of the heads of departments. In the professions, college men are slowly but surely leavening the Negro church, are healing and preventing the devastations of disease, and beginning to furnish legal protection for the liberty and property of the toiling masses. All this is needful work. Who would do it if Negroes did not? How could Negroes do it if they were not trained carefully for it? If white people need colleges to furnish teachers, ministers, lawyers, and doctors, do black people need nothing of the sort?

If it be true that there are an appreciable number of Negro youth in the land capable by character and talent to receive that higher training, the end of which is culture, and if the two and a half thousand who have had something of this training in the past have in the main proved themselves useful to their race and generation, the question then comes, What place in the future development of the South might the Negro college and college-bred man to occupy? That the present social separation and acute race sensitiveness must eventually yield to the influences of culture as the South grows civilized is clear. But such transformation calls for singular wisdom and patience. If, while the healing of this vast sore is progressing, the races are to live for many years side by side, united in economic effort, obeying a common government, sensitive to mutual thought and feeling, yet subtly and silently separate in many matters of deeper human intimacy—if this unusual and dangerous development is to progress amid peace and order, mutual respect and growing intelligence, it will call for social surgery at once the most delicate[6] and nicest in modern history. It will demand broadminded, upright men both white and black, and in its final accomplishment American civilization will triumph. So far as white men are concerned, this fact is today being recognized in the South, and a happy renaissance of university education seems imminent. But the very voices that cry Hail! to this good work are, strange to relate, largely silent or antagonistic to the higher education of the Negro.

Strange to relate! for this is certain, no secure civilization can be built in the South with the Negro as an ignorant, turbulent proletariat. Suppose we seek to remedy this by making them laborers and nothing more: they are not fools, they have tasted of the Tree of Life, and they will not cease to think, will not cease attempting to read the riddle of the world. By taking away their best equipped teachers and leaders, by slamming the door of opportunity in the faces of their bolder and brighter minds, will you make them satisfied with their lot, or will you not rather transfer their leading from the hands of men taught to think to the hands of untrained demagogues? We ought not to forget that despite the pressure of poverty, and despite the active discouragement and even ridicule of friends, the demand for higher training steadily increases among Negro youth: there were, in the years from 1875 to 1880, twenty-two Negro graduates from Northern colleges; from 1885 to 1895 there were forty-three, and from 1895 to 1900, nearly 100 graduates. From Southern Negro colleges there were, in the same three periods, 143, 413, and over 500 graduates. Here, then, is the plain thirst for training; by refusing to give this Talented Tenth the key to knowledge can any sane man imagine that they will lightly lay aside their yearning and contentedly become hewers of wood and drawers of water?

No. The dangerously clear logic of the Negro's position will more and more loudly assert itself in that day when increasing wealth and more intricate social organization preclude the South from being, as it so largely is, simply an armed camp for intimidating black folk. Such waste of energy cannot be spared if the South is to catch up with civilization. And as the black third of the land grows in thrift and skill, unless skillfully guided in its larger philosophy, it must more and more brood over the red past and the creeping, crooked present, until it grasps a gospel of revolt and revenge and throws its new-found energies athwart the current of advance. Even today the masses of the Negroes see all too clearly the anomalies of their position and the moral crookedness of yours. You may marshal strong indictments against them, but their counter-cries, lacking though they be in formal logic, have burning truths within them which you may not wholly ignore, O Southern Gentlemen! If you deplore their presence here, they ask, Who brought us? When you shriek, Deliver us from the vision of intermarriage, they answer, that legal marriage is infinitely better than systematic concubinage and prostitution. And if in just fury you accuse their vagabonds of violating women, they also in fury quite as just may wail: the rape which your gentlemen have done against helpless black women in defiance of your own laws is written on the foreheads of two millions of mulattoes, and written in ineffaceable blood. And finally, when you fasten crime upon this race as its peculiar trait, they answer that slavery was the arch-crime, and lynching and lawlessness its twin abortion; that color and race are not crimes, and yet they it is which in this land receive most unceasing condemnation, North, East, South, and West.

I will not say such arguments are wholly justified—I will not insist that there is no other side to the shield; but I do say that of the nine millions of Negroes in this nation, there is scarcely one out of the cradle to whom these arguments do not daily present themselves in the guise of terrible truth. I insist that the question of the future is how best to keep these millions from brooding over the wrongs of the past and the difficulties of the present, so that all their energies may be bent toward a cheerful striving and cooperation with their white neighbors toward a larger, more just,[7] and fuller future. That one wise method of doing this lies in the closer knitting of the Negro to the great industrial possibilities of the South is a great truth. And this the common schools and the manual training and trade schools are working to accomplish. But these alone are not enough. The foundations of knowledge in this race, as in others, must be sunk deep in the college and university if we would build a solid, permanent structure. Internal problems of social advance must inevitably come,—problems of work and wages, of families and homes, of morals and the true valuing of the things of life; and all these and other inevitable problems of civilization the Negro must meet and solve largely for himself, by reason of his isolation; and can there be any possible solution other than by study and thought and an appeal to the rich experience of the past? Is there not, with such a group and in such a crisis, infinitely more danger to be apprehended from half-trained minds and shallow thinking than from over-education and over-refinement? Surely we have wit enough to found a Negro college so manned and equipped as to steer successfully between the dilettante and the fool. We shall hardly induce black men to believe that if their bellies be full it matters little about their brains. They already dimly perceive that the paths of peace winding between honest toil and dignified manhood call for the guidance of skilled thinkers, the loving, reverent comradeship between the black lowly and black men emancipated by training and culture.

The function of the Negro college then is clear: it must maintain the standards of popular education, it must seek the social regeneration of the Negro, and it must help in the solution of problems of race contact and cooperation. And finally, beyond all this, it must develop men. Above our modern socialism, and out of the worship of the mass, must persist and evolve that higher individualism which the centers of culture protect; there must come a loftier respect for the sovereign human soul that seeks to know itself and the world about it; that seeks a freedom for expansion and self-development; that will love and hate and labor in its own way, untrammeled alike by old and new. Such souls aforetime have inspired and guided worlds, and if we be not wholly bewitched by our Rhine-gold, they shall again. Herein the longing of black men must have respect: the rich and bitter depth of their experience, the unknown treasures of their inner life, the strange rendings of nature they have seen, may give the world new points of view and make their loving, living, and doing precious to all human hearts. And to themselves in these the days that try their souls the chance to soar in the dim blue air above the smoke is to their finer spirits boon and guerdon[8] for what they lose on earth by being black.

I sit with Shakespeare, and he winces not. Across the color line I move arm in arm with Balzac and Dumas, where smiling men and welcoming women glide in gilded halls. From out the caves of Evening that swing between the strong-limbed earth and the tracery of the stars, I summon Aristotle and Aurelius and what soul I will, and they come all graciously with no scorn nor condescension. So, wed with Truth, I dwell above the Veil. Is this the life you grudge us, O knightly America? Is this the life you long to change into the dull red hideousness of Georgia? Are you so afraid lest peering from this high Pisgah, between Philistine and Amalekite, we sight the Promised Land?

Notes

1. *Editor's note*: This essay originally appeared in the September issue of *The Atlantic Monthly* 90 (1902): 289-297. Undergoing only minor modifications, this essay appeared as "Of the Training of Black Men" in *The Souls of Black Folk* (1903). This essay was the last of four essays originally published in *The Atlantic Monthly* to be incorporated into *The Souls of Black Folk*.

2. *Editor's note*: For a discussion of the meaning of this expression, please see the second note at the end (pages 71–2) of Reading 7.

3. *Editor's note*: This is a German expression meaning the "spirit of the age or tome." The term is often used to describe a nation or group's cultural or intellectual climate. See "*Zeitgeist*." http://en.wikipedia.org/wiki/Zeitgeist.

4. *Editor's note*: It appears that Du Bois meant to use the word "ne'er-do-well" here.

5. *Editor's note*: This is a French word meaning "tactless." See "*Gaucherie*." http://www.merriam-webster.com/dictionary/gaucherie.

6. *Editor's note*: In place of "most delicate" Du Bois originally employed the word, "delicatest."

7. *Editor's note*: Du Bois used "juster" rather than "more just."

8. *Editor's note*: Boon is a synonym for "benefit" while guerdon is a synonym for "compensation." See "Boon." http://thesaurus.com/browse/boon and "Guerdon." http://thesaurus.com/browse/guerdon.

Part 2:
Contextual Sociological Essays:
1897–1900

Reading 9

The Negro in Business: Results of the Investigation[1]

1. *Scope of the Inquiry.* —The general idea of the Atlanta Conferences is to select among the various and intricate questions arising from the presence of the Negro in the South certain lines of investigation which will be at once simple enough to be pursued by voluntary effort, and valuable enough to add to our scientific knowledge. At the same time the different subjects studied each year have had a logical connection, and will in time form a comprehensive whole. The starting point was the large death-rate of the Negroes; this led to a study of their condition of life, and the efforts they were making to better that condition. These efforts, when studied, brought clearly to light the hard economic struggle through which the emancipated slave is today passing.

The general method of making these inquiries is to distribute among a number of selected persons throughout the South, carefully prepared schedules. Care is taken to make the questions few in number, simple and direct, and, so far as possible, incapable of misapprehension. The investigators to whom these blanks are sent are usually well-educated Negroes, long resident in the communities; by calling on the same persons for aid year after year, a body of experienced correspondents has been gradually formed, numbering now about fifty.

In this investigation the object was to find in each locality, the number and kind of Negro business men. The following blank was sent out:[2]

Figure 9.1. Schedule of Negro Business Men and Negro Businesses, 1899

1. Negro merchants in _____.
2. State of _____.
3. Reported by _____.
4. Name _____.
5. Street and number _____.
6. Kind of business _____.
7. Years in business _____.
8. Capital _____.

87

With this was sent an explanatory letter defining the term "business man," and urging particular care in getting at the capital invested. Thus a large number of reports were secured. Then some of the chief merchants reported were written to and more particular inquiry made into their lives and experiences. The returns represent, therefore, the reports of business men themselves, interpreted and commented upon by an intelligent investigator of some experience. They can, therefore, on the whole, be depended upon as substantially accurate. The item of "capital invested" is naturally apt to contain the largest amount of errors since it is in most cases an estimate. Yet the estimate was either made by a disinterested person on data furnished by the merchant, or given directly by the merchant. In some cases the amount may have been exaggerated from motives of pride, in others underestimated for fear of taxes or jealousy. All doubtful estimates have been omitted when discovered.

It is hardly possible to place too great stress on the deep significance of business ventures among American Negroes. Physical emancipation came in 1863, but economic emancipation is still far off. The great majority of Negroes are still serfs bound to the soil or house-servants. The nation which robbed them of the fruits of their labor for two and a half centuries, finally set them adrift penniless. It would not have been wonderful or unprecedented if the Freedman had sunk into sluggish laziness, ignorance and crime after the war. That he did not wholly, is due to his own vigor and ambition, and the crusade of education from the North. What have these efforts, seconded by the common-school and to a limited extent the college, been able to accomplish in the line of making the Freedman a factor in the economic re-birth of the South?

Of the various answers that might be made to this question, none is more interesting than that which shows the extent to which the Negro is engaging in the various branches of business. Naturally business, of all vocations, was furthest removed from slavery. Even the ante-bellum plantation owner was hardly a good business man, and his slaves were at best careless sharers in a monarchical communism and, at worst, dumb driven cattle.

For a Negro then to go into business means a great deal. It is, indeed, a step in social progress worth measuring. It means hard labor, thrift in saving, a comprehension of social movements and ability to learn a new vocation—all this taking place, not by concerted guided action, but spontaneously here and there, in hamlet and city, North and South. To measure such a movement is difficult, and yet worth the trial. We need to know accurately the different kinds of business venture that appear, the order of their appearance, their measure of success and the capital invested in them. We need to know what sort of men go into business, how long they have been engaged and how they managed to get a start. Finally, we should know where this economic advance is being most strongly felt, and what the present tendencies are.

2. *Territory Covered by the Inquiry.*—In the census of 1890, the following Negro business men are returned:[3]

Hotel-keepers	420
Saloon-keepers	932
Livery-stable Keepers	390
Druggists	135
Grocers	1,829
Retail Merchants, unspecified	4,490
Publishers	20
Total	8,216

There are many obvious errors in these returns; the first three items are greatly exaggerated without doubt, containing many lodging-houses misnamed "hotels;" employees in saloons erroneously returned as "saloon-keepers;" and hostlers returned as "livery-stable keepers." The unspecified retail merchants also probably include some clerks, hucksters and restaurant-keepers. With some allowances for these errors, it is probable that there are in the United States at least 5,000 Negro business men. Of these the following study has returns from something less than one-half, living in 30 different states and territories as follows:

Table 9.1 Negro Business Men by States, 1899[4]

State	Number	State	Number
Alabama	136	Maryland	49
Arkansas	94	Mississippi	78
California	43	Missouri	49
Colorado	8	New Jersey	36
Delaware	16	New York	80
District of Columbia	50	North Carolina	98
Florida	78	Ohio	14
Georgia	324	Oklahoma	7
Indiana	4	Pennsylvania	47
Indian Territory	7	South Carolina	123
Illinois	23	Tennessee	131
Kansas	30	Texas	159
Kentucky	72	Virginia	105
Louisiana	11	Washington	10
Massachusetts	14	West Virginia	9
Total			1,906

Condensing this table we have reported from:

The north, east of the Mississippi	218
The south, east of the Mississippi	1,281
West of the Mississippi	407
Total	1,906

The value of this comparison is somewhat spoiled by the fact that the Negroes in the states of Georgia and Alabama and the middle South were more thoroughly canvassed than those in other parts of the country, since the Conference had more correspondents there. Nevertheless, it is clear that it is density of Negro population in the main that gives the Negro business man his best chance.

There were, of course, wide gaps and large omissions in such an inquiry. Small towns in considerable numbers, and country stores, were not returned, and many minor enterprises in larger towns. Of the large cities, the most important omission was the city of New Orleans from which returns came too late for insertion. With the latter exception it would seem, after careful inquiry, that the returns represent fully 75% of the more important business enterprises among Negroes, and consequently give a fair picture of their economic advance in this line.

2. *Kinds of Business Enterprise.*—The term "bussiness man" in this study has been interpreted to include all with stocks of goods to sell, and also all other persons who have at least $500 of capital invested; for instance, while the ordinary barber should be classed as an artisan, a man with $500 or more invested in a shop, with several hired assistants, is a capitalist rather than an artisan, and 162 such men have been classed as business men. So, too, it seemed best to include 31 blacksmiths and wheelwrights who had considerable capital invested and kept stocks of wagons or other goods on sale. In several other cases there was some difficulty in drawing a line between artisans and business men, and the decision had to be more or less arbitrary, although the investment of considerable capital directly in the business was the usual criterion.

The different kinds of business reported were as follows:

Table 9.2. Negro Business Men According to Occupations, 1899[5]

Occupation	Number	Occupation	Number
Grocers	432	Builders and Contractors	48
General merchandise dealers	166	Dealers in meat	47
Barbers with $500 or more invested	162	Merchant tailors	40
Publishers and job printers	89	Dealers in fuel	27[8]
Undertakers	80	Dealers in real estate	36
Saloon-keepers	68	Wagon-makers / blacksmiths	32
Druggists	64	Hotels	30
Restaurant-keepers	61	Green grocers, dairymen, etc.	30
Hackmen[6] and expressmen,[7] owning		Livery-stable keepers	26
outfits	53	Confectioners	25

Table 9.2. Negro Business Men According to Occupations, 1899
(*continued*)

Occupation	Number	Occupation	Number
Caterers	24	Crockery-stores	4
Plumbing, tinware, and hardware		Carpet-cleaning works	4
shops	17	Upholstering shops	3
Shoe dealers and repairers	17	Hair goods stores	3
Fish dealers	15	Lumber mills	3
Furniture dealers	13	Cleaning and dyeing shops	3
Building and loan associations	13	Brick contractors	3
Jewelers	11	Dealers in cotton	3
Market gardeners and planters	11	Ice-cream depots	2
Clothing-dealers	10	Wire goods manufacturers	2
Wall-paper and paint-shops	10	Dressmaking shops	2
Bakers, with shops	10	Private cemeteries	2
Dry-goods dealers	9	Bicycle-stores	2
Cotton gin proprietors	9	Mechanics with shops	2
Steam laundries	8	Shirt factory	1
Proprietors of machine shops	8	Toilet supply shop	1
Cigar manufacturers	8	Broom manufactory	1
Photographers	8	Cotton mill	1
Brokers and money lenders	8	Assembly hall	1
Dealers in feed	7	Naval stores dealer	1
Dealers in fruit	6	School of music	1
Milliners	5	Fan manufactory	1
Banks	4	Carpet manufactory	1
Second-hand stores	4	Handle factory	1
Harness-shops	4	Rubber goods shop	1
Employment agencies	4	Book-store	1
Florists	4	Miscellaneous, undesignated	82
Total	1,906		

It must be remembered in scanning these figures, that on most lines of business here reported, only establishments of considerable size and success have been reported. There are, for instance, large numbers of ice-cream dealers, pool-rooms, cleaning and dyeing shops, employment agencies, and the like among Negroes; most of these however are small and short lived and only a few well-established businesses in these lines have been reported. Again, under the method employed in gathering these facts, it is hardly possible that the real proportion between the different kinds of businesses is correctly pictured, and there are doubtless large omissions here and there.

Perhaps the most instructive way of studying these businesses would be in the light of their historic evolution from the past economic condition of the Negro. For example, it is easy to see how the Barber, the Caterer and the Restaurant keeper were the direct economic progeny of the House-servant, just as the Market-Gardener; the Sawmill Proprietor, and the Florist were descended from the Field-hand. We may, indeed, divide the business men in the above table as follows:

(a) HOUSE SERVANT CLASS: Barbers, Restaurant-keepers, Expressmen, Butchers, Caterers, Liverymen, Bakers, Milliners, etc.,—462.
(b) FIELD-HAND CLASS: Market-Gardeners, Green-grocers, Dairymen. Cotton-gin owners, Florists, Lumber-mill owners, etc.,—l.
(c) PLANTATION MECHANIC CLASS: Builders and Contractors, Blacksmiths, Brick-makers, Jewelers, Shoe-dealers and Repairers, Machinists, Cigar manufacturers, Tinners, Paperhangers and Painters, Harness dealers, Upholsterers, etc.,—176.
(d) THE TRADERS: Grocers, General merchants and Dealers in Fuel, Fish, Clothing, Furniture, Feed and Dry-goods, and Second Hand Dealers,—695.
(e) THE CAPITALISTS: Banks, Real Estate dealers, Money-lenders, Building and Loan Associations, etc.,—67.
(f) THE MANUFACTURERS: Makers of Shirts, Brooms, Fans, Carpets, Handles and Rubber Goods; and the Cotton Mill,—9.
(g) CO-OPERATIVE EFFORTS: Undertakers, Druggists, Publishers, Cemetaries, Printers, etc.,—189.
(h) EFFORTS FOR AMUSEMENT: Saloons, Pool-rooms, Photographers, Bicycle dealers, etc.,—101.

No economic development is altogether accidental—previous occupation, enforced co-operation, the natural instinct to barter, and the efforts for recreation, explain among American Negroes, as among other people, their present occupations. Let us take up the classes in order as indicated above.

34. *House Servant Class.*—It is a well-known fact that the aristocracy of the plantation slaves were the house servants—those who, for appearance, ability and intelligence, were selected from the mass of the slaves to perform household duties at their master's house. Often such servants were educated and skillful; sometimes they were the natural children of their masters, and at all times they were the class which, when emancipation came, made the first steps toward independent livelihood. The master's valet set up his barber-shop in town and soon had a lucrative trade; the cook became proprietor of a small eating-stand or restaurant, or, if he was exceptionally efficient and noted for certain dishes, he became a caterer. It was in this way that the famous guild of black caterers arose in Philadelphia. In similar ways, but more slowly, a little saving of capital transformed the driver into the expressman, the coachman into the livery-stable keeper, the laundress into the proprietress of a public laundry. The most successful of these ventures hitherto have been those of the barber, the restaurant-keeper, the caterer, and the expressman. There were, in 1890, some 7,480 Negro barbers reported. Most of these were journeymen working for wages and the rest were

largely proprietors of small shops, either entirely without assistants or with one helper on Saturday nights. Neither of these classes would come under consideration here. There are, however, a number of barbers, 162 of whom are reported here, and whose actual number may be 300 or more, who are really business men. They own large, elegant shops with costly furniture, hire from three to eight assistants and do a lucrative business. The 162 reported have nearly $200,000 capital invested as follows:

```
$500–1,000 ................................................................... 60
$1,000–2,500 ............................................................... 63
$2,500–5,000 ............................................................... 12
$5,000–10,000 .............................................................. 3
Others over $500 .......................................................... 24
```

Of the restaurant-keepers 19 had from $1,000–2,500 invested, and 12 from $2,500 to $5,000; 14 had from $500 to $1,000. The caterers, as a class, are well-to-do men of intelligence. It is difficult to discriminate in these cases between their capital and their accumulated wealth. Their reported capital is:

```
$100–500 ...................................................................... 1
$500–1,000 ................................................................... 1
$1,000–2,500 ............................................................... 5
$2,500–5,000 ............................................................... 5
$5,000–10,000 .............................................................. 4
$10,000–50,000 ............................................................ 2
Unknown ...................................................................... 6
```

The expressmen and hackmen have considerable business in several southern cities. The fifty reported had capital as follows:

```
$500–1,000 ................................................................... 8
$1,000–2,500 ............................................................... 16
$2,500–5,000 ............................................................... 20
$5,000–10,000 .............................................................. 9
```

This whole class represented directly after the war, and up until about ten or fifteen years ago, the most prosperous class of Negroes. The caterers, barbers and stewards were leaders in all social movements among Negroes, and held the major part of the accumulated wealth. Lately, however, the class has lost ground. The palatial hotel and large restaurant have displaced the individual caterer in business, both white and black; the cab and transfer lines are crowding the single hackmen and in many other lines of work the influence of aggregated capital has proven disastrous to the emancipated house-servant. The barbering business has fallen into dislike among Negroes, partly because it had so long the stigma of race attached, and nearly all barbers were Negroes, and especially because the Negro barber was compelled to draw the color-line.

35. *Field Hand Class.*—The great mass of the slaves were field hands driven to the most unskilled kinds of agriculture. This, today, forms the great unrisen horde of freedmen who swarm in the country districts of the South, and whose social development and economic emancipation has scarcely begun. In a few cases some of them own large plantations and have money invested in cotton gins, plantation stores, market-gardening, and shipping to northern markets. Possibly they might be called business men. Eleven such are so denominated in this study, and have capital invested as follows:

$ 500–1,000	1
$1,000–2,500	2
$2,500–5,000	2
$6,000–10,000	4
$50,000 and over	1
Unknown	1

Of course this does not take account of those who are simply large land owners and farmers. These eleven and scores of others like them, not reported in this query, represent a sort of border-class—the first turning of the field-hand from pure agriculture to something like merchandising. The green grocers, dairymen, and the like, have gone a step further and established market stalls or stores for the sale of the products of their farms. Thirty of these are reported, which does not include the numerous small hucksters:

$100–500	7
$500–1,000	6
$1,000–2,500	12
$2,500–5,000	3
$5,000–10,000	2

The other callings which have developed logically from this class are few in number, and of importance chiefly as indicating tendencies. The three lumber mills have an aggregate capital of $10,000, and the four florists, $6,200. Much future interest attaches to the economic development of the former field-hand and present metayer.[9] There is, as yet, no trace of house industries or domestic manufacturers of any sort, although it would seem that theoretically the economic hope of the black South lies there.

36. *Plantation Mechanic Class.*—The *elite* of the field-hands were the slave mechanics—a class which, in some respects, rivaled the house-servants in importance During slavery they were the artisans of the South, and although emancipation brought the severe competition of better trained mechanics, and complicated the situation by drawing the color-line, still Negro mechanics continue to do a large amount of work in the South. Moreover, some, by saving money,

have become capitalists on a considerable scale, especially is this true of carpenters and builders. It is difficult to estimate the invested capital of a contractor as it varies so from job to job, and from season to season. Forty-one contractors are reported as follows:

$500–1,000 10
$1,000–2,500 14
$2,500–5,000 4
$5,000–10,000 8
$10,000–50,000 5

One large brickmaker has $10,000 invested. The tin-shops usually have small investments under $2,500. Three have over $5,000. The eleven jewelers are watch and clock repairers with small stocks of goods. They have sums varying from $100 to $5,000 invested. Nearly all the other vocations mentioned as belonging to this class have small capital, and are but a step removed from the journeyman mechanic. The shoe-making business some years ago had a considerable number of large enterprises making shoes to order. The ready-made machine shoe has driven all but a few of these shops out of business, leaving only the small repair shops. A few of the older shops, of which six are reported, still do a large custom business, and to these are now being added regular shoe-stores of which eleven are here reported. The great industrial schools are trying to make these enterprises, and the mechanical industries whence they sprung, their especial field of work and, eventually, their efforts will undoubtedly bear fruit. As yet there is, however, little trace of this movement.

37. *The Traders.* So far we have considered three great classes of business venture, the logical origin of which are plainly seen in the house-servant, the field-hand and the slave-mechanic. Of course this does not say that every individual green-grocer was a field-hand before the war, or every barber a house-servant. It merely serves as a rough indication of a social evolution, and is true when applied to the great mass of the Negroes.

We now come to the traders—the merchants proper. The African Negro is a born trader, and despite the communism of the slave plantation, considerable barter went on among the slaves, and between them and the whites. The Negroes, under the better class of masters, enjoyed a *peculium*[10] earned by working over-time, and expended as they wished. In some cases they owned quite a little property and were able to buy their freedom. In most cases they merely kept themselves in a little pocket money.

While then trade and property was not unknown to slaves, yet the Negro merchant is distinctly a *post-bellum* institution. The Negro grocery and general merchandise store is the direct descendant of the "store-house" on the old plantation. Here the "rations" were distributed every Saturday to the assembled slaves. After emancipation these "rations" became "supplies" advanced to the black tenant, and the "store-house" developed into a store with a variety of goods. Finally, merchants outside the plantations began to furnish supplies for the various plantations round about. In this development, the Negro who had saved a little capital was easily attracted into the grocery and general merchandise business; if he had tenants on his own farm, he set up a little store to "furnish" them. If not, he set up a little store in town and caught the transient trade of farmers and laborers. In this way the business has spread until there is scarcely a town or hamlet in the South which has not its grocer. The 598 grocers and general merchants reported here form, therefore, only a small part of the total merchants thus engaged. The 6,319 retail merchants reported by the census of 1890 perhaps approximates the truth.

Combining the grocers and general merchants we find that those reported represent a total investment of $1,828,243, in sums as follows:[11]

Table 9.3. Investment Capital for Grocers and General Merchants, 1899

Capital Invested	Number	Percentage
Under $500	174	32
$500–1,000	164	30
$1,000–2,500	171	31
$2,500–5,000[a]	23	7[b]
$5,000 and over	15	
Total	547	100

Notes: [a] The category range printed in the original table was $2,500–5,900. This appears to be a misprint and has been corrected.

[b] Du Bois combined these capital investment categories.

A little less than a third of these stores are small shops with a few hundred dollars worth of shelf goods bought on credit. Another third are stores worth $1,000 to $2,500 invested in a considerable variety of goods. They have Negro clerks and usually make a good appearance. Seven percent are large ventures. It is a question as to what, under present conditions, is to be the future of such stores. Certainly it would seem that they may form a very important field of enterprise in the future, especially when the black peasant becomes emancipated, and the present cry of "Negro money for Negro merchants" continues to grow louder.

The other merchants deal principally in wood and coal, fish, new and second-hand furniture and clothing, dry-goods, feed and fruit. Taking the dealers in these eight articles, we find they have $251,994 invested as follows:

Under $500	15
$500-1,000	17
$1,000-2,500[12]	32
$2,500-5,000	13
$5,000 and over	14
Unknown	8

It would seem probable that we might expect a considerable increase in these minor businesses among Negroes in the future. The great drawback is the little knowledge of business methods among Negroes. Their whole training, their idealistic temperament is against them. Moreover, it is difficult to overcome these defects because it is so hard to get openings for Negro youth to learn business methods. Even in the North how many firms stand ready to allow a bright black boy to come into their counting-rooms and learn the difficult technique of modern commercial life?

38. *The Capitalist.*—It is a difficult thing for those unused to the notion of property to learn to save. Moreover the national crime perpetrated in the mismanagement of the Freedman's Rank had wide-spread influence in discouraging the saving habit. As it is today, there is not among all these millions any far-reaching movement to encourage or facilitate saving except such local efforts as have arisen among themselves. While their extravagance and carelessness in the expenditure of their incomes is characteristic of the race, and will be for some time, yet there is some considerable saving even now, and much money is invested. Land and houses are naturally favorite investments, and there are a number of real estate agents. It is difficult, to separate capital from accumulated wealth in the case of many who live on the income from rents or buy and sell real estate for a profit. Thirty-six such capitalists have been reported with about $750,000 invested. There are four banks,—in Washington, DC, Richmond, VA., and Birmingham, AL, and several large insurance companies which insure against sickness and death, and collect weekly premiums. There are a number of brokers and money-lenders springing up here and there, especially in cities like Washington where there is a large salaried class.

The most gratifying phenomenon is the spread of building and loan associations, of which there are thirteen reported:

Philadelphia, PA	8
Washington, DC	1
Hampton, VA	1
Ocala, FL	1
Sacramento, CA	1
Wilmington, NC	2
Augusta, GA	1
Little Rock, AR	1
Portsmouth, VA	1
Anderson, SC	1

There are probably several more of these associations not reported. The crying need of the future is more agencies to encourage saving among Negroes. Penny savings banks with branches in the country districts, building and loan associations and the like would form a promising field for philanthropic effort. The Negroes, themselves, have as yet too few persons trained in handling and investing money. They would, however, co-operate with others, and such movements well-started would spread.

39. *The Manufacturer.*—If the general training of the Negro was unfavorable to general business enterprise, it was even more ill-suited to imparting the technical knowledge which the manufacturer needs. It will, therefore, be many years before the Negro will enter this field. Still there are even now some interesting ventures which must be regarded as experiments. There is the Coleman Cotton Mill, spoken of in the Atlanta University Publications, No.4. During the past year machinery has been installed, but the mill has not started yet. The foundry described among the contributed papers is small but successful, and looks as though it might survive. There are several broom factories, one of which is reported here, and a number of minor manufactures which partake something of the nature of handicrafts. As yet there is little or no trace of house industries. Here is another field for philanthropic effort. If, throughout the South, the Negro peasant proprietor could eke out the scanty earnings of the farm by home manufactures it would solve many vexed problems: it would establish the country home, elevate the Negro womanhood from the rough unsexing work of the field, lessen the temptation to migrate to cities, and decrease idleness and crime. Lack of profitable congenial occupation for the rising middle class of Negroes is the central economic problem of the South today, and house industries would, in a measure, solve it.

310. *Co-operative Efforts.*—Under co-operative effort have been grouped a number of business ventures whose existence is due primarily to the peculiar environment of the Negro in this land. Segregated as a social group, there are many semi-social functions in which the prevailing prejudice makes it pleasanter that he should serve himself if possible. Undertakers, for instance, must come in close and sympathetic relations with the family. This has led to Negroes taking up this branch of business, and in no line have they had greater success. Twenty-three of those reported had over $5,000 in capital invested, and there are, in fact, many more than this. Probably $500,000 is invested by Negroes in this business. Then, too, the demand for pomp and display at funerals has compelled these undertakers to equip their establishments unusually well. In Philadelphia, Baltimore, Atlanta, and other cities, there are Negro undertaking establishments equal in most of their appointments to the best white establishments. The advent of the Negro physician and undertaker naturally called for the drug-store. Sixty-four drug-stores are reported, forty-seven of which have over $1,000 invested. They are especially popular in the South for the social feature of the soda fountain and for their business partnership with sick-benefit societies. They are usually neat and well conducted, and are a favorite venture for young Negro

physicians. There are many private cemeteries owned by companies and societies, only two of which are reported here. They arose from the color line in burial and the poor condition of the public burial grounds for colored people. Finally, a demand for news and books among themselves has led to the establishment
of many hundred newspapers, of which over a hundred still survive, and to three
or four publishing houses. The more successful publishing houses are connected
with the large Negro church organizations, as the African Methodist at Philadelphia and Nashville, the Methodist Zion at Charlotte, NC, and the Baptist at
Nashville. These publish denominational literature, papers and books. They own
four buildings in all, and the largest has a plant valued at $45,000. There are
some other small publishing establishments of no great importance. The newspapers are dealt with in another place.[13]

These enterprises are peculiar instances of the "advantage of the disadvan-
tage"—of the way in which a hostile environment has forced the Negro to do for
himself. On the whole he has begun to supply well some of the needs thus
created.

311. *Efforts for Amusement.*—Efforts to supply the large social demand for
recreation and amusement are a large part of the co-operative efforts noted
above. The Negro church has, until recently, been the chief purveyor of amusement to the mass of Negroes, and even now it supplies by far the larger part of
social intercourse and entertainment for the masses. At the same time, there is a
large unsatisfied demand for recreation natural to a light-hearted people who
work hard. The saloon and the pool-room supply a part of this demand, and of
the 68 saloons reported, 54 have over $1,000 invested. The abuse of alcoholic
liquors is not one of the especial offenses of the Negro, and yet he spends considerable in this way, especially during the Christmas holidays. The saloon among
these people, even more than among the Irish and other city groups, is a distinct
social centre. In the country towns of the black belt, the field-hands gather there
to gossip, loaf, and joke. In the cities a crowd of jolly fellows can be met there
and in the adjacent pool-rooms. Consequently, the business has attracted Negroes with capital in spite of the fact that the Negro church distinctly frowns on
the vocation, which means some social ostracism for the liquor dealer. Next to
saloons in importance come the traveling Negro vaudeville shows. None of
these are reported here, for having no permanent headquarters they were difficult to reach; but there are known to be some three or four successful companies
of this sort traveling about the country. Most of them are compelled to have
white managers in order to get entrée into the theatres, but they are largely under
Negro control, and represent a considerable investment of Negro capital. Other
caterers to amusements are the bicycle dealers, photographers, and the like.

There is a large field for development here, and for considerable education
and social uplifting. Few people, for instance, have stronger dramatic instincts
than Negroes, and yet the theatre is almost unknown among them. Much could
be done to elevate and enlighten the masses by a judicious catering to their unsa-

tisfied demand for amusement. Here is a chance for philanthropy and five percent for black and white capitalists.

Notes

1.   *Editor's note*: This excerpt is taken from pages 4–15 of *The Negro in Business*. Atlanta: Atlanta University Press, 1899. Du Bois edited this Atlanta University Conference final report. The selected pages are part of Du Bois' executive summary, "Results of the Investigation."

2.   *Editor's note*: This schedule has been slightly modified by the editor to enhance clarity. Essentially Du Bois' chart format is replaced with a question format. The figure title has been provided by the editor.

3.   Eleventh Census, Population, Vol. II, pp 355, ff.

4.   *Editor's note*: The editor has renumbered the table and altered the table title slightly. The variable headings have been supplied by the editor also.

5.   *Editor's note*: The table title and the display of the data have been altered slightly by the editor to promote clarity. These data have not been altered in any way.

6.   *Editor's note*: A hackman was a person who could be employed as a carriage driver. See "Hackmen." http://www.yourdictionary.com/hackmen.

7.   *Editor's note*: An expressman was a train worker. It was this person's responsibility to insure that cargo arrived at its destination safely. This person would also pack cargo and could be placed in charge of guarding the train's safe. See "Expressman." http://en.wikipedia.org/wiki/Expressman.

8.   *Editor's note*: Du Bois provides this figure, but since the number of persons in each business category was presented in descending order, this figure could be a misprint. This being the case the correct number would be 37. On the other hand, the category could be misclassified. When the numbers presented in the table as is are added, the total is 1,891 businessmen. Even if one adds ten additional persons to the "Dealers in fuel" category, the total only come to 1,901. Since the total number of businessmen provided by Du Bois is 1,906, it is possible that one or more business categories were omitted from the original table.

9.   *Editor's note*: The metayer was an agricultural worker who worked a landlord's land in exchange for a portion of the crop's harvest. The landlord would provide tools and seed. The metayer was a sharecropper and an integral part of the crop-lien system. See "Metayer." http://www.thefreedictionary.com/metayer.

10.   *Editor's note*: The *peculium* is a Latin term which is derived from Roman law. The expression was used to reference property that could be held by a son, a wife, or a slave. See "*Peculium*." http://www.thefreedictionary.com/peculium.

11.   *Editor's note*: The table title, headings and the total line have been provided by the editor.

12.   *Editor's note*: In the original report, this capital investment range was identified as 1,000–2,505, and the dollar sign was missing.

13.   *Editor's note*: One of the papers submitted to the conference that was included in the third section of the conference final report was by Du Bois. The paper is found on pages 72–75. The paper title is "The Negro Newspaper." In this paper Du Bois compiled lists of publications produced by African Americans. The publications were grouped by the following types: magazines, daily papers, weekly papers, and school and college pa-

pers. The weekly papers were listed by state, and the total number of publications by all types was 153 publications.

Reading 10

The Negro and Crime[1]

THE development of a negro criminal class after emancipation was to be expected. It is impossible for such a social revolution to take place without giving rise to a class of men, who, in the new stress of life, under new responsibilities, would lack the will and power to make a way, and would consequently sink into vagrancy, poverty, and crime. Indeed it is astounding that a body of people whose family life had been so nearly destroyed, whose women had been forced into concubinage, whose labor had been enslaved and then set adrift penniless, that such a nation should in a single generation be able to point to so many pure homes, so many property-holders, so many striving law abiding citizens. "The vast majority of the colored people," says *The Atlanta Constitution*, "would no more commit heinous crime than would the corresponding white class," and the Rev. Dr. Hoss declares in the Nashville *Christian Advocate*, of which he is editor:

> The negroes on the whole have done astonishingly well. Their record since the war has been almost as honorable as the one they made while the conflict was raging. To hold the entire race responsible for the outrages committed by a few thousands, or a few score thousands of its members, is not just or right.

In the town of Palmetto, where the recent disturbance began, it was only last December that a Methodist conference declared:

> We observe with gratitude the sympathetic and cordial relations between the white and colored people of this village and community, and the mutual co-operation between them in Christian work and in civil life.

If one thing is certain, then, it is that the negro criminal in no Southern community represents the mass of the race, or can rightly be mistaken for it. Even in the matter of sexual crime the most prominent paper in the South declared editorially that "ninety-five percent" of the negro men "are as respectful toward white women as any people on earth." And whenever the terrible crime of rape has been beyond reasonable doubt proven upon a negro, he has been

103

found to be among the most ignorant and degraded of his people. The sexual looseness among the negroes themselves, which the nation that taught them now taunts them with, is slowly but surely disappearing. The rate of illegitimacy among them is probably less than in Austria or Italy, and it would be still smaller if law and public opinion in the South gave the defenseless black girl half the protection it throws about the white girl.

Granting then, as every fair-minded man must, that "in almost all the elements of civilization the race, as a whole, has made distinct and gratifying progress," to quote Dr. W. W. Landrum, Pastor First [white] Baptist Church of Atlanta, GA, the question then comes—and this is the crucial question—What is chiefly responsible for crime among Southern negroes, outside the economic effects of emancipation?

The first and greatest cause of negro crime in the South is the convict-lease system. States which use their criminals as sources of revenue in the hands of irresponsible speculators, who herd girls, boys, men and women promiscuously together without distinction or protection, who parade chained convicts in public, guarded by staves and pistols, and then plunge into this abyss of degradation the ignorant little black boy who steals a chicken or a handful of peanuts—what can such States expect but a harvest of criminals and prostitutes? Does it not seem natural that the State which produced Sam Hose is guilty, as *The Atlanta Constitution* declared March 22, of "the burning shame of converting our penal establishments into schools for crime?" and we are prepared to hear, notwithstanding the awful revelations of Governor Atkinson's prison commission:

> Georgia has not even made a beginning yet in the right direction. The provision of our new penal law will prove the veriest sham. We must get at the issue straight and separate juvenility from crime.

The next greatest cause of negro crime in the South is the attitude of the courts. The Southern courts have erred in two ways: One, in treating the crime of whites so leniently that red-handed murderers walk scot-free and the public has lost faith in methods of justice. The other, in treating the crimes and misdemeanors of negroes with such severity that the lesson of punishment is lost through pity for the punished. When, therefore, the number of negroes in Southern penal institutions is cited as evidence of their lawlessness, students must not forget this double standard of justice, which can best be illustrated by the following clippings from The Atlanta Constitution of January 22nd:

> Egbert Jackson [colored], aged thirteen, was given a sentence of $50, or ten months in the chain gang for larceny from the house. . . . The most affecting scene of all was the sentencing of Joe Redding, a white man, for the killing of his brother, John Redding. . . . Judge —— is a most tender-hearted man, and heard the prayers and saw the tears, and tempered justice with moderation, and gave the modern Cain two years in the penitentiary.

Of course Jackson could pay no such fine and went to the chain gang.

The third cause of crime is the increasing lawlessness and barbarity of mobs. Let a negro be simply accused of any crime from barn-burning to rape and he is liable to be seized by a mob, given no chance to defend himself, given neither trial, judge, nor jury, and killed. Passing over the acknowledged fact that many innocent negroes have thus been murdered, the point that is of greater gravity is that lawlessness is a direct encouragement to crime. It shatters the faith of the mass of negroes in justice; it leads them to shield criminals; it makes race hatred fiercer; it discourages honest effort; it transforms horror at crime into sympathy for the tortured victim; and it binds the hands and lessens the influence of those race leaders who are striving to preach forbearance and patience and honest endeavor to their people. It teaches eight million wronged people to despise a civilization which is not civilized.

Finally, the last cause of negro crime is the exaggerated and unnatural separation in the South of the best classes of whites and blacks. A drawing of the color line, that extends to street-cars, elevators, and cemeteries, which leaves no common ground of meeting, no medium of communication, no ties of sympathy between two races who live together and whose interests are at bottom one—such a discrimination is more than silly, it is dangerous. It makes it possible for the mass of whites to misinterpret the aims and aspiration of the negroes, to mistake self-reliance for insolence, and condemnation of lynch-law for sympathy with crime. It makes it possible for the negroes to believe that the best people of the South hate and despise them, and express their antipathy in proscribing them, taunting them and crucifying them. Such terrible misapprehensions are false, and the sooner some way is made by which the best elements of both races can sympathize with each other's struggles, and in a calm Christian spirit discuss them together—the sooner such conferences can take place all over the South the sooner lynch-law will disappear and crime be abated.

Note

1. *Editor's note*: This essay was originally published in 1899 in the *Independent*. The article appeared on pages 1355–57 of volume 51. Following the title, Du Bois was identified as the author. The citation read "By Prof. W.E. Burghardt Du Bois, of Atlanta University." After this citation the editor of the publication provided a comment enclosed in brackets. The comment was as follows, "Professor Du Bois is well known as the leading writer among the colored people of this country on social questions affecting his race." Du Bois' status as a sociologist can be inferred from this comment.

Reading 11

The American Negro at Paris[1]

On the banks of the Seine, opposite the *Rue des Nations*, stands a large, plain white building, where the promoters of the Paris Exposition have housed the world's ideas of sociology. As a matter of fact, anyone who takes his sociology from theoretical treatises would be rather disappointed at the exhibit; for there is little here of the "science of society." On the other hand, those who have followed historically the development, out of the old Political Economy, of a miscellaneous body of knowing chiefly connected with the larger aspects of human benevolence, will here find much of interest: the building and mutual-aid societies of France; the working-man's circles of Belgium; the city governments of Sweden; the Red Cross Society; the state insurance of Germany,—are all here strikingly exhibited by charts, statistics, models, and photographs.

The United States section of this building is small, and not, at first glance, particularly striking. There are, in the center, well-made tenement-house models; in one corner a small exhibit of the American Library Association, and elsewhere sets of interesting maps and photographs showing the work of factory inspectors and typical industrial plants. All these exhibits, are, unfortunately, rather fragmentary, and do scant justice to the wonderful social and economic development of America.

In the right-hand corner, however, as one enters, is an exhibit which, more than most others in the building, is sociological in the larger sense of the term— that is, is an attempt to give, in as systematic and compact a form as possible, the history and present condition of a large group of human beings. This is the exhibit of American Negroes, planned and executed by Negroes, and collected and installed under the direction of a Negro special agent, Mr. Thomas J. Calloway.

In this exhibit there are, of course, the usual paraphernalia for catching the eye—photographs, models, industrial work, and pictures. But it does not stop here; beneath all this is a carefully thought-out plan, according to which the exhibitors have tried to show:

(a) The history of the American Negro.

(b) His present condition.
(c) His education.
(d) His literature.

The history of the Negro is illustrated by charts and photographs; there is, for instance, a series of striking models of the progress of the colored people, beginning with the homeless freedman and ending with the modern brick schoolhouse and its teachers. There are charts of the increase of Negro population, the routes of the African slave-trade, the progress of emancipation, and the decreasing illiteracy. There are pictures of the old cabins, and, in three great manuscript volumes, the complete black code of Georgia, from colonial times to the end of the nineteenth century. Not the least interesting contribution to history is the case given to Negro medal-of-honor men in the army and navy—from the man who "seized the colors after two color-bearers had been shot down and bore them nobly through the fight" to the black men in the Spanish War who "voluntarily went ashore in the face of the enemy and aided in the rescue of their wounded comrades." It was a Massachusetts lawyer who replied to the Patent Office inquiry, "I never knew a negro to invent anything but lies;" and yet here is a record of 350 patents granted to black men since 1834.

The bulk of the exhibit, is naturally, an attempt to picture present conditions. Thirty-two charts, 500 photographs, and numerous maps and plans form the basis of this exhibit. The charts are in two sets, one illustrating conditions in the entire United States and the other conditions in the typical State of Georgia. At a glance one can see the successive steps by which the 220,000 Negroes of 1750 had increased to 7,500,000 in 1890; their distribution throughout the different States; a comparison of the size of the Negro population with European countries bringing out the striking fact that there are nearly half as many Negroes in the United States as Spaniards in Spain. The striking movement by which the 4 2/5 percent of Negroes living in the cities in 1860 has increased to 12 percent in 1890 is shown, as is also the fact that recognized mulattoes have increased 50 percent in 30 years, even in the defective census returns. Twenty percent of the Negroes are shown to be home-owners, 60 percent of their children are in school, and their illiteracy is less than that of Russia, and only equal to that of Hungary.

It was a good idea to supplement these very general figures with a minute social study in a typical Southern State. It would hardly be suggested, in the light of recent history, that conditions in the State of Georgia are such as to give a rose-colored picture of the Negro; and yet Georgia, having the largest Negro population, is an excellent field of study. Here again we have statistics: the increase of the black population in a century from 30,000 to 860,000, the huddling in the Black Belt for self-protection since the war, and a comparison of the age distribution with France showing the wonderful reproductive powers of the blacks. The school enrollment has increased from 10,000 in 1870 to 180,000 in 1897, and the Negroes are distributed among the occupations as follows:

In agriculture, 62 percent; in domestic and personal service, 28 percent; in manufacturing and mechanical industries, 5 percent; in trade and transportation, 4 1/2 percent; in the professions, 1/2 per cent.

They own 1,000,000 acres of land and pay taxes on $12,000,000 worth of property—not large, but telling figures; and the charts indicate, from year to year, the struggle they have had to accumulate and hold this property. There are several volumes of photographs of typical Negro faces, which hardly square with conventional American ideas. Several maps show the peculiar distribution of the white and black inhabitants in various towns and counties.

The education of the Negro is illustrated in the work of five great institutions—Fisk, Atlanta, and Howard Universities, and Tuskegee and Hampton Institutes. The exhibit from Fisk illustrates, by photographs and examination papers, the work of secondary and higher education. Atlanta University shows her work in social study and the work of her college and normal graduates; Howard University shows the work of her professional schools, especially in medicine, theology, and law. From Hampton there is an especially excellent series of photographs illustrating the Hampton idea of "teaching by doing," and from Tuskegee there are numerous specimens of work from the manual-training and technical departments.

Perhaps the most unique and striking exhibit is that of American Negro literature. The development of Negro thought—the view of themselves which these millions of freedmen have taken—is of intense psychological and practical interest. There are many who have scarcely heard of a Negro book, much less read one; still here is a bibliography made by the Library of Congress containing 1,400 titles of works written by Negroes; 200 of these books are exhibited on the shelves. The Negroes have 150 periodicals, mostly weekly papers, many of which are exhibited here.

We have thus, it may be seen, an honest, straightforward exhibit of a small nation of people, picturing their life and development without apology or gloss, and above all made by themselves. In a way this marks an era in the history of the Negroes of America. It is no new thing for a group of people to accomplish much under the help and guidance of a stronger group; indeed, the whole Palace of Social Economy at the Paris Exposition shows how vast a system of help and guidance of this order is being carried on today throughout the world. When, however, the inevitable question arises, What are these guided groups doing for themselves? there is in the whole building no more encouraging answer than that given by the American negroes, who are here shown to be studying, examining, and thinking of their own progress and prospects.[2]

Notes

1.   *Editor's note*: This essay originally appeared on pages 575–77 of the November 1900 issue of *The American Monthly Review of Reviews*. The article was included in

volume 22. A condensed version of this essay appeared on pages 620–21 of the November 1900 issue of *Public Opinion*. The abridged version of the essay appeared in volume 29 with the title, "The Sociological Exhibit of American Negroes."

    2.   *Editor's note*: A summary statement of the list of awards earned by the participants in the American Negro Exhibit individually and collectively was attached to Du Bois' original article. The list was provided by the American Negro Exhibit director, Thomas J. Calloway. The American Negro Exhibit collectively was awarded a Grand Prix, and Du Bois received a Gold Medal as collaborator and compiler of a social study on African American life in Georgia. "The Georgia Negro Exhibit: A Social Study" appears as Reading 16 in *The Sociological Souls of Black Folk*.

Reading 12

The Conservation of Races[1]

THE AMERICAN NEGRO has always felt an intense personal interest in discussions as to the origins and destinies of races: primarily because back of most discussions of race with which he is familiar, have lurked certain assumptions as to his natural abilities, as to his political, intellectual and moral status, which he felt were wrong. He has, consequently, been led to deprecate and minimize race distinctions, to believe intensely that out of one blood God created all nations, and to speak of human brotherhood as though it were the possibility of an already dawning tomorrow.

Nevertheless, in our calmer moments we must acknowledge that human beings are divided into races; that in this country the two most extreme types of the world's races have met, and the resulting problem as to the future relations of these types is not only of intense and living interest to us, but forms all epoch in the history of mankind.

It is necessary, therefore, in planning our movements, in guiding our future development, that at times we rise above the pressing, but smaller questions of separate schools and cars, wage-discrimination and lynch law, to survey the whole question of race in human philosophy and to lay, on a basis of broad knowledge and careful insight, those large lines of policy and higher ideals which may form our guiding lines and boundaries in the practical difficulties of every day. For it is certain that all human striving must recognize the hard limits of natural law, and that any striving, no matter how intense and earnest, which is against the constitution of the world, is vain. The question, then, which we must seriously consider is this: What is the real meaning of Race; what has, in the past, been the law of race development, and what lessons has the past history of race development to teach the rising Negro people?

When we thus come to inquire into the essential difference of races we find it hard to come at once to any definite conclusion. Many criteria of race differences have in the past been proposed, as color, hair, cranial measurements and language. And manifestly, in each of these respects, human beings differ widely. They vary in color, for instance, from the marble-like pallor of the Scandinavian to the rich, dark brown of the Zulu, passing by the creamy Slav, the yellow Chinese, the light brown Sicilian and the brown Egyptian. Men vary, too, in the texture of hair from the obstinately straight hair of the Chinese to the obstinately tufted and frizzled hair of the Bushman. In measurement of heads, again, men vary; from the broad-headed Tartar to the medium-headed European and the narrow-headed Hottentot; or, again in language, from the highly-inflected Roman tongue to the monosyllabic Chinese, All these physical characteristics are patent enough, and if they agreed with each other it would be very easy to classify mankind. Unfortunately for scientists, however, these criteria of race are most exasperatingly intermingled. Color does not agree with texture of hair, for many of the dark races have straight hair; nor does color agree with the breadth of the head, for the yellow Tartar has a broader head than the German; nor, again, has the science of language as yet succeeded in clearing up the relative authority of these various and contradictory criteria. The final word of science, so far, is that we have at least two, perhaps three, great families of human beings—the whites and Negroes, possibly the yellow race. That other races have arisen from the intermingling of the blood of these two. This broad division of the world's races which men like Huxley and Raetzel have introduced as more nearly true than the old five-race scheme of Blumenbach, is nothing more than an acknowledgment that, so far as purely physical characteristics are concerned, the differences between men do not explain all the differences of their history. It declares, as Darwin himself said, that great as is the physical unlikeness of the various races of men their likenesses are greater, and upon this rests the whole scientific doctrine of Human Brotherhood.

Although the wonderful developments of human history teach that the grosser physical differences of color, hair and bone go but a short way toward explaining the different roles which groups of men have played in Human Progress, yet there are differences—subtle, delicate and elusive, though they may be—which have silently but definitely separated men into groups. While these subtle forces have generally followed the natural cleavage of common blood, descent and physical peculiarities, they have at other times swept across and ignored these. At all times, however, they have divided human beings into races, which, while they perhaps transcend scientific definition, nevertheless, are clearly defined to the eye of the Historian and Sociologist.

If this be true, then the history of the world is the history, not of individuals, but of groups, not of nations, but of races, and he who ignores or seeks to override the race idea in human history ignores and overrides the central thought of all history. What, then, is a race? It is a vast family of human beings, generally of common blood and language, always of common history, traditions and impulses, who are both voluntarily and involuntarily striving together for the accomplishment of certain more or less vividly conceived ideals of life.

Turning to real history, there can be no doubt, first, as to the widespread, nay, universal, prevalence of the race idea, the race spirit, the race ideal, and as to its efficiency as the vastest and most ingenious invention for human progress. We, who have been reared and trained under the individualistic philosophy of the Declaration of Independence and the laissez-faire philosophy of Adam Smith, are loath to see and loath to acknowledge this patent fact of human history. We see the Pharaohs, Caesars, Toussaints, and Napoleons of history and forget the vast races of which they were but epitomized expressions. We are apt to think in our American impatience, that while it may have been true in the past that closed race groups made history, that here in conglomerate America *nous avons changer tout cela*—we have changed all that,[2] and have no need of this ancient instrument of progress. This assumption, of which the Negro people are especially fond, cannot be established by a careful consideration of history.

We find upon the world's stage today eight distinctly differentiated races, in the sense in which History tells us the word must be used. They are, the Slavs of eastern Europe, the Teutons of middle Europe, the English of Great Britain and America, the Romance nations of Southern and Western Europe, the Negroes of Africa and America, the Semitic people of Western Asia and Northern Africa, the Hindus of Central Asia, and the Mongolians of Eastern Asia. There are, of course, other minor race groups, as the American Indians, the Esquimaux and the South Sea Islanders; these larger races, too, are far from homogeneous; the Slav includes the Czech, the Magyar, the Pole, and the Russian; the Teuton includes the German, the Scandinavian, and the Dutch; the English include the Scotch, the Irish, and the conglomerate American. Under Romance nations the widely-differing Frenchman, Italian, Sicilian, and Spaniard are comprehended. The term Negro is, perhaps, the most indefinite of all, combining the Mulattoes and Zamboes of America and the Egyptians, Bantus, and Bushmen of Africa. Among the Hindus are traces of widely differing nations, while the great Chinese, Tartar, Corean, and Japanese families fall under the one designation—Mongolian.

The question now is: What is the real distinction between these nations? Is it the physical differences of blood, color and cranial measurements? Certainly we must all acknowledge that physical differences play a great part, and that, with wide exceptions and qualifications, these eight great races of today follow the cleavage of physical race distinctions; the English and Teuton represent the white variety of mankind; the Mongolian, the yellow; the Negroes, the black. Between these are many crosses and mixtures, where Mongolian and Teuton have blended into the Slav, and other mixtures have produced the Romance nations and the Semites. But while race differences have followed mainly physical race lines, yet no mere physical distinctions would really define or explain the deeper differences—the cohesiveness and continuity of these groups. The deeper differences are spiritual, psychical, differences—undoubtedly based on the physical, but infinitely transcending them. The forces that bind together the Teuton nations are, then, first, their race identity and common blood; secondly, and more important, a common history, common laws and religion, similar habits of thought and a conscious striving together for certain ideals of life. The whole process which has brought about these race differentiations has been a growth, and the great characteristic of this growth has been the differentiation of spiritual and mental differences between great races of mankind and the integration of physical differences.

The age of nomadic tribes of closely related individuals represents the maximum of physical differences. They were practically vast families, and there were as many groups as families. As the families came together to form cities the physical differences lessened, purity of blood was replaced by the requirement of domicile, and all who lived within the city bounds became gradually to be regarded as members of the group; i.e., there was a slight and slow breaking down of physical barriers. This, however, was accompanied by an increase of the spiritual and social differences between cities. This city became husbandmen, this, merchants, another warriors, and so on. The *ideals of life* for which the different cities struggled were different. When at last cities began to coalesce into nations there was another breaking down of barriers which separated groups of men. The larger and broader differences of color, hair and physical proportions were not by any means ignored, but myriads of minor differences disappeared, and the sociological and historical races of men began to approximate the present division of races as indicated by physical researches. At the same time the spiritual and physical differences of race groups which constituted the nations became deep and decisive. The English nation stood for constitutional liberty and commercial freedom; the German nation for science and philosophy; the Romance nations stood for literature and art, and the other race groups are striving, each in its own way, to develop for civilization its particular message, its particular ideal, which shall help to guide the world nearer and nearer that perfection of human life for which we all long, that "one far off Divine event."

This has been the function of race differences up to the present time. What shall be its function in the future? Manifestly some of the great races of today—particularly the Negro race—have not as yet given to civilization the full spiritual message which they are capable of giving. I will not say that the Negro race has as yet given no message to the world, for it is still a mooted question among scientists as to just how far Egyptian civilization was Negro in its origin; if it was not wholly Negro, it was certainly very closely allied. Be that as it may, however, the fact still remains that the full, complete Negro message of the whole Negro race has not as yet been given to the world: that the messages and ideal of the yellow race have not been completed, and that the striving of the mighty Slavs has but begun. The question is, then: How shall this message be delivered; how shall these various ideals be realized? The answer is plain: By the development of these race groups, not as individuals, but as races. For the development of Japanese genius, Japanese literature and art, Japanese spirit, only Japanese, bound and welded together, Japanese inspired by one vast ideal, can work out in its fullness the wonderful message which Japan has for the nations of the earth. For the development of Negro genius, of Negro literature and art, of Negro spirit, only Negroes bound and welded together, Negroes inspired by one vast ideal, can work out in its fullness the great message we have for humanity. We cannot reverse history; we are subject to the same natural laws as other races, and if the Negro is ever to be a factor in the world's history—if among the gaily-colored banners that deck the broad ramparts of civilization is to hang one uncompromising black, then it must be placed there by black hands, fashioned by black heads and hallowed by the travail of 200,000,000 black hearts beating in one glad song of jubilee.

For this reason, the advance guard of the Negro people—the 8,000,000 people of Negro blood in the United States of America—must soon come to realize that if they are to take their just place in the van of Pan-Negroism, then their destiny is not absorption by the white Americans. That if in America it is to be proven for the first time in the modern world that not only Negroes are capable of evolving individual men like Toussaint, the Savior, but are a nation stored with wonderful possibilities of culture, then their destiny is not a servile imitation of Anglo-Saxon culture, but a stalwart originality which shall unswervingly follow Negro ideals.

It may, however, be objected here that the situation of our race in America renders this attitude impossible; that our sole hope of salvation lies in our being able to lose our race identity in the commingled blood of the nation; and that any other course would merely increase the friction of races which we call race prejudice, and against which we have so long and so earnestly fought. Here, then, is the dilemma, and it is a puzzling one, I admit. No Negro who has given earnest thought to the situation of his people in America has failed, at some time in life, to find himself at these cross-roads; has failed to ask himself at some time: What, after all, am I? Am I an American or am I a Negro? Can I be both? Or is it my duty to cease to be a Negro as soon as possible and be an American? If I strive as a Negro, am I not perpetuating the very cleft that threatens and separates Black and White America? Is not my only possible practical aim the subduction of all that is Negro in me to the American? Does my black blood place upon me any more obligation to assert my nationality than German, or Irish or Italian blood would?

It is such incessant self-questioning and the hesitation that arises from it, that is malting the present period a time of vacillation and contradiction for the American Negro; combined race action is stifled, race responsibility is shirked, race enterprises languish, and the best blood, the best talent, the best energy of the Negro people cannot be marshaled to do the bidding of the race. They stand back to make room for every rascal and demagogue who chooses to cloak his selfish deviltry under the veil of race pride.

Is this right? Is it rational? Is it good policy? Have we in America a distinct mission as a race—a distinct sphere of action and an opportunity for race development, or is self-obliteration the highest end to which Negro blood dare aspire?

If we carefully consider what race prejudice really is, we find it, historically, to be nothing but the friction between different groups of people; it is the difference in aim, in feeling, in ideals of two different races; if, now, this difference exists touching territory, laws, language, or even religion, it is manifest that these people cannot live in the same territory without fatal collision; but if, on the other hand, there is substantial agreement in laws, language, and religion; if there is a satisfactory adjustment of economic life, then there is no reason why, in the same country and on the same street, two or three great national ideals might not thrive and develop, that men of different races might not strive togeth-er for their race ideals as well, perhaps even better, than in isolation. Here, it seems to me, is the reading of the riddle that puzzles so many of us. We are Americans, not only by birth and by citizenship, but by our political ideals, our language, our religion. Farther than that, our Americanism does not go. At that point, we are Negroes, members of a vast historic race that from the very dawn of creation has slept, but half awakening in the dark forests of its African father-land. We are the first fruits of this new nation, the harbinger of that black to-morrow which is yet destined to soften the whiteness of the Teutonic today. We are that people whose subtle sense of song has given America its only American music, its only American fairy tales, its only touch of pathos and humor amid its mad money-getting plutocracy. As such, it is our duty to conserve our physical powers, our intellectual endowments, our spiritual ideals; as a race we must strive by race organization, by race solidarity, by race unity to the realization of that broader humanity which freely recognizes differences in men, but sternly deprecates inequality in their opportunities of development.

For the accomplishment of these ends we need race organizations: Negro colleges, Negro newspapers, Negro business organizations, a Negro school of literature and art, and an intellectual clearing house, for all these products of the Negro mind, which we may call a Negro Academy. Not only is all this necessary for positive advance, it is absolutely imperative for negative defense. Let us not deceive ourselves at our situation in this country. Weighted with a heritage of moral iniquity from our past history, hard pressed in the economic world by foreign immigrants and native prejudice, hated here, despised there and pitied everywhere; our one haven of refuge is ourselves, and but one means of ad-vance, our own belief in our great destiny, our own implicit trust in our ability and worth. There is no power under God's high heaven that can stop the ad-vance of eight thousand thousand honest, earnest, inspired and united people. But—and here is the rub—they *must* be honest, fearlessly criticizing their own faults, zealously correcting them; they must be *earnest*. No people that laughs at itself, and ridicules itself, and wishes to God it was anything but itself ever wrote its name in history; it *must* be inspired with the Divine faith of our black mothers, that out of the blood and dust of battle will march a victorious host, a mighty nation, a peculiar people, to speak to the nations of earth a Divine truth that shall make them free. And such a people must be united; not merely united for the organized theft of political spoils, not united to disgrace religion with whoremongers and ward-heelers; not united merely to protest and pass resolu-tions, but united to stop the ravages of consumption among the Negro people, united to keep black boys from loafing, gambling and crime; united to guard the purity of black women and to reduce that vast army of black prostitutes that is today marching to hell; and united in serious organizations, to determine by careful conference and thoughtful interchange of opinion the broad lines of poli-cy and action for the American Negro.

This, is the reason for being which the American Negro Academy has. It aims at once to be the epitome and expression of the intellect of the black-blooded people of America, the exponent of the race ideals of one of the world's great races. As such, the Academy must, if successful, be

(*a*). Representative in character.
(*b*). Impartial in conduct.
(*c*). Firm in leadership.

It must be representative in character; not in that it represents all interests or all factions, but in that it seeks to comprise something of the *best* thought, the most unselfish striving and the highest ideals. There are scattered in forgotten nooks and corners throughout the land, Negroes of some considerable training, of high minds, and high motives, who are unknown to their fellows, who exert far too little influence. These the Negro Academy should strive to bring into touch with each other and to give them a common mouthpiece.

The Academy should be impartial in conduct; while it aims to exalt the people it should aim to do so by truth—not by lies, by honesty—not by flattery. It should continually impress the fact upon the Negro people that they must not expect to have things done for them—they MUST DO FOR THEMSELVES; that they have on their hands a vast work of self-reformation to do, and that a little less complaint and whining, and a little more dogged work and manly striving would do us more credit and benefit than a thousand Force or Civil Rights bills.

Finally, the American Negro Academy must point out a practical path of advance to the Negro people; there lie before every Negro today hundreds of questions of policy and right which must be settled and which each one settles now, not in accordance with any rule, but by impulse or individual preference; for instance: What should be the attitude of Negroes toward the educational qualification for voters? What should be our attitude toward separate schools? How should we meet discriminations on railways and in hotels? Such questions need not so much specific answers for each part as a general expression of policy, and nobody should be better fitted to announce such a policy than a representative honest Negro Academy.

All this, however, must come in time after careful organization and long conference. The immediate work before us should be practical and have direct bearing upon the situation of the Negro. The historical work of collecting the laws of the United States and of the various States of the Union with regard to the Negro is a work of such magnitude and importance that nobody but one like this could think of undertaking it. If we could accomplish that one task we would justify our existence.

In the field of Sociology an appalling work lies before us. First, we must unflinchingly and bravely face the truth, not with apologies, but with solemn earnestness. The Negro Academy ought to sound a note of warning that would echo in every black cabin in the land: *Unless we conquer our present vices they will conquer us*; we are diseased, we are developing criminal tendencies, and an alarmingly large percentage of our men and women are sexually impure. The Negro Academy should stand and proclaim this over the housetops, crying with Garrison: *I will not equivocate, I will not retreat a single inch, and I will be heard.* The Academy should seek to gather about it the talented, unselfish men, the pure and noble-minded women, to fight an army of devils that disgraces our manhood and our womanhood. There does not stand today upon God's earth a race more capable in muscle, in intellect, in morals, than the American Negro, if he will bend his energies in the right direction; if he will

> Burst his birth's invidious bar
> And grasp the skirts Of happy chance,
> And breast the blows of circumstance,
> And grapple with his evil star.

In science and morals, I have indicated two fields of work for the Academy. Finally, in practical policy, I wish to suggest the following *Academy Creed*:

1. We believe that the Negro people, as a race, have a contribution to make to civilization and humanity, which no other race can make.

2. We believe it the duty of the Americans of Negro descent, as a body, to maintain their race identity until this mission of the Negro people is accomplished, and the ideal of human brotherhood has become a practical possibility.

3. We believe that, unless modern civilization is a failure, it is entirely feasible and practicable for two races in such essential political, economic, and religious harmony as the white and colored people of America, to develop side by side in peace and mutual happiness, the peculiar contribution which each has to make to the culture of their common country.

4. As a means to this end we advocate, not such social equality between these races as would disregard human likes and dislikes, but such a social equilibrium as would; throughout all the complicated relations of life, give due and just consideration to culture, ability, and moral worth, whether they be found under white or black skins.

5. We believe that the first and greatest step toward the settlement of the present friction between the races—commonly called the Negro Problem—lies in the correction of the immorality, crime, and laziness among the Negroes themselves, which still remains as a heritage from slavery. We believe that only earnest and long continued efforts on our own part can cure these social ills.

6. We believe that the second great step toward a better adjustment of the relations between the races, should be a more impartial selection of ability in the economic and intellectual world, and a greater respect for personal liberty and worth, regardless of race. We believe that only earnest efforts on the part of the white people of this country will bring much needed reform in these matters.

7. On the basis of the foregoing declaration, and firmly believing in our high destiny, we, as American Negroes, are resolved to strive in every honorable

way for the realization of the best and highest aims, for the development of strong manhood and pure womanhood, and for the rearing of a race ideal in America and Africa, to the glory of God and the uplifting of the Negro people.

Notes

1.   *Editor's note*: This essay was originally published in 1897 as the second "Occasional Paper" of the American Negro Academy.

2.   *Editor's note*: Du Bois provided his own English translation of this French idiom. See "*Nous avons changer tout cela*." http://www.merriam-webster.com/dictionary /nous%20avons.

Reading 13

Careers Open to College-Bred Negroes[1]

TO THE YOUNG ears that hearken behind college walls at the confused murmur of the world beyond, there comes at times a strangely discordant note to mar the music of their lives. Men tell them that college is a play world—the mirage of real life; the place where men climb or seek to climb heights whence they must sooner or later sink into the dust of real life. Scarcely a commencement season passes but what, amid congratulation and rejoicing, amid high resolve and lofty sentiment, stalks this pale, half-mocking ghost, crying to the new born bachelor in arts: You have played—now comes work. And, therefore, students of the class of '98, I have thought to take this oft-repeated idea and talk with you in this last hour of your college days about the relation which, in your lives, a liberal education bears to bread-winning.

And first, young men and women, I heartily join in congratulating you to whom has been vouchsafed the vision splendid—you who stand where once I stood,

> "When meadow, grove, and stream,
> The earth, and every common sight,
> To me did seem
> Apparelled in celestial light,
> The glory and the freshness of a dream."

And yet, not a dream, but a mighty reality—a glimpse of the higher life, the broader possibilities of humanity, which is granted to the man who, amid the rush and roar of living, pauses four short years to learn what living means. The vision of the rich meaning of life, which comes to you as students, as men of culture, comes dimly or not at all to the plodding masses of men, and even to men of high estate it comes too often blurred and distorted by selfishness and greed. But you have seen it in the freshness and sunshine of youth; here you have talked with Aristotle and Shakespeare, have learned of Euclid, have heard the solemn drama of a world, and thought the thoughts of seers and heroes of the world that was. Out of such lore, out of such light and shade, has the vision of the world appeared before you: you have not all comprehended it; you have, many of you, but glanced at its brilliant hues, and have missed the speaking splendor of the background.

I remember how once I stood near the ancient cathedral at Berne, looking at the Alps; I heard the rushing waters below and knew their music; I saw the rolling fields beyond and thought them pretty; then I saw the hills and the towering masses of dark mountains; they were beautiful, and yet I saw them with a tinge of disappointment, but even as I turned away, I glanced toward the sky, and then my heart leaped—for there above the meadows and the waters, above the hills and the mountains, blazed in the evening sunshine, the mighty, snow-clad peaks of the high Alps, glistening and glorious with the hues of the rainbow, in spotless purity and awful majesty. And so many a man to whom opportunity has unveiled some revelation of the broader, truer world, has turned away from it, half seen and half known.

But some have seen the vision, have comprehended all the meaning of a liberal education; and now, as you turn away half-regretfully, half gladly, what relation has this day of transfiguration to the hard, cold paths of the world beyond these walls? Is it to be but a memory and a longing, or if more than this, how much more?

I presume that few of you have fully realized that with tomorrow morning you begin to earn your own bread and butter; that today is the commencement of a new life on which you are to find self-support by daily toil. And I am glad if you have not given this matter too much thought or worry, for, surely, if you have done well your college work you have had other things to think of, problems of life and humanity far broader than your own single destiny; not that you have neglected dreams and plans of parts that you might play in life, but that you have scarce thought out its dry details. And, therefore, to most of you the nearness of real life dawned this morning with a certain suddenness; with something of that dark dismay with which the human creator faces his own creature—with some thought, too, half of rebellion and an aimless asking: Why must I turn from so pleasant a life to one hard and matter of fact? Why must I leave the pleasures of study and dear companionship and high inspiration to "bear the whips and scorns of time, the oppressor's wrong, the proud man's contumely?"

Today the paradox of life rises over you as never before, and you wonder why you, of all men, should not have been born rich and privileged, not to see the vision of the world and all the glory that shall be, fade into some distant future, leaving long paths of dirt and rocks between. All these questions you have asked, I have asked, and all men have asked, who, whether on the college rostrum or with the pick and shovel, have, on a commencement morning, turned from study to deeds, from ideals to realization, from thought to life.

All this I cannot answer plainly, and yet the shadow of answer falls on us all; for why should the sun rise if there be neither noon nor evening, and what is a life that is all beginning? And have not these, your college days, been all the happier for the promise and prophecy of a life to come?

Three universal laws underlie the necessity of earning a living: the law of work, the law of sacrifice, the law of service. The law of work declares that to live one must toil, continuously, zealously; the apple may hang ripe upon the tree, but to eat we must pick it; grain will sprout and grow, but not till we plant it; houses will shelter us and clothes cover us only as we build and weave. Sometimes, to be sure, it may seem that enjoyment came without work and sacrifice—but it is not so. Someone toils, someone delves, and though we may shift our burden on the bowed shoulders of others—yet that is the necessity of the sick, or the shame of the lazy, or the crime of the coward.

Blind toil alone, however, will not satisfy the wants of aught but the lowest and simplest culture; the greater satisfaction comes from the sacrifice of today's enjoyment that tomorrow's may be greater; of this year's consumption to increase next year's production; of the indulgence of youth to the vigor of old age, of the pleasure of one life to the richer heritage of humanity; this is the law of sacrifice, and we see it everywhere: in the fruit we save to ripen, in the fields that lie fallow, in the years given to training and education, and in the self-sacrifice of a Socrates, a Darwin, or a David Livingstone.

Even this does not complete the laws of life as we find it in the twilight of the nineteenth century. We must not only work and sacrifice for ourselves and others, but also render each other mutual service. The physician must heal not himself, but all men; the tailor must mend the whole village; the farmer must plant for all. Thus in the civilized world each serves all, and all serve each, and the binding force is faith and skill, and the skill is bounded only by human possibility and genius, and the faith is faithful even to the untrue.

Such are the laws of that life, young people, which you enter today. And upon these laws have been built through the ages, in sweat of brow and sorrow of soul, all that fair world whose darkly glorious vision has made its study sweet to you, and its knowledge precious.

While these be the laws of universal life, their application differs in each age, and an equipment in life suitable to one century may be fatally unsuited to another. Therefore, you must not make the mistake of misunderstanding the age in which you live; and I especially warn you here, because as American Negroes, in the strange environment and unusual conditions of life which surround you, it will be peculiarly easy for you to fail to catch the spirit of the times; to distort the proportions of life, to seek to do what others have done better, and to seek quickly to undo what cannot legally be undone. I have often feared that the failure of many a promising young Negro was due largely to this natural ignorance. Young Negroes are born in a social system of caste that belongs to the middle ages; they inherit the moral looseness of a sixteenth century; they learn to lisp the religious controversies of the seventeenth century; they are stirred by discussions of the rights of man that belong to the eighteenth century, and it is not wonderful if they hardly realize that they live upon the threshold of the twentieth century. You, men of Fisk, must not misunderstand your age; you must know that the world does not feel the injustice of caste as it once did, but rather sees in it some antidote for a vulgar democracy; you must remember that there are central elementary moral precepts which the world utterly refuses to excuse or palliate; you must realize that the controversies of Methodists and Baptists chiefly interest antiquarians and not active Christians of today; that we insist today on men's duties rather than their rights, and that the spirit of the century in which you will work is service not indulgence.

And surely no century more richly deserves understanding than the nineteenth. It has not the romantic interest of the fifteenth, when the world rose in a dream and wandered in the sunshine of its new discovered self, and poetry and art and tales from overseas; it has not the rugged might of that sixteenth century, when the dark monk faced the emperor of all the world, daring to be honest rather than orthodox, and crying, "Here I stand. God help me! I cannot waver."

But whatever the nineteenth century may lack in romantic or striking interest, it repays and more than repays in human opportunity; in the broadness of its conception of humanity, in the wonderful organization of effort to serve humanity. Never before have work and sacrifice and service meant so much, never before were there so many workers, such widespread sacrifice, such world-service. In the business of governing men, never before did so many take part. The issue is not altogether successful, and yet its measure of success far exceeds the wildest dreams of the world of long ago.

Never before have so many hands and heads joined to make the earth yield her increase, to make glad the waste places of the earth, to ply the loom, and whirl the spindle, and transform the useless and the worthless. On our breakfast table lies each morning the toil of Europe, Asia, and Africa, and the isles of the sea; we sow and spin for unseen millions, and countless myriads weave and plant for us; we have made the earth smaller and life broader by annihilating distance, magnifying the human voice and the stars, binding nation to nation, until today, for the first time in history, there is one standard of human culture as well in New York as in London, in Cape Town as in Paris, in Bombay as in Berlin.

Is not this, then, a century worth living in—a day worth serving? And through toil, hard, heavy toil, be the price of life, shall we not, young men and women, gladly work and sacrifice and serve

> "That one, far off, divine event,
> Toward which the whole creation moves"?

And we serve first for the sake of serving—to develop our own powers, gain the mastery of this human machine, and come to the broadest, deepest self-realization. And then we serve for real end of service, to make life no narrow, selfish thing, but to let it sweep as sweeps the morning—broad and full and free for all men and all time, that you and I and all may earn a living and earn, too, much more than that—a life worth living.

This, fellow-workers, is the veil of toil that hangs before the vision glorious. And yet, when on commencement morning, we leave behind the vivid hues of this, our inspiration, believe me, it is not easy to guard the sacred image, to keep alive the holy fire that lights and lightens life; to hold amid the toil and turmoil of living those old ideals fixed and tranquil before the soul. How often do we see young collegians enter life with high resolve and lofty purpose and then watch them shrink and shrink and shrink into sordid, selfish, shrewd plodders, full of distrust and sneers. Woe to the man, who, with the revelation of the world once before him, as it stands before you now, has let it fade and whiten into common day—life is death.

But you who, firm and inspired, turn toward the work of living, undismayed, knowing the world that was, loving the world that is, and believing in the world that is to be, just what can you do—what careers may you follow to realize the ideals and hopes of this day?

You cannot surely be knights and kings and magicians, but you can choose careers fully as wonderful and much more useful. You look about you in the world and see servants, they whose function it is to help the helpless, the weak and the busy—to cook, that Washington may command armies; to sweep, that Edison may have time to think. You see the laborer, that wizard who places his weak shoulders against the physical world and overturns mountains and pushes away forests, and guides the rivers, and garners the harvests. You see the manufacturer guiding the laborer with brains and with capital: he is the alchemist in whose alembic dirt turns to houses, grass to coats, and stones to food. The merchant you see standing beside him, the prophet who enables us to laugh at famine, and want, and waste, by bringing together buyer and seller, maker and user, reader and writer. There is the teacher, the giver of immortal life, the one who makes the child to start where his fathers left off, that the world may think on with one mind. Yonder stands the physician with the long sought elixir of life, the lawyer clothed in justice, the minister who seeks to add to justice righteousness, and to life ideals higher than life. Your restless eye may easily overlook the corner where sits the scientist seeking the truth that shall make us free, or the other, where the artist dies that there may live a poem or painting or a thought.

All these ways of earning a living you may see in the world, and many more. But it does not follow that you may idly or thoughtlessly choose one as you pick a flower on a summer's day. To choose a life calling is a serious thing: first, you must consider not so much what you want to do as what wants to be done; secondly, you cannot wander at will over all the world of work that wants workers, but duty and privilege and special advantage calls to the work that lies nearest your hands. The German works for Germany, the Englishman serves England, and it is the duty of the Negro to serve his blood and lineage, and so working, each for each, and all for each, we realize the goal of each for all.

The concrete question, then, that faces you of the class of '98, is What part can I best take in the striving of the eight million men and women who are bound to me by a common sorrow and a common hope, that through the striving of the Negro people this land of our fathers may live and thrive?

The most useful, and universal work, and the type of all other work, is that of the servant and common laborer. The ordinary, unskilled part of this work I pass over—it is useful, it is honorable, but you have been trained for skilled work, and it is throwing away the money of this institution if its college graduates are to become Pullman porters. Even the higher branches of house-service, as cooking and nursing, and the great field of skilled labor, are rather for different training, and you will rightly leave them to the skilled graduates of our great industrial schools, with the sincere hope that so useful and promising avenues will soon be filled by able and honest artisans.

The first field that opens itself to you is the calling of the farmer. I do not mean the farm hand or the milkmaid, nor even the agricultural scientist. I mean the man who, by rational methods and business sense, with a knowledge of the world market, the methods of transportation, and the possibilities of the soil, will make this land of the South to bloom and blossom like Belgium and Holland, France and Germany; who will transform the slipshod, wasteful, happy-go-lucky farming of the South into the scientific business methods of New England and the West. There is little more reason for leaving farming to people without brains or culture than there would be in thus abandoning the other great fields of industry. Especially, however, do the Negro people need the country gentleman—the man of air and health and home and morals; and today we have an unparalleled chance to supply such an aristocracy. Throughout Tennessee and Georgia and Virginia, where the young people are hurrying to the industries of the cities, stand the fine old abandoned farms and decaying mansions of a gentry that has passed. You are the ones to buy these farms at a nominal price, start a new agriculture; and a balance for the sickly crowding of cities and to furnish the food and material which these cities increasingly demand, and thus help to solve some of the most intricate of our social problems.

The next great field open to you is that of the merchant, where again there is among Negroes no discouraging competition, and a broad field for development.

Those Negroes who urge the blight of color prejudice as a barrier to their entering mercantile pursuits, quite forget that they have before them an undeveloped market of eight million souls, and that these millions spend every year $150,000,000 to $300,000,000, and that a part of this expenditure, at least, could be made through Negro merchants, if well trained, educated, active men would only enter this field and cultivate it. Of course, the training of slavery was most unfortunate for business qualities. There linger among the freedmen's sons habits of laziness, of being perpetually five minutes behind time, of inattention to detail, which are fatal to modern business methods. All this can and must be unlearned, and the college man who, making himself familiar with the best business methods of a business age, starts in to open this field, will not only earn and deserve a living for himself, but will make it easier for thousands to follow his example.

And this brings me to a thought that I want especially to impress upon college men: The time has come when the American Negro is being expected to take care of himself, and not much longer to depend on alms and charity; he must become self-supporting—a source of strength and power instead of a menace and a burden to the nation; the hindrance that today prevents him from fulfilling this expectation with reasonable quickness is his anomalous economic condition—his lack of remunerative employment. And you, young men and women, are the ones to supply this lack. We have workers enough, brawny and willing; we have some skill, and the industrial schools are furnishing more; moreover, a people that have today more than $26,000,000 invested in church property alone, and who spend at least $10,000,000 each year in those churches, have capital enough to collect in savings banks and put into industrial enterprises. But what we do lack, and what schools like this must begin to supply in increasing numbers is the captain of industry, the man who can marshal and guide workers in industrial enterprises, who can foresee the demand and supply it—note the special aptitude of laborers and turn it to advantage—so guide with eye and brain the work of these black millions, that, instead of adding to the poverty of the nation and subtracting from its wealth, we may add to the wealth of the land and make Negro poverty no longer a by-word.

Here is a field for development such as few ages offer—a body of willing workers such as few nations furnish. And this field calls not for mere money-makers, or those who would ape the silly display and ostentation of certain classes of Americans; nor does it call for men narrowed and shrunk by the soul destroying commercialism of the hour, that philosophy which imagines men made for industry and not industry for men; but rather here is a chance to set a nation working, to make their work more effective, to build and fortify Negro homes, to educate Negro children, to establish institutions of protection, reform, and rescue, and to make the Negro people able to help others even as others have helped us.

Let us turn now to the professional class and ask about the openings there for college-bred men. As to the demand in one department there can be no doubt. If ever a nation needed the gospel of health presented to them, it is the negro race, with its alarming death rate, its careless habits, its widows and orphans, and its sick and maimed. For the well trained physician, as distinguished from the quack, and the man who is too hurried to learn, there is a large and important work. The remuneration which a poor people can pay will not be large, but the chance for usefulness and far-reaching influence on the future of our race and country can scarcely be over-estimated. Especially is the calling open to young women, who ought to find here congenial, useful employment, and employment, perhaps, next in nobility to that of the noblest and best—motherhood.

When we come to the profession of law we have a narrower and less obvious field, one in which there is plenty of room for success, but against the peculiar difficulties of which, young people need warning and advice. These difficulties arise from the fact that, first, the Negro himself furnishes little important or lucrative law business, and, secondly, even among the whites, the profession is overcrowded, and only men of ability or some wealth and much influence can expect much success. Thus, many changes must come before the handicap of color prejudice will allow Negroes to start in this profession with an even chance. Yet, here as elsewhere, blood will tell.

For thirty years the chief function of the Negro college has been that of furnishing teachers for the Negro schools, and the extraordinary success and value of this work has not yet been adequately recognized. Nevertheless, it is evident that this work has already passed through many phases and is about to pass through others. Fisk University at first furnished common school teachers, then teachers of schools that teach common school teachers; finally, teachers of men who teach the teachers; with each of these steps comes, to be sure, a demand for better quality, but also for a smaller quantity. The field for teaching, therefore, open to the class of '98, is smaller than that open to former classes and more exacting in its demands. What is true now is apt to be emphasized in the future; specially trained teachers of high attainments will ever find some demand for their services. On the other hand, most college graduates will slowly turn to other work. Hereafter, when Negro education is more firmly founded, the better trained college men will be more in demand. This, then, is a field still open—of broad usefulness and demanding the very best in character, and the better in training and knowledge, only the competition is sharp, and is destined to be sharper.

I now turn to the Christian ministry with something of diffidence. The development of the Negro church has been so extraordinary, and of such deep sociological interest that its future course is a matter of great concern. As it is now, churches organized among Negroes are, for the most part, curiously composite institutions, which combine the work of churches, theaters, newspapers, homes, schools, and lodges. As a social and business institution, the church has had marvelous success and has done much for the Negro people. As a religious institution, also, it has played some part, but it is needless to say that its many other activities have not increased the efficiency of its function as a teacher of morals and inspirer to the high ideals of Christianity. An institution so popular that there is now in the United States one organization for every sixty Negro families, has, naturally, already attracted to its leadership a vast army of men. Moreover, the severest charge that can be brought against the Christian education of the Negro in the South during the last thirty years, is the reckless way in which sap-headed young fellows, without ability, and, in some cases, without character, have been urged and pushed into the ministry. It is time now to halt. It is time to say to young men like you: Qualifications that would be of no service elsewhere are not needed in the church; a general desire to be good, joined to a glib tongue, is not the sort of combination that is going to make the Negro people stop stealing and committing adultery. And, instead of aimless, wholesale invitations to enter this calling of life, we need to put our hands kindly on the shoulders of some young candidates, and tell them firmly that they are not fitted to be heads of the church of Christ. What we need is not more but fewer ministers, but in that lesser number we certainly need earnest, broad, and cultured men; men who do a good deal more than they say; men of brood plans and farseeing thought; men who will extend the charitable and rescue work of the churches, encourage home getting, guard the children of the flock, not on Sundays, but on week days, make the people use savings banks, and, in fine, men who will really be active agents of social and moral reform in their communities. There, and there only, is the soil which will transform the mysticism of Negro religion into the righteousness of Christianity.

There is then an opening for college men in this field, but it is a field to be entered with more care than others, not with less; to be chosen by men of more stable character than others, not of less; and it is the one field where the man who doubts his fitness had best give the world the benefit of the doubt. But to those consecrated men who can and will place themselves today at the head of Negro religious life and guide this wavering people to a Christianity pure and holy and true—to those men in the day of reckoning shall surely come the benediction of a useful life, and the "Well done!" of the Master.

Finally, I come to the field of the scientist and the artist—of the men who seek to know and create. And here little can be said of openings or of hindrances—for the way of such men is the dim and unfenced moor that wends its path beyond the world into the unknown; the man who enters here must expect long journeys, poor and unknown and often discouraged. To do in science and literature today anything worth the doing, anything that is really good and lasting, is hard to anyone, impossible to many. And here the young Negro so often forgets that "art is long, and time is fleeting." The first applause of his good-natured race too often turns his head; lets him rest on his oars, and instead of pursuing more doggedly the faint chance of doing some little masterpiece, he lingers upon his notoriety, and puts his picture and biography in the papers. For the man who will work, and dig, and starve, there is a chance to do here incalculable good for the Negro race; for the woman in whose soul the divine music of our fathers has touched some answering chord of genius, there is a chance to do more than follow the masters; to all of you in whom the tragedy of life, or its fitful comedy, has created a tale worth the telling, there is a chance to gain listeners who will know no color line. Everywhere there is work to be done; in physical and social science, in literature, painting and architecture, in music and sculpture, in every place where genius and toil will unite and strive.

Let me now briefly review these fields of work:

A broad field of scientific, business-like farming.

The uncultivated but promising field of the Negro merchant, with a constituency of eight millions.

The pressing demands for captains of industry to employ the labor, to direct the work, and develop the capacity of Negro workmen by industrial enterprise.

The large field for well trained physicians.

Some small demand for lawyers.

A considerable field for specially trained teachers.

The pressing necessity for fewer ministers of better type and more thorough devotion.

An ever open field for talent and application in literature, science, and art.

Such are some of the paths that open before you, class of '98, and along these you go toward the goal you have set for yourselves. Which path you will take you must choose, and the choice is difficult. Nevertheless, it cannot be long put off—for no choice is a choice. And when you have chosen, stand by it, for the man who ever is wavering and choosing again is wasting God's time. Choose, then, remembering that failure is the lot of many men, and that no success will be so marvelous but what it beckons to greater goals beyond.

And with the life work chosen, remember that it can become, as you will it, drudgery or heroism, prosaic or romantic, brutal or divine. Who of the world to-day cares whether Washington was a farmer or a merchant? Who thinks of Lincoln as a country lawyer, or reads of St. Peter, the fisherman, prays to Jesus Christ, the carpenter? If you make the object of your life calling food and drink, food and drink it will yield you grudgingly—but if above and beyond mere existence you seek to play well your part because it is worth playing—to do your duty because the world thirsts for your service, to perform clean, honest, thorough work, not for cheap applause, but because the work needs to be done, then is all your toil and drudgery transfigured into divine service and joins the mighty lives that have swept beyond time into the everlasting world. In this sense, is it, young men and women, that the vision of life you have gained here is truer and holier and more real than the narrow, sordid views of life which you meet on the streets and in the homes of smaller souls. Cling to those ideals, cherish them, and in travail and sorrow, if need be, make them more true.

It is now ten years since I stood amid these walls on my commencement morning, ten years full of toil and happiness and sorrow, and the full delight of hard work. And as I look back on that youthful gleam, and see the vision splendid, the trailing clouds of glory that lighted then the wide way of life, I am ever glad that I stepped into the world guided of strong faith in its promises, and inspired by no sordid aims. And from that world I come back to welcome you, my brothers and my sisters. I cannot promise you happiness always, but I can promise you divine discontent with the imperfect. I cannot promise you success—'tis not in mortals to command success.

But as you step into life I can give you three watchwords: First, you are Negroes, members of that dark, historic race that from the world's dawn has slept to hear the trumpet summons sound through our ears. Cherish unwavering faith in the blood of your fathers, and make sure this last triumph of humanity. Remember next, that you are gentlemen and ladies, trained in the liberal arts and subjects in that vast kingdom of culture that has lighted the world from its infancy and guided it through bigotry and falsehood and sin. As such, let us see in you an unfaltering honesty wedded to that finer courtesy and breeding which is the heritage of the well trained and the well born. And, finally, remember that you are the sons of Fisk University, that venerable mother who rose out of the blood and dust of battle to work the triumphs of the Prince of Peace. The mighty blessing of all her sons and daughters encompass you, and the sad sacrifice of every pure soul, living and dead, that has made her what she is, bend its dark wings about you and make you brave and good! And then through the weary striving and disappointment of life fear not for the end, even though you fail:

> "Truth forever on the scaffold,
> Wrong forever on the throne,
> Yet that scaffold sways the future,
> And behind the dim unknown
> Standeth God within the shadow,
> Keeping watch above his own."[2]

Notes

1. *Editor's note*: This essay was the June 1898 commencement address for Fisk University graduates. Du Bois received his B.A. from Fisk in 1888. This address was originally published in *Two Addresses Delivered by Alumni of Fisk University, in connection with the Anniversary Exercises of their Alma Mater, June, 1898*. This address was published by Fisk University in 1898.

2. *Editor's note*: In the original publication of this essay, the phrase, "Commencement Address, Fisk University, June 1898," appeared at the end of the address.

Reading 14

The Problem of Amusement[1]

I wish to discuss with you somewhat superficially a phase of development in the organized life of American Negroes which has hitherto received scant notice. It is the question of the amusements of Negroes—what their attitude toward them is, what institutions among them conduct the recreations, and what the tendency of indulgence is in amusements of various sorts. I do not pretend that this is one of the more pressing of the Negro problems, but nevertheless it is destined as time goes on to become more and more so; and at all times and in all places, the manner, method, and extent of a people's recreation is of vast importance to their welfare.

I have been in this case especially spurred to take under consideration this particular one of the many problems affecting the Negroes in cities and in the country because I have long noted with silent apprehension a distinct tendency among us, to depreciate and belittle and sneer at means of recreation, to consider amusement as the peculiar property of the devil, and to look upon even its legitimate pursuit as time wasted and energy misspent. I have heard sermon after sermon and essay after essay thunder warnings against the terrible results of pleasure and the awful end of those who are depraved enough to seek pleasure. I have heard such a fusillade of "don'ts" thrown at our young people: don't dance, don't play cards, don't go to the theatre, don't drink, don't smoke, don't sing songs, don't play kissing games, don't play billiards, don't play football, don't go on excursions—that I have not been surprised, gentlemen and ladies, to find in the feverish life of a great city, hundreds of Negro boys and girls who have listened for a life-time to the warning, "Don't do this or you'll go to hell," and then have taken the bit between their teeth and said, "Well, let's go to hell."

If you go out through the country side of Virginia, to the little towns and hamlets, the first thing you will note is the scarcity of young men and women. There are babies aplenty, and boys and girls up to fifteen, sixteen, and seventeen—then suddenly the supply seems to stop, and from eighteen to thirty there is a great gap. Where are these young people? They are in Norfolk, Richmond, Baltimore, Washington, Philadelphia, and New York. In one ward of Philadelphia young people between the ages of sixteen and thirty form over a third of the population; the Negro population of the whole city of Philadelphia, which has increased fully one hundred per cent since 1860, has received its main element

133

of increase from these young boys and girls. Why have they gone? Primarily, their migration is, of course, but a belated ripple of that great wave city-ward which is redistributing the population of England, France, Italy, Germany, and the United States, and draining the country districts of those lands of their bone and sinew. The whole movement is caused by that industrial revolution which has transferred the seat of human labor from agriculture to manufacturing and concentrated manufacturing in cities, thus by higher wages attracting the young people. This is the primary motive, but back of this is a powerful and in some cases even more deciding motive; and that is the thirst for amusement. You, who were born and reared amid the kaleidoscopic life of a great city, scarcely realize what an irresistible attraction city life has for one who has long experienced the dull, lifeless monotony of the country. When now that country life has been further shorn of the few pleasures usually associated with it, when the public opinion of the best class of Negroes in the country districts distinctly frowns, not only upon most of the historical kinds of amusements usual in a peasant community, but also to some extent upon the very idea of amusement as a necessary, legitimate pursuit, then it is inevitable that you should have what we are seeing today, a perfect stampede of young Negroes to the city.

When now a young man has grown up feeling the trammels of precept, religion, or custom too irksome for him, and then at the most impressionable and reckless age of life, is suddenly transplanted to an atmosphere of excess, the result is apt to be disastrous. In the case of young colored men or women, it is disastrous, and the story is daily repeated in every great city of our land, of young men and women who have been reared in an atmosphere of restricted amusement, throwing off when they enter city life, not one restriction, not some restrictions, but almost all, and plunging into dissipation and vice. This tendency is rendered stronger by two circumstances peculiar to the condition of the American Negro: the first is his express or tacit exclusion from the public amusements of most great cities; and second, the little thought of fact that the chief purveyor of amusement to the colored people is the Negro church, which in theory is opposed to most modern amusements. Let me make this second point clear, for much of the past and future development of the race is misunderstood from ignorance of certain fundamental historic facts. Among most people the primitive sociological group was the family or at least the clan. Not so among American Negroes: every vestige of primitive organization among the Negro slaves was destroyed by the slave ship; in this country the first distinct voluntary organization of Negroes was the Negro church. The Negro church came before the Negro home, it antedates their social life, and in every respect it stands today as the fullest, broadest expression of organized Negro life.

We are so familiar with churches, and church work is so near to us, that we have scarce time to view it in perspective and to realize that in origin and functions the Negro church is a broader, deeper, and more comprehensive social organism than the churches of white Americans. The Negro church is not simply an organism for the propagation of religion; it is the center of the social, intellectual, and religious life of an organized group of individuals. It provides social intercourse, it provides amusements of various kinds, it serves as a newspaper and intelligence bureau, it supplants the theatre, it directs the picnic and excursion, it furnishes the music, it introduces the stranger to the community, it serves as a lyceum, library, and lecture bureau—it is, in fine, the central organ of the organized life of the American Negro for amusement, relaxation, instruction, and religion. To maintain its preeminence the Negro church has been forced to compete with the dance hall, the theatre, and the home as an amusement-giving agency; aided by color proscription in public amusements, aided by the fact mentioned before, that the church among us is older than the home, the church has been peculiarly successful, so that of the ten thousand Philadelphia Negroes whom I asked, "Where do you get your amusements?" fully three-fourths could only answer, "From the churches."

The minister who directs this peculiar and anomalous institution must not be criticized with full knowledge of his difficult role. He is in reality the mayor, the chief magistrate of a community, ruling to be sure, but ruling according to the dictates of a not over-intelligent town council, according to time-honored custom and law; and above all, hampered by the necessities of his budget; he may be a spiritual guide, he must be a social organizer, a leader of actual men; he may desire to enrich and reform the spiritual life of his flock, but above all he must have church members; he may desire to revolutionize church methods, to elevate the ideals of the people, to tell the hard, honest truth to a people who need a little more truth and a little less flattery—but how can he do this when the people of this social organism demand that he shall take from the purely spiritual activities of his flock, time to minister to their amusement, diversion, and physical comfort; when he sees the picnic masquerading as a camp-meeting, the revival becoming the social event of the season, the day of worship turned into a day of general reception and dining out, the rival church organizations plunging into debt to furnish their houses of worship with an elegance that far outruns the financial ability of a poverty stricken people; when the church door becomes the trysting place for all the lovers and Lotharios[2] of the community; when a ceaseless round of entertainments, socials, and necktie parties chase the week through—what minister can be more than most ministers are coming to be, the business managers of a picnic ground?

This is the situation of the Negro church today—I do not say of all Negro churches, but I mean the average church. It is rather the misfortune than the fault of the church. With the peculiar development we have had in this country, I doubt if the Negro church could have more nobly fulfilled its huge and multi-form task; if it totters beneath its burden, it nevertheless demands respect as the first demonstrator of the ability of the civilized Negro to govern himself. Notwithstanding all this, the situation remains, and demands—peremptorily demands—reform. On the one hand we have an increasingly restless crowd of young people who are always demanding ways and means of recreation; and every moment it is denied them is a moment that goes to increase that growth of a distinct class of Negro libertines, criminals, and prostitutes which is growing among us day by day, which fills our jails and hospitals, which tempts and taints our brothers, our sisters, and our children, and which does more in a day to tarnish our good name than Hampton can do in a year to restore it. On the other hand we have the Negro church seeking to supply this demand for amusement—and doing so to the detriment and death of its true, divine mission of human inspiration.

Under such circumstances two questions immediately arise: first, Is this growing demand for amusement legitimate? and second, Can the church continue to be the center of amusements?

Let us consider the first question; and ask, What is amusement? All life is rhythm—the right swing of the pendulum makes the pointer go round, but the left swing must follow it; the down stroke of the hammer welds the iron, and yet the hammer must be lifted between each blow; the heart must beat and yet between each beat comes a pause; the day is the period of fulfilling the functions of life and yet the prelude and end of day is night. Thus throughout nature, from the restless beating of yonder waves to the rhythm of the seasons and the whirl of comets, we see one mighty law of work and rest, of activity and relaxation, of inspiration and amusement. We might imagine a short sighted philosopher arguing strongly against the loss of time involved in the intermittent activities of the world—arguing against the time spent by the hammer in raising itself for the second blow, against the unnecessary alternate swing of the pendulum, against sleep that knits up the raveled sleeve of care, against amusements that reinvigorate and recreate and divert. With such a philosophy the world has never agreed, the whole world today is organized for work and recreation. Where the balance between the two is best maintained we have the best civilization, the best culture; and that civilization declines toward barbarism where, on the one hand, work and drudgery so predominate as to destroy the very vigor which stands behind them, or on the other hand, where relaxation and amusement become dissipation instead of recreation.

I dwell on these simple facts because I fear that even a proverbially joyous people like the American Negroes are forgetting to recognize for their children the God-given right to play; to recognize that there is a perfectly natural and legitimate demand for amusement on the part of the young people, and that no people can afford to laugh at, sneer at, or forcibly repress the natural joyousness and pleasure-seeking prosperity[3] of young womanhood and young manhood. Go into a great city today and see how thoroughly and wonderfully organized its avenues of amusements are; its parks and play grounds, its theatres and galleries, its music and dancing, its excursions and trolley rides represent an enormous proportion of the expenditure of every great municipality. That the matter of amusement may often be overdone in such centers is too true, but of all the agencies that contribute to its overdoing none are more potent than undue repression. Proper amusement must always be a matter of careful reasoning and ceaseless investigation, of nice adjustment between repression and excess; there is not a single means of amusement from church socials to public balls, or from checkers to horse racing that may not be carried to harmful excess; on the other hand it would be difficult to name a single amusement which if properly limited and directed would not be a positive gain to any society; take, for instance, in our modern American society, the game of billiards; I suppose, taken in itself, a more innocent, interesting, and gentlemanly game of skill could scarcely be thought of, and yet, because it is today coupled with gambling, excessive drinking, lewd companionship, and late hours, you can hear it damned from every pulpit from San Francisco to New York as the straight road to perdition; so far as present conditions are concerned the pulpit may be right, but the social reformer must ask himself: Are these conditions necessary? Was it not far sighted prudence for the University of Pennsylvania to put billiard tables in its students' club room? Is there any valid reason why the Y.M.C.A. at Norfolk should not have a billiard table among its amusements? In other words, is it wise policy to surrender a charming amusement wholly to the devil and then call it devilish?

If now there is among rational, healthy, earnest people a legitimate demand for amusement, and if from its peculiar history and constitution the Negro church has undertaken to furnish this amusement to American Negroes, is it fairly to be supposed that the church can be successful in its attempt? Of the answer to this question there is one unfailing sign: if the young people are flocking into the church then the church has accomplished its double task; but as matter of fact the young people are leaving the church; in the forty Negro churches of Philadelphia I doubt if there are two hundred young men who are effective, active church members; there are to be sure, two thousand young men who meet their sweethearts there Sunday nights—but they are not pillars of the church. The young women are more faithful but they too are dropping away; in the country, this tendency is less manifest because the young people have no other place to go, but even there it is found increasingly difficult to reach the young people. This simply means that the younger generation of Negroes are tired of the limited and hackneyed amusements the church offers, and that the spiritual message of the church has been dulled by too indistinct and inopportune reiteration.

And then there is another reason, deeper and more subtle, and therefore more dangerous than these; and that is, the recoil of young, honest souls against a distinct tendency toward hypocrisy in the apparent doctrine and the practice of the Negro church. The Methodist and Baptist and nearly all the churches which the slaves joined, had at the time of their introduction into America, felt the full impulse of a spiritual recoil against excessive amusement. The dissipations of an age of debauchery, of display, of license, had led those churches to preach the earnestness of life, and the disgrace of mere pleasure-seeking as a life work.

Transported to America this religion of protest became a wholesale condemnation of amusements, and a glorification of the ascetic ideal of self-inflicted mi-
sery. In this tongue the Negro church first began to lisp; its earliest teaching was
that the Christian stood apart from and utterly opposed to a world filled with
pleasures, and that to partake of those pleasures was sinful. When now in these
days the church speaks in those same tones and invites healthy and joyous
young people from the back seats to renounce the amusements of this world for
a diet of fasting and prayer, those same young people in increasing numbers are
positively, deliberately, and decisively declining to do any such thing; and they
are pointing to the obvious fact that the very church that is preaching against
amusement is straining every nerve to amuse them; they feel that there is an
essential hypocrisy in this position of the church and they refuse to be hypocrites.

As a matter of fact you and I know that our church is not really hypocritical
on this point; she errs only in using antiquated and unfortunate phraseology.
What the Negro church is trying to impress upon young people is that Work and
Sacrifice is the true destiny of humanity—the Negro church is dimly groping for
that divine word of Faust:

"*Entbehren sallst du, sollst entbehren.*"
"Thou shalt forego, shalt do without."

But in this truth, properly conceived, properly enunciated, there is nothing in-
compatible with wholesome amusement, with true recreation—for what is true
amusement, true diversion, but the re-creation of energy which we may sacrifice
to noble ends, to higher ideals, while without proper amusement we waste or
dissipate our mightiest powers? If the Negro church could have the time and the
opportunity to announce this spiritual message clearly and truly; if it could con-
centrate its energy and emphasis on an encouragement of proper amusement
instead of on its wholesale denunciation; if it could cease to dissipate and chea-
pen religion by incessant semi-religious activity then we would, starting with a
sound religious foundation, be able to approach the real question of proper
amusement. For believe me, my hearers, the great danger of the best class of
Negro youth today is not that they will hesitate to sacrifice their lives, their
money, and their energy on the altar of their race, but the danger is lest under
continuous and persistent proscription, under the thousand little annoyances and
petty insults and disappointments of a caste system, they lose the divine faith of
their fathers in the fruitfulness of sacrifice; for surely no son of the nineteenth
century has heard more plainly the mocking words of "Sorrow, cruel fellowship!"

There has been no time in the history of American Negroes when they had a
more pressing need of spiritual guidance of the highest type; when amid the petty cares of social reform and moral reaction, there was wider place for a divine
faith in the high destiny and marvelous might of that vast historic Negro race

whose promise and first-fruits we of America are. There are creeping in among us low ideals of petty hatred, of sordid gain, of political theft, of place hunting and immodest self-praise, that must be stifled lest they sting to death our loftier and nobler sentiments.

Thus far I have sought to show; first, that the problem of proper amusement for our young people is rapidly coming to be a pressing one; second, that the Negro church, from its historic development has become the chief center of our amusements, and has been forced into the untenable position of seeming to deny the propriety of worldly amusements and dissipating at the same time its spiritual energy in furnishing them for its members.

I now wish to insist that the time has come when the activities of the Negro church must become differentiated and when it must surrender to the school and the home, and social organizations, those functions which in a day of organic poverty it so heroically sought to bear. The next social organism that followed the church among the Negroes was the school, and with the slow but certain up building of the Negro home, we shall at last become a healthy society. Upon the school and the home must rest the burden of furnishing amusements for Negro youth. This duty must not be shirked—it must not be an after-thought—it must not be a spasmodic activity but a careful, rational plan. Take the boys and girls of the primary schools: I want to impress the fact upon every school teacher here who has children from six to thirteen under her care that oversight over the amusements of those children is just as important as oversight over their studies. And first of all, let the children sing, and sing songs, not hymns; it is bad enough on Sunday to hear the rude vigor and mighty music of the slave songs replaced by that combination of flippant music and mediocre poetry which we call gospel hymns. But for heaven's sake, let us not further tempt Providence by using these not only for hymns but for day-school purposes. Buy good song books—books that sing of earth and air and sky and sea, of lovers, birds, and trees, of everything that makes God's world beautiful. Set the Southland to singing Annie Laurie, the Lorelei, Santa Lucia, and "My Heart's in the Hielands" let the children yodel, whistle, and clap their hands—they will get more real religion out of one healthy, wholesome folk-song than out of an endless repetition of hymns on all occasions, with sour faces, and forced reverence. Again, make the observance of recess as compulsory as that of work. In work time make the pupils work and work hard and continuously, and at recess time make them play and play hard and joyously; join in and direct their games, their "I Spy," and "King Consello" and "Grey Wolf" and the thousand and one good old games which are known from England to China. Watch that boy who after a morning's work will not play; he is not built right. Watch that girl who can mope and sleep at recess time; she needs a physician. In these schools of primary grade especial attention should be paid to athletic sports; boys and girls should be encouraged if not compelled to run, jump, walk, row, swim, throw, and vault. The school picnic

with a long walk over hill and dale and a romp under the trees in close communion with Mother Nature is sadly needed. In fine, here should be developed a
capacity for pure, open-hearted enjoyment of the beautiful world about us, and
woe to the teacher who is so bigoted and empty-headed as to suggest to innocent
laughing hearts that play is not a divine institution which ever has and ever will,
go hand in hand with work.

When the child grows up, in the momentous years from fourteen to eighteen, the problem of amusements becomes graver, and because it is graver it
demands not less attention but more; generally the last thing that is thought of in
the organization of a great school is: How are we to furnish proper amusement
of these two or three hundred young people of all ages, tastes, and tempera-
ments? And yet, unless that school does amuse, as well as instruct those boys
and girls, and teach them how to amuse themselves, it fails of half its duty and it
sends into the world men and women who can never stand up successfully in the
awful moral battle which Negro blood is today waging for humanity. Here again
athletic sports must in the future play a larger part in the normal and mission
schools of the South, and we must rapidly come to the place where the man all
brain and no muscle is looked upon as almost as big a fool as the man all muscle
and no brain; and when the young woman who cannot walk a couple of good
country miles will have few proposals of marriage. The crucial consideration at
this age of life, between fourteen and eighteen, is really the proper social intercourse of the sexes; it is a grave question because its mistaken answer today
coupled with an awful social history compels us to plead guilty to the shameful
fact that sexual impurity among Negro men and Negro women of America is the
crying disgrace of the American republic. The Southern school which can so
train its sons and daughters that they can mingle in pure and chaste conversation,
and thoroughly enjoy the natural love they have for each other's companionship;
which can amuse and interest them and at the same time protect them with a
high sense of honor and chastity—that school will be the greatest of Negro
schools and the mightiest of American institutions. On the other hand, the school
which seeks to build iron walls between the sexes, which discourages honest,
open intercourse, which makes it a business to set the seal of disapproval upon
sensible and joyous amusement, that school is filling the bawdy houses and
gambling halls of our great cities with its most hopeless inmates.

I wish to take but one illustration to make clear my meaning in this crucial
question; and I take two common amusements which bring the sexes together—
dancing and accompanying young ladies home from church Sunday night. I
never shall forget a dance I attended in Eisenach, Germany; contrary to my very
elaborate expectation the young men did not accompany the girls to the dance;
the girls went with their fathers and mothers; the boys went alone. In the pretty,
airy hall the mothers seated themselves in a circle about the sides of the room
and drew up their daughters beside them; fathers and elder brothers looked on
from the doorway. Then we danced under the eyes of mothers and fathers, and
we got permission to dance from those parents; we felt ourselves to be trusted

guests in the bosom of families; three hours glided by in pure joyousness until, finally, long tables were brought in; we sat down, and cooled off and drank coffee and sang. Then the mothers took their daughters home, and the young men took themselves. I have had many good times in life, but not one to which I look back with more genuine pleasure and satisfaction. When now we compare the amusement thus conducted with the universal custom among us of allowing our daughters, unattended and unwatched, to be escorted at night, through great cities or country districts by chance acquaintances unknown to parents, with no rational diversion, but frivolous conversation and aimless nonsense, I have no hesitancy in saying I would rather have a daughter of mine dance her head off under her mother's eye, than to throw her unguarded and uncared for into the hands of unwatched strangers. The cases I have cited are of course extreme—all escorting of girls from church is not improper, and all dancing is not carried on as at Eisenach, but I wish to leave this one query with you. Is it not possible for us to rescue from its evil associations and conditions, so pleasant, innocent, and natural an amusement as dancing?

I have already talked too long and have but half exhausted a fertile and peculiarly interesting subject; the whole question of home pleasures and of diversions for older people remains untouched. I wish to leave you with a reiteration of what I desire to be the central thought of this paper, it is not a defense of particular amusements or a criticism of particular prohibitions, but an insistence on the fact that amusement is right, that pleasure is God-given, and that the people that seek to deny it and to shut the door upon it, simply open wide the door to dissipation and vice. I beg you to strive to change the mental attitude of the race toward amusement for the young, from a wholesale negative to an emphatic positive. Instead of warning young people so constantly against excess of pleasure, let us rather inspire them to unselfish work, and show them that amusement and recreation are the legitimate and necessary accompaniments of work, and that we get the maximum of enjoyment from them when they strengthen and inspire us for renewed effort in a great cause; and above all, let us teach them that there can be no greater cause than the development of Negro character to its highest and holiest possibilities.

Notes

1. *Editor's note*: This essay was originally published in the September 1897 issue of *The Southern Workman*. The essay appeared on pages 181–84 of volume 27.

2. *Editor's note*: Lothario was a major character in the 1703 tragedy, *The Fair Penitent*, by Nicholas Rowe. Lothario was a seducer of women. The name has become a

synonym for a libertine or a seducer. See "Lothario." http://www.thefreedictionary.com/
Lotharios. Du Bois was commenting on the fact that in some instances the church was
reduced to becoming a meeting place for potential lovers.

    3.   *Editor's note*: Perhaps Du Bois intended to use the word "propensity" here.

Reading 15

The Negro in the Black Belt: Some Social Sketches[1]

The studies of Negro economic development here presented are based mainly on seminary notes made by members of the senior class of Atlanta University. These young persons, born and bred under the conditions which they describe, have unusual facilities for first-hand knowledge of a difficult and intricate subject. They are also somewhat more experienced in life than corresponding classes in Northern institutions, being in school for the most part through their own exertions and teaching in various communities in vacation time.

Six small groups, containing a total of 920 Negroes, have been studied, all but one of which are situated in Georgia. The groups, however, differ greatly from each other and are designed to represent the development of the Negro from country to city life, from semi-barbarism to a fair degree of culture. The first sketch, for instance, is of 11 families in a small country district of Georgia, and the second of 16 families in a small village of the same State. Here we get a glimpse of the real Negro problem; of the poverty and degradation of the country Negro, which means the mass of Negroes in the United States. Next our attention is called to two towns, both county seats and centers of trade. To such towns both the energetic and listless class of country Negroes are migrating. In these towns are taken up the condition of 83 families, which are mostly, though not entirely, families of the better class and represent the possibilities of the town Negroes. Finally we consider two groups of 85 families, in two small cities, who represent distinctly the better class of Negroes—the class that sends its children to Atlanta, Fisk, and Tuskegee.

Thus it will be seen that there is here no attempt at a complete study of the Negro in the Black Belt, but rather a series of sketches, whose chief value lies in their local color.

A COUNTRY DISTRICT IN DEKALB COUNTY, GEORGIA.

Seventeen miles east of Atlanta is a small village of less than 500 persons called Doraville; 21 miles southeast is a bit of country without a special name.

There are in these two localities between 60 and 75 Negro families, of whom 11 fairly representative ones have been chosen for this study.

In general these Negroes are a degraded set. Except in two families, whisky, tobacco, and snuff are used to excess, even when there is a scarcity of bread. In other respects also the low moral condition of these people is manifest, and in the main there is no attempt at social distinctions among them.

In these 11 families there are 131 individuals, an average of nearly 13 persons to a family. In size the families rank as shown in the following table:

Table 15.1. Number of Persons in 11 Selected Families of a County District of DeKalb County, Georgia, by Size of Families[2]

Size of Family	Number of Families	Number of Individuals
7 persons	1	7
9 persons	1	9
10 persons	2	20
11 persons	1	11
12 persons	2	24
13 persons	3	39
21 persons	1	21
Total	11	131
Average		11.9

The fecundity of this population is astonishing. Here is one family with 19 children:—14 girls and 5 boys, ranging in age from 6 to 25 years. Another family has one set of triplets, two sets of twins, and 4 single children. The girls of the present generation, however, are not marrying as early as their mothers did. Once in a while a girl of 12 or 13 runs off and marries, but this does not often happen. Probably the families of the next generation will be smaller.

Four of the 11 heads of families can read and write. Of their children, a majority, possibly two-thirds, can read and write a little. Five of the families own their homes. The farms vary from 1 to 11 acres in extent, and are worth from $100 to $400. Two of these farms are heavily mortgaged. Six families rent farms on shares paying one-half the crop. They clear from $5 to $10 in cash at the end of a year's work. They usually own a mule or two and sometimes a cow.

Nearly all the workers are farm hands, women and girls as well as men being employed in the fields. Children as young as 6 are given light tasks, such as dropping seed and bringing water. The families rise early, often before daylight, working until breakfast time and returning again after the meal. One of the men is a stonecutter. He earns $1.50 a day, owns a neat little home, and lives comfortably. Most of the houses are rudely constructed of logs or boards, with one large and one small room. There is usually no glass in the openings which serve as windows. They are closed by wooden shutters. The large room always contains several beds and homemade furniture, consisting of tables, chairs, and chests. A few homes had three rooms, and one or two families had sewing machines, which, however, were not yet paid for.

These families raise nearly all that they eat—corn, wheat, pork, and molasses. Chickens and eggs are used as currency at the country store to purchase cloth, tobacco, coffee, etc. The character of the home life varies with the different families. The family of 21 is a poverty-stricken, reckless, dirty set. The children are stupid and repulsive, and fight for their food at the table. They are poorly dressed, sickly, and cross. The table dishes stand from one meal to another unwashed, and the house is in perpetual disorder. Now and then the father and mother engage in a hand-to-hand fight.

In some respects this family is exceptionally bad, but several others are nearly as barbarous. A few were much better, and in the stonecutter's five-room house one can find clean, decent family life, with neatly dressed children and many signs of aspiration. The average of the communities, however, was nearer the condition of the family first described than that of the latter one.

In religion the people are sharply divided into Baptists and Methodists, who are in open antagonism; and have separate day schools. The Baptists are the more boisterous and superstitious, and their pastor is ignorant and loud-mouthed, preaching in his shirt sleeves and spitting tobacco juice on either side of the pulpit as he works his audience up to the frenzy of a "shouting." Outside the churches there is a small, women's beneficial society for sickness and death, under the presidency of the stonecutter's wife. Many of the members are in arrears with their payments. There is also a lodge of Odd Fellows. The schools run only 3 months in the year, the wretched schoolhouses and the system of child labor preventing a longer term.

On the whole, a stay in this community has a distinctly depressing effect. There are a few indications of progress, but those of listlessness and stagnation seem more powerful.

A SMALL VILLAGE: LITHONIA, DEKALB COUNTY, GA.

Lithonia is 24 miles east of Atlanta, and has a population of perhaps 800. There are in the town two dry goods stores, a drug store, three grocery stores, a barber shop, and a millinery shop conducted by white persons, and a blacksmith shop and a barber shop conducted by Negroes. Nearly all the workingmen of the town are employed in the three rock quarries, which furnish the chief business of the village. The Negro stonecutters here used to earn from $10 to $14 a week, but now they receive from $5 to $8.50 a week. There are many "scabbers"[3] outside the union who work for still less. They now include the majority of the Negro laborers. Some Negroes are also employed in domestic service and at the large boarding house.

Less than a dozen homes are owned by the Negroes; they rent for the most part small, two-room tenements, at $4 a month. The whites have a private and a public school, giving them a term of 8 or 9 months. The Negro schools are divided into a Methodist and a Baptist school, each of which has a term of 3 months. The school buildings are old and dilapidated and scarcely fit to teach in; they will not accommodate nearly all the Negro children of school age.

Sixteen of these Negro families have been especially studied; they represent the average of the village. The families by size are shown in the following table:

Table 15.2. Number of Persons in 16 Selected Families of Lithonia, GA by Size of Families

Size of Family	Number of Families	Number of Individuals
2 persons	1	2
4 persons	1	4
5 persons	4	20
6 persons	4	24
7 persons	3	21
9 persons	1	9
10 persons	1	10
11 persons	1	11
Total	16	101
Average		6.3

The next table shows the number of persons in these families, by age and sex:

Table 15.3. Number of Persons in 16 Selected Families of Lithonia, GA, by Age and Sex

Age	Males	Females	Total
Under 15 years	21	21	42
15 to 40 years	27	20	47
40 years or over	5	7	12
Total	53	48	101

Most of these persons were born in the State; 6 were born in Virginia, 6 in Alabama, and 3 in South Carolina. Of those 10 years of age or over, 8 out of 63, or 13 percent, were illiterate.

Six of these families owned their homes. The following table shows the condition of each family:

Table 15.4. Condition of 6 Selected Families Owning Homes in Lithonia, GA[4]

Family ID	Size of Family	Rooms in House	Wage Earners	Occupation	Wages per Week	Weeks Employed	Yearly Wages	Family Earnings
1	5	3	3	Stonecutter	$8.50	48	$408	$752
				Stonecutter	5.00	48	240	
				Hotel waiter	2.00[a]	52	104	
2	11	4	5	Drayman (1)	b	b	250[c]	550[c]
				Farm hands (4)	b	b	300[d]	
3	6	3	1	Stonecutter	15–20[e]	b	200	200
4	6	2	1	Stonecutter	5.00[f]	b	200	200
5	6	2	1	Stonecutter	5.00[f]	b	200	200
6	5	4	1	Stonecutter	6.50	48	312	312

Notes: [a] And board.
[b] Not reported.
[c] Approximate.
[d] Approximate total for 4 farm hands.
[e] Per month.
[f] Or less.

Besides a house of 3 rooms, family No. 1 owned 6 acres of farm land, the hotel waiter earned his board in addition to $2 a week wages. Family No. 2 owned a four-room house with a lot 150 by 35 feet. In this family there were 5 daughters, who helped on the farm, besides the 4 male farm hands. Family No.3 saved from $20 to $30 a year out of earnings of $200. They owned a three-room house and a lot 150 by 50 feet. Families Nos. 4 and 5 each owned a two-room house with lots, and family No. 6 owned a four-room house with a large lot.

The remaining 10 families investigated at Lithonia rented houses, and the size of such houses and the rent paid are shown in the following table:

Table 15.5. Rent Paid by 10 Selected Families Renting Houses in Lithonia, GA, by Size of Houses

Size of House	Rent Paid per Month	Families Renting
2 rooms	$4.00	5
2 rooms	a	1
3 rooms	4.00	1
3 rooms	4.50	1
3 rooms	5.00	1
4 rooms	5.00	1

Note: [a] Two bales of cotton per year.

In these 16 families there is an average of 2.75 rooms to a family and a little over 2 persons to a room. The following table presents the 16 families by size of family and classified income:

Table 15.6. Classified Income of 16 Selected Families of Lithonia, GA, by Size of Families

Income per Family	Persons per Family[5]								Total Families
	2	4	5	6	7	9	10	11	
Under $200	1	0	1	1	1	0	1	0	5
$200 to $300	0	0	1	3	0	0	0	0	4
$300 to $400	0	1	1	0	1	0	0	0	3
$400 to $500	0	0	0	0	1	1	0	0	2
$500 or over	0	0	1	0	0	0	0	1	2
Total	1	1	4	4	3	1	1	1	16

The morals of the colored people in the town are decidedly low. They dress and live better than the country Negroes, however, and send their children more regularly to school. The union stonecutters are nearly all members of a local branch of the Odd Fellows. The women have a beneficial society. There are three churches—two Baptist and one Methodist—whose pastors are fairly intelligent.[6]

A COUNTY SEAT: COVINGTON, NEWTON COUNTY, GA.

Covington is in the center of one of the smaller counties of the State, and is 41 miles southeast of Atlanta. Being the principal town, it carries on an extensive trade, especially on Saturdays, with the people of Newton, Jasper, and Morgan counties. On such days the main square, formed by the intersection of the two principal streets, is filled with country folk, white and black, in all sorts of conveyances, from the carryall to the ox cart. Here they spend their money, make debts, eat, talk, and are happy. Tasting thus the larger life of the town, large numbers of country people are being constantly tempted to leave their farms and move to town. At the same time, Covington boys and girls are pushing on to Macon and Atlanta. This immigration to Covington has been greatly stimulated by the recent extension of the Georgia Railway to the town, so that the village of 1,415 persons in 1880 had 1,823 in 1890, and possibly 3,000 in 1898.

The chief business of the town is retailing supplies for the farmers, selling rope and thread, which is manufactured nearby, handling and ginning cotton, handling farm products, etc. There are about 50 retail stores.

Between 250 and 300 Negro families live in the town, representing all conditions. From these have been chosen 50 families for the purposes of this investigation. These families represent the better class of Negroes, and are rather above the average for the town. Their condition shows the general development of the more favorably, situated Negroes in a thriving country town. At the same time some notice of general conditions has been taken. The 50 families, according to size, are as follows:

Table 15.7. Number of Persons in 50 Selected Families of Covington, GA, by Size of Families[7]

Size of Family	Families
2 persons	15
3 persons	12
4 persons	9
5 persons	10
7 persons	1
9 persons	1
10 persons	2
Total	50

The total number of members of these families was 188, making the average size of the families 3.76 members. In the following table is shown the number of members of these families, by age and sex:

Table 15.8. Number of Persons in 50 Selected Families of Covington, GA, by Age and Sex

Age	Males	Females	Total
Under 15 years	31	40	71
15 to 40 years	35	37	72
40 years or over	19	26	45
Total	85	103	188

The conjugal condition is shown in the following table:

Table 15.9. Conjugal Condition of Persons 15 Years of Age or Over in 50 Selected Families of Covington, GA

	Males			Females		
Age	Single	Married	Widowed	Single	Married	Widowed
15 to 40 years	8	24	3	12	25	0
40 years or over	0	16	3	4	15	7
Total	8	40	6	16	40	7

In the general Negro population of the town the average family is larger than in these families, still it does not approach the average size of the country families. This is partly because only the smaller families move to the city, and partly because of the postponing of marriage.

There is a public school for Negroes open 9 months in the year. It has 3 teachers and an average of 250 scholars. The male principal receives $50 a month, and his 2 female assistants $30. The schoolhouse is small and in bad repair, but it is expected a new one will be built sometime. Many girls and some of the boys are sent to Atlanta and Augusta to school. The illiteracy among the 50 families does not exceed 10 percent.

The number of males 10 years of age or over in each of the occupations represented in the 50 families was as follows: Eight porters, 6 teachers, 6 barbers, 5 carpenters, 4 laborers, 3 gardeners, 3 office boys, 2 mail agents, 2 drivers, 2 draymen, 2 grocers, 2 ministers, 2 waiters, 1 bartender, 1 butcher, 1 farmer, 1 quarryman, 1 contractor, and 1 brick mason, making a total of 53 in the various occupations.

Of the females 10 years of age or over there were 11 teachers, 10 seamstresses, 6 cooks, 3 washerwomen, 1 boarding-house keeper, and 1 housekeeper, a total of 32.

Among the mass of the Negro population the distribution of employments is quite different. There is practically no work for colored girls except domestic service, in which consequently most of them are engaged. The majority of the men are laborers, with a sprinkling of artisans and men in higher walks.

COMMON AND DOMESTIC LABOR.—The men are porters in stores, janitors, draymen, drivers, general servants, waiters, common laborers, and farm hands. They usually earn from $10 to $12 a month, besides board, and often help in other ways. The women are employed as cooks, nurses, milkmaids, and general servants. They receive from $4 to $6 a month for cooking, $1.50 to $3 a month for nursing, $1 a month per cow for milking, etc. The number engaged in domestic service is large, but it is an unpopular calling, and those who can possibly escape from it do so. A great many girls and women do day's work for families, such as sewing, washing, scrubbing, etc. They receive 40 to 50 cents a day for this, and one or two meals. Those who take in washing receive from 60 cents to $1 for a family wash. Female farm hands receive from 35 to 50 cents a day.

THE TRADES.—Among skilled laborers are found a few Negro painters, shoemakers, blacksmiths, brick masons, plasterers, and carpenters, and one wheelwright. Most of these live in the town, although a few live in the surrounding country. White and Negro mechanics work together without apparent friction, and usually receive the same pay.

FARMING.—Four of the town families, besides their regular vocations, conduct farms in the Country. Much interest is taken in gardens for family use, and a good deal is sold out of them. Many Negro gardeners earn 50 cents or more a day by taking care of gardens for white families.

BUSINESS ENTERPRISE.—Although few Negroes have ventured into the management of businesses, those that have demand especial attention. Negroes are represented in the following enterprises: Two grocery stores, 2 meat markets, 3 restaurants, 1 watchmaker, 5 contractors in building and painting, and 2 furniture makers. Besides these there are the following artisans, who own their establishments: Four barbers, 4 blacksmiths, and 3 shoemakers.

The grocery stores each do a business of from $20 to $30 a week. At first Negroes did not patronize them much, but now they are beginning to. They are three or four years old. Of the 4 meat markets in the town, 2 are conducted by Negroes, and one of these has been in business 13 years. He is the leading meat dealer in the town, furnishing fully one-half the meat consumed; he has driven many competitors out of business, and owns considerable property in town and country. Three of the four restaurants are conducted by Negroes. The most successful is that of a Negro. He has an ice-cream parlor in addition, with separate eating rooms for the two races. He hires 2 men, and is said to have about $8,000 in property. The watch repairer is always busy. The contractors do a great deal of work in the town and surrounding country. The 2 furniture makers build nearly all the coffins used by Negroes. The barbers, blacksmiths, and shoemakers seem to be well patronized. There are no white barbers.

THE PROFESSIONS.—There are 4 Negro preachers. They average about $400 a year and house rent. They have fair English training, but none of them is a graduate of a theological school. In character they are far superior to those in the country districts. A few young women and men teach in the town and in the county schools. The latter schools pay from $15 to $30 a month and run 5 months or less.

The only clerical work of importance performed by Negroes is in the Railway Mail Service, where 2 Negroes have positions gained by civil-service examination. One has had this work 5 years.

UNEMPLOYED AND CRIMINAL CLASSES.—There is a great deal of idleness and loafing, arising partly from the fact that the common work is abundant at certain seasons and scarce at others, and arising, also, in part from shiftlessness and crime. Many boys and girls become discouraged at the narrow opportunities open to them, and there results emigration, idleness, or vicious habits. On the outskirts of the town are many dives and gambling dens where liquor may be had. Here, especially on Saturday nights, crowds gather and carouse, drunkenness and fighting ensue, and many arrests are made.

The mass of the Negroes are hard-working people with small wages. Many, however, manage to buy homes with their savings. It is interesting to watch the more thrifty. They pay a little each month until a lot is bought; then they build perhaps a single room which stands alone until it is black and weather-beaten; then the frame of a second room is added and pieced up board by board. So the home grows, until after years of toil a house of three or more rooms stands finished. A majority of the better class of Negroes are thus buying property, and a family is considered "low" which is not making some efforts.

The yearly income of the mass of Negroes is between $100 and $300. The incomes of the 50 selected families may be estimated as follows:

Table 15.10. Classified Income of 50 Selected Families of Covington, GA, by Size of Families

Income per Family	Persons per Family							Total Families
	2	3	4	5	7	9	10	
Under $200	4	2	1	0	0	0	0	7
$200 to $300	6	3	0	0	0	0	0	9
$300 to $500	2	3	6	6	0	0	0	17
$500 to $750	1	3	1	3	0	1	1	10
$750 to $1,000	0	1	1	0	1	0	1	4
$1000 or over	2	0	0	1	0	0	0	3
Total	15	12	9	10	1	1	2	50

The average income of a Negro family of the better class is thus seen to be between $300 and $500. Three typical families will best illustrate this:

The first of these was a family of 5 persons. The annual income was $400. The father was a barber, earning $6 a week. The mother was a seamstress and earned from $1 to $4 per week. Two young daughters were in school, and one child was at home. The family owned their home.

The second family was composed of 4 persons and the annual income was $400. The father, who was a carpenter, worked part of the year at $10 a week. The mother averaged $1 a week from outside work, in addition to her work as a housewife. The family owned their home and had 2 children in school.

The third family comprised 9 persons, had an annual income of $450, and owned their home. The father earned $3 a week as a gardener, the mother $2 a week as a washerwoman, one son $2 a week as a porter, and another son from $2 to $3 a week as a gardener. This family also had 2 daughters and 2 sons in school and one child at home.

The majority of these 50 families own their homes, as is shown in the following table:

Table 15.11. Homes Owned and Rented by 50 Selected Families of Covington, GA, by Size of Homes

Homes	Families occupying homes of—					Total Families
	2 rooms.	3 rooms.	4 rooms	5 rooms.	6 rooms.	
Owned	9	8	13	9	2	41
Rented	0	6	1	1	1	9
Total	9	14	14	10	3	50

In the community at large the number of home owners is naturally much less; nevertheless the percentage is considerable. The degree of comfort in the homes can be roughly gauged by a comparison of the size of families with the number of rooms occupied, as shown in the following table:

Table 15.12. Size of Families and of Homes Compared, for 50 Selected Families of Covington, GA

Size of Family	Families occupying homes of—					Total Families	Total Individuals	Total Rooms Occupied
	2 rooms.	3 rooms.	4 rooms.	5 rooms.	6 rooms.			
2 persons	9	6	0	0	0	15	30	36
3 persons	0	7	5	0	0	12	36	41
4 persons	0	0	9	0	0	9	36	36
5 persons	0	0	0	10	0	10	50	50
7 persons	0	1	0	0	0	1	7	3
9 persons	0	0	0	0	1	1	9	6
10 persons	0	0	0	0	2	2	20	12
Total	9	14	14	10	3	50	188	184

This table shows that there is an average of nearly 4 rooms to a family and of nearly 1 room to an individual. Among the mass of the population there are still a few one-room cabins. Most of the tenements rented in the town have 2 rooms, and probably the average Negro family occupies 2 or 3 rooms. The houses are all one story, and a common type is that of two rooms united by a hall, and in some cases a small kitchen in the rear. Sometimes a front porch is added.

As a rule the Negroes live in neighborhoods by themselves. In the surrounding country there are many small communities composed entirely of Negroes, which form clans of blood relatives. A few of these settlements are thrifty and neat, but most of them have a dirty, shiftless air, with one-room cabins and numbers of filthy children. Such communities are furnishing immigrants to the town. In Covington there is some tendency among the Negro population to group itself according to social classes. Many streets and neighborhoods are thus respectable and decent, while others are dirty and disreputable.

There are four Negro churches; a beneficial society twenty years old, which owns some property; a lodge of Masons, and one of Odd Fellows.[8]

A COUNTY SEAT: MARION, PERRY COUNTY, AL

Marion is in the midst of the Black Belt of Alabama, in a county the Negroes outnumber the whites 4 to 1. In the town itself, the 2,000 inhabitants are about equally divided. Thirty-three of the perhaps 250 Negro families in the town have been chosen for this study. Here, again, these families represent the better class of the community rather than the average. The number of families of each size was as follows:

Table 15.13. Number of Persons in 33 Selected Families of Marion, AL, by Size of Families[9]

Size of Family	Families
2 persons	1
3 persons	5
4 persons	6
5 persons	11
6 persons	1
7 persons	3
8 persons	2
9 persons	4
Total	33

The average family is 5.3 persons. The age classification of the 175 members is as follows:

Table 15.14. Number of Persons in 33 Selected Families of Marion, AL, by Age and Sex

Age	Males	Females	Total
Under 15 years	18	22	40
15 to 40 years	46	39	85
40 years or over	22	28	50
Total	86	89	175

Among the persons from 15 to 40 years of age there is a noticeable lack of young people between 20 and 30 years of age, as so many of these have left the town in search of work. As shown in the following table, nearly all of these selected families own their homes:

Table 15.15. Homes Owned and Rented by 33 Selected Families of Marion, AL, by Size of Homes

Homes	Families occupying homes of—						Total Families
	2 rooms.	3 rooms.	4 rooms	5 rooms.	6 rooms.	8 rooms	
Owned	2	15	6	3	1	1	28
Rented	0	2	2	1	0	0	5
Total	2	17	8	4	1	1	33

The size of the home is compared with the size of the families in the following table:

Table 15.16. Size of Families and of Homes Compared, for 33 Selected Families of Marion, AL

Size of Family	Families occupying homes of—					Total Families	Total Individuals	Total Rooms Occupied
	2 rooms.	3 rooms.	4 rooms.	5 rooms.	6 rooms.			
2 persons	0	1	0	0	0	1	2	3
3 persons	0	1	3	1	0	5	15	20
4 persons	2	4	0	0	0	6	24	16
5 persons	0	7	3	1	0	11	55	38
6 persons	0	0	1	0	0	1	6	4
7 persons	0	0	1	2	0	3	21	14
8 persons	0	0	0	0	2[a]	2	16	14
9 persons	0	4	0	0	0	4	36	12
Total	2	17	8	4	2	33	175	121

Editor's Note: [a] One family with eight persons was living in a six-room home, and another family with eight persons was living in an eight-room home. In the original table Du Bois provided a column for families occupying six and eight rooms.

Among the mass of the Negro population there are a number who own their homes. Most of the Negroes live in two-room houses, and a few in one-room cabins.

The occupations of the males 10 years of age or over and the number in each occupation were as follows for the 83 families: Seven farmers, 6 ministers, 5 barbers, 5 carpenters, 4 bakers, 3 masons, 2 undertakers, 2 merchants, 2 clerks, 2 teachers, 1 mail agent, 1 drayman, 1 Government employee, 1 missionary, 1 plumber, 1 porter, 1 sailor, 1 nurse, and 1 gardener, making a total of 47 in the various occupations.

Of the females 10 years of age or over, there were 7 teachers, 2 nurses, 2 cooks, 1 merchant, 1 seamstress, and 1 washerwoman, a total of 14.

Taking a general survey of employments among Negroes, we find in the better-paid vocations 2 blacksmiths, who average from $3 to $5 a day. There were also 2 Negro barber shops, the only ones in town; 2 grocery stores, and a large bakery with a half dozen or more employees and an unusually successful business. One of the black merchants not only owns his store, but rents apartments to a white merchant. There are several carpenters, masons, and other artisans who earn from $1.50 to $2.50 a day.

The mass of the colored folks are farmers, laborers, and servants. The farmers as a rule own their own farms, but they are not generally very successful; they do not seem to know how to manage and economize. The young men are mostly porters, waiters, and farm hands. The young women wash, cook, and nurse. They receive very small wages and spend much of their wages for dress.

Compared with the surrounding county, Marion has good school facilities, and consequently a more favorable rate of illiteracy. Of the 135 persons 15 years of age or over in the selected families 34 were illiterate. Only one of these illiterates, however, was under 40 years of age. The public school is poor, but there are 3 missionary schools, one of which, under the American Missionary Association, is very efficient.

There are 4 churches—Methodist, Baptist, and Congregational. The first two originated in slavery times and were for a long time branches of white churches. The Congregational Church is 30 years old, and the more intelligent Negroes attend it; the majority of the selected families are members. There may be distinguished among Marion Negroes three pretty clearly differentiated classes—the class we have studied; the mass of laborers, servants, and farmers, who are usually goodhearted people; but not energetic nor always strictly moral; finally, the slum elements, among whom sexual looseness, drunkenness, and crime are prevalent. It is appalling to see the large number of young people who drift into this lowest class, some of them being intelligent and well reared. Poor home life is responsible for this.[10]

A LARGE TOWN: MARIETTA, COBB COUNTY, GA

Marietta is situated in a county where one-third of the inhabitants are Negroes. It is a place of something over 4,000 inhabitants, lying in north Georgia, 23 miles northwest of Atlanta. It has a Negro population of at least 1,500, of whom 162 persons, or 11 percent, composing 40 families, have been selected for this study. They represent, on the whole, the better class. Twenty-eight of the 162 persons, or 17 percent, cannot read or write. The public schools of the town are fair. Some scholars have been sent away to school, 5 have been graduated from the normal course of Atlanta University, 2 from the theological department of the Atlanta Baptist Seminary, and 2 from Tuskegee Institute.

Twenty-six of the 40 families own their homes. Most of these homes have 3 rooms, although they vary from 2 to 7 rooms. The lots are usually large enough for front and back yards. The occupations of the heads of the selected families and the number in each occupation are as follows; Four painters, 4 porters, 4 barbers, 3 drivers, 3 carpenters, 3 hostlers, 3 chair factory employees, 3 teachers, 2 grocers, 2 brick masons, 2 shoemakers, 2 blacksmiths, 2 farmers, 1 laborer, 1 gardener, and 1 butler.

Marietta has a number of industries in which Negroes are employed. Two large chair factories employ colored workmen almost exclusively. The work is light and much of it is done in the homes. The hands earn from 50 to 75 cents a day. There are also 2 marble mills, a paper mill, a foundry, and railway shops where numbers of Negroes work. The chief trades of the Negroes are painting, blacksmithing, bricklaying, and carpentry. There are 2 grocery stores.

The proprietors own the buildings and hire no clerks. One of the stores is in the center of the town among the white merchants, and has business enough to employ a delivery wagon. This store does a business of from $40 to $50 a week. The other store, which is out of the business section of the town, does a business of from $20 to $25 a week. There are a few farmers on the outskirts of the town who may be included in the town population.

The Negro draymen earn from $4.50 to $5 a week. The mass of the Negroes are laborers earning from 75 to 80 cents a day, or domestic servants.

The average Negro family can live on from $2 to $4 a week. A two-room house rents from $3 to $4 a month; a three-room house for from $5 to $6. Soft coal costs $3 a ton; wood, $1.75 a cord. Many families raise their own vegetables. Meat sells for from 4 to 10 cents a pound.

There are 3 churches. The Baptist and Methodist ministers are not very well educated, and there is still a demand for noise and demonstration in the services. There is a lodge of Odd Fellows and a beneficial society for women. The latter society owns a large building. In 1897 a weekly newspaper was started; it soon failed, but has recently been revived. The amusements of the people are furnished largely by the churches. The lower elements indulge in dancing and minstrel shows, which are frequently scenes of excess and disorder.[11]

A GROUP OF CITY NEGROES IN ATHENS, CLARKE COUNTY, GA

Athens is a city of 10,000 or 12,000 inhabitants, of whom possibly one-third are Negroes. Of these we notice especially 163 persons, or about 4 percent, composing 45 families. As in the other cases, they form a small selected group of the better class of colored folks. In size these families range as follows:

Table 15.17. Number of Persons in 45 Selected Families of Athens, GA, by Size of Families

Size of Family	Number of Families	Number of Individuals
1 person	1	1
2 persons	13	26
3 persons	11	33
4 persons	4	16
5 persons	13	65
7 persons	2	14
8 persons	1	8
Total	45	163

This shows a small average family of 3.6 persons. In age and sex these persons range thus:

Table 15.18. Number of Persons in 45 Selected Families of Athens, GA, by Age and Sex

Age	Males	Females	Total
Under 15 years	14	17	31
15 to 40 years	40	41	81
40 years or over	25	26	51
Total	79	84	163

Late marriages and the migration of young people would seem to be the cause of the small families. The conjugal condition may thus be tabulated:

Table 15.19. Conjugal Condition of Persons 15 Years of Age or Over in 45 Selected Families of Athens, GA

Age	Males			Females			Total
	Single	Married	Widowed	Single	Married	Widowed	
15 to 40 years	27	13	0	22	18	1	81
40 years or over	0	23	2	0	18	8	51
Total	27	36	2	22	36	9	132

Of the 132 persons, 10 or 15 percent are illiterate. There are 4 Negro schools in the city. Two are missionary schools and are not very efficient. The 2 public schools, on the other hand, are unusually well conducted.

As shown in the following table, most of these 45 families own their homes:

Table 15.20. Homes Owned and Rented by 45 Selected Families of Athens, GA, by Size of Homes

Homes	Families occupying homes of—							Total Families
	2 rooms.	3 rooms.	4 rooms.	5 rooms.	6 rooms.	7 rooms.	8 rooms.	
Owned	5	10	5	10	3	2	4	39
Rented	1	0	0	3	1	0	1	6
Total	6	10	5	13	4	2	5	45

The occupations of this little group are as follows for males 10 years of age or over: Six drivers, 5 teachers, 3 barbers, 3 blacksmiths, 3 in United States mail service, 2 waiters, 2 shoemakers, 2 carpenters, 2 tailors, 2 physicians, 2 ministers, 1 office boy, 1 clerk, 1 bookkeeper, 1 merchant, 1 editor, 1 restaurant keeper, 1 real estate agent, 1 pharmacist, 1 plasterer, 1 cook, 1 expressman, 1 farmer, and 1 plumber, making a total of 45 in the various occupations.

Of females in different occupations, there were 12 teachers, 11 washerwomen, 6 seamstresses, 2 boarding-house keepers, and 2 cooks, a total of 33.

The income of these families can be given only approximately; it is about as follows:

Table 15.21. Classified Income of 45 Selected Families of Athens, GA, by Size of Families

Income per Family								Total Families
	1	2	3	4	5	7	8	
$100 to $150	1	0	0	0	0	0	0	1
$150 to $200	0	0	2	0	1	0	0	3
$200 to $250	0	4	1	0	1	0	0	6
$300 to $500	0	3	1	0	2	0	0	6
$500 to $750	0	6	2	2	4	2	0	16
$750 or over	0	0	5	2	5	0	1	13
Total	1	13	11	4	13	2	1	45

The great mass of the Athens Negroes is made up largely of immigrants from the country, and a stream is still pouring in. These countrymen replace the town laborers in many employments by accepting lower wages, and thus lowering the standard of life which the town group is striving to raise.[12] Naturally the following more or less well-defined social classes arise from this situation: The small class of the better conditioned Negroes, like those we have studied; the large class of working people and servants; the great number of ignorant countrymen who are common laborers; finally, a substratum of the vicious and criminal. This latter class is small in Athens, and there has not been much serious crime there.

There are 8 Negro churches in the place. Three of the Baptist churches are: First Baptist, founded in 1865, having property valued at $6,000, and a membership of 425 persons; Ebenezer Baptist, founded in 1885, whose property is valued at $2,000, and whose membership is 326; Bill's Chapel, founded in 1895, owning property worth $1,000, and numbering 150 members. Besides these there are 3 Methodist churches, 1 Congregational, and 1 Primitive Baptist. There are a large number of Negro organizations, especially secret and beneficial organizations.[13]

From these incomplete sketches few general conclusions can be drawn. Nevertheless, they have a distinct value. First, they are the impressions of lifelong residents, not of hurried investigators; secondly, in the widely separated communities there are certain striking resemblances and lessons. The communities fall easily into three classes: A country district of 131 persons and 11 families; a small village of 101 persons and 16 families; town and city groups of 688 persons and 168 families. In the first class is had a glimpse of the deepest of the Negro problems, that of the country Negro, where the mass of the race still lives in ignorance, poverty, and immorality, beyond the reach of schools and other agencies of civilization for the larger part of the time. Small wonder that the Negro is rushing to the city in an aimless attempt to change, at least, if not to better, his condition. Perhaps, on the whole, this is best; certainly it is if this influx can be balanced by a counter migration of the more intelligent and thrifty Negroes to the abandoned farms and plantations. In the second class we catch a glimpse of the small village life with one industry, more material prosperity, but traces of shiftlessness and thrift, immorality and a better family life, curiously intermingled. In both these classes the sketches furnished are, unfortunately, meager. In the third class we have a wider field of observation—4 thriving Southern towns—but here, again, there is a limitation. We have studied that part of the population which has succeeded best in the struggle of town life, and have seen little of the crime, squalor, and idleness of some of the rest of the Negro population. Nevertheless, these 168 families have a peculiar interest. They represent, so far as they go, a solution of the Negro problem, in that they are law-abiding, property-holding people, marrying with forethought, careful of their homes, working hard in new lines of economic endeavor, and educating their children. They are, to be sure, comparatively small in number, and yet in them lies the hope of the American Negro, and—shall we not say—to a great extent, the hope of the Republic.

Notes

1.   *Editor's note*: This study was originally published in May of 1899 in the U.S. Department of Labor's *Bulletin*. The report appeared on pages 401–17 of volume 4, number 22. The study was published by the Government Printing Office. Following the title, Du Bois was identified as the author. The citation read, "By W.E. Burghardt Du Bois, Ph.D."

2.   *Editor's note*: The table numbers in this essay have been supplied by the editor.

3.   *Editor's note*: "Scabber" is a prejudicial term used to describe a strikebreaker. "Scabbers" were workers who were hired to replace union workers who were striking. See "Scab." http://en.wikipedia.org/wiki/Scab.

4.   *Editor's note*: The variable headings have been altered slightly by the editor, but the data remain unchanged. The original variable headings were: family number, size of family, rooms in house, wage earners in family, occupation of wage earners, wages per week, weeks employed per year, yearly wages of wage earners, and yearly earnings of families.

5.   *Editor's note*: This heading was modified slightly by the editor. In the body of the table, the editor utilized 0s in place of —. The practice of replacing a — with a 0 is continued throughout the remaining tables. Note also that in this table and in tables 15.10 and 15.21 the income categories overlap. The income categories are not mutually exclusive.

6.	The data on which the two studies on conditions in a country district in DeKalb County and in the small village of Lithonia, GA, are based were furnished by Miss Aletha Howard, a graduate of Atlanta University, who has been the school-teacher in these communities.

7.	*Editor's note*: The table number, title, and headings have been supplied by the editor.

8.	The study of conditions in Covington, GA is based on data furnished by Miss T.B. Johnson, who was born in the town and has always lived there.

9.	*Editor's note*: The table number, title, and headings have been supplied by the editor.

10.	Miss J. G. Childs, a graduate of Atlanta University, furnished data for this study of Marion, AL. She was born and reared in Marion.

11.	W. A. Rogers, a senior in Atlanta University, furnished the notes for this study of conditions in Marietta, GA; he is a native of the town.

12.	*Editor's note*: Here Du Bois is documenting the fact that groups migrating into an area will often work for less. In more recent times, Bonacich (1972) has argued that several factors contribute to this phenomenon. Groups working for less may be earning more at the new location than they did at their previous location. Groups moving into a new area may not be aware that they are working for less, and they may also lack political representation. Finally, the members of the migrating group may be working to meet an immediate need and may relocate once the need is met. The presence of groups willing to work for less can be a source of conflict among established workers and new workers.

13.	Notes for this study of conditions in Athens, GA, were furnished by Miss C. E. Brydie, a native of Athens, and at present a senior in Atlanta University.

Reading 16
The Georgia Negro: A Social Study –
Editor's Reconstruction

The 1900 Paris Exhibition (*Exposition Universelle*) was held April 15 through November 12. The "The Georgia Negro: A Social Study" was prepared by Du Bois with the assistance of some of his Atlanta University students and was included as part of "The Negro Exhibit" (see Reading 11). Du Bois made reference to this project in *The Autobiography of W.E.B. Du Bois* ([1968] 2007). He perceived the international exhibition as providing an opportunity to present his ongoing work on the empirical study of "the Negro problems" to a larger audience. Du Bois ([1968] 2007: 140) maintained, "The great world's Fair at Paris was being planned and I thought I might put my findings into plans, charts and figures, so one might see what we were trying to accomplish."

What follows is a reconstruction of Du Bois' study by the editor. The original study includes a title page followed by sixty-two pages of charts, maps, and tables addressing the quality of life of African Americans residing in Georgia and the United States.[1] Each page of the study is described and, where possible, findings are presented in tabular form. In a few instances the information is no longer clearly discernable. Each chart, map, or table title was supplied by Du Bois. The data chart numbers have been supplied by the editor. Du Bois' original page numbers appeared at the bottom right hand corner of each page of the exhibit. The number was placed in brackets and appears to have been handwritten. In this reconstructed version of the exhibit, Du Bois' numbering system appears in parentheses beside the "Title Page" and each "Data Chart" designation. The page number is supplied with each chart number to avoid confusion between the reconstructed data chart number and the original exhibit page number.

Title Page (Page 1): The exhibit title and the author's name were centered at the top of the page. The title reads "The Georgia Negro: A Social Study" by W.E. Burghardt Du Bois. Two circular maps of the world are presented in the center of the title page. North, Central, and South America are presented on the left, and the rest of the world is depicted on the right. The heading above the two maps reads, "distribution of the Negro race." Arrows connecting the two maps indicate the "routes of the African slave trade." The legend includes an identifier for the state of Georgia. Two captions are centered on the bottom fourth of the page. The first caption states, "This case is devoted to a series of charts, maps and other devices designed to illustrate the development of the American Negro in a single typical state of the United States." One then has the second known instance of Du Bois' well-known phrase, "The problem of the 20th century is the problem of the color-line."

   Data Chart 1 (Page 2): A map of the United States at the turn of the twentieth century is placed in the center of this chart. The title of this chart is, "Relative Negro Population of the States of the United States." A color-coded legend identified the various population ranges. Ten population categories were identified. The categories are: 750,000 Negroes and over, 600,000–750,000, 500,000–600,000, 300,000–500,000, 200,000–300,000, 100,000–200,000, 50,000–100,000, 25,000–50,000, 10,000–25,000, and under–10,000. The reader will note that the categories overlapped and were not mutually exclusive. Neither the date nor the source of the data was identified, but it appears that Du Bois was relying on census data. The data were probably based on the 1890 census. The states with the largest number of African Americans in the total population included Georgia, Texas, Arkansas, Tennessee, Kentucky, Illinois, Ohio, Maryland, Delaware, and New York. These states have not been listed by the editor according to the size of each state's African American population.

   Data Chart 2 (Page 3): This chart contains a bar graph with what appears to be the absolute number of African Americans residing in each state listed. The chart caption reads, "The States of the United States According to Their Negro Population." The fifteen states with the largest number of African American residents listed in descending order are: Georgia, Mississippi, South Carolina, Alabama, Virginia, North Carolina, Louisiana (*sic.*), Texas, Tennessee, Arkansas, Kentucky, Maryland, Florida, Missouri, and Pennsylvania. A bar for all other states is included at the end of the table. Since a population scale was not provided, it is not possible to gauge what size population each bar length represents. The data source was not stated, but it is again assumed that the 1890 census data were probably utilized.

   Data Chart 3 (Page 4): The original data presented in this chart were portrayed in a bar chart. The chart presents the growth of the African American population for the state of Georgia for 1790–1890. Census data were probably used. Except where noted it is assumed throughout this exhibit reconstruction that Du Bois was utilizing census data. The source was not provided for any of the charts included in the exhibit. These data originally portrayed in this bar chart are now presented in tabular form. One will note that the African American population of Georgia more than doubled from 1790 to 1800. Du Bois verified this in a later chart (see *Chart 6*, Page 7). Georgia's African American population doubled again by 1820 and then again by 1850 and 1890.

Table 16.1. Negro Population of Georgia

Year	Negro Population
1790	29,662
1800	60,423
1810	107,019
1820	151,417
1830	220,017
1840	283,697
1850	384,613
1860	465,698
1870	545,142
1880	725,133
1890	858,815

Chart 4 (Page 5): This chart displays a county-level map of the African American population of Georgia by county for 1890. The title of the map is "Negro Population of Georgia by Counties. 1890." The legend designated eight different population categories ranging from under 1,000 to over 30,000 Negroes. As before the population categories overlap. The intervals are also uneven. The eight population intervals in descending order are: over 30,000 Negroes, between 20,000 and 30,000, 15,000 to 20,000, 10,000 to 15,000, 5,000 to 10,000, 2,500 to 5,000, 1,000 to 2,500, and under 1,000.

Chart 5 (Page 6): The data presented on this chart are similar to the previous chart. Here the African American population of Georgia for 1880 and 1870 was presented on two county-level maps. The 1870 map was presented first. The heading for the chart is "Negro Population of Georgia by Counties," and the population legend provided applies to both maps. The seven overlapping population categories are: between 20,000 and 30,000, 15,000 to 20,000, 10,000 to 15,000, 5,000 to 10,000, 2,500 to 5,000, 1,000 to 2,500, and under 1,000.

Chart 6 (Page 7): The title of this chart is "Comparative Increase of White and Colored Population of Georgia." Two lines were plotted on the graph. The solid line traced the percentage increase of the "Colored" population on a decennial basis from 1790 to 1890. The dashed line provided the same information for the White population. A percentage increase scale ranging from 0 to 100 percent was provided at the base of the line chart. Given the way the lines were plotted, it is not possible to determine the exact percentage growth for each race for each time period. However, it is clear that the largest percentage growth for African Americans and Whites occurred between 1790 and 1800. During this ten year period, it appears that the African American population grew by approximately 103 percent while the White population appears to have grown by around 92 percent.

Chart 7 (Page 8): Two maps addressing the topic of African American migration in and out of Georgia were provided on this chart. The title reads, "Migration of Negroes. 1890." The top map documented African American outmigration from Georgia. The following label was placed under the map: "Present Dwelling Place of Negroes Born in Georgia." The number of African Americans who were originally born in Georgia and were currently living in another state was written in each state's borders; however, the data for each state are no longer clearly distinguishable. Likewise, the second map documented African American in-migration into Georgia. The label under this map reads "Birth Place of Negroes Now resident in Georgia." The number of African Americans now living in Georgia who were originally born in another state was identified within that state's borders, but once again, these data for each state are not clearly distinguishable.

Chart 8 (Page 9): A bar graph was utilized to compare the age distribution of Georgia's African American population to that for the general population of France. Neither the date nor the source of the data was identified. The material was originally published as a bar graph but has now been reconstructed by the editor in tabular form. Some of the variable headings have been altered slightly, and a "total" line has been added by the editor.

Table 16.2. Age Distribution of Georgia Negroes Compared with France

Age Group	Georgia Negroes (Percent)	France (Percent)
Ages under 10	30.1	17.6
10–20	26.1	17.4
20–30	17.3	16.3
30–40	10.6	13.8
40–50	6.8	12.3
50–60	4.6	10.1
60–70	a	7.6
70 and over	a	5.0
Total	95.5	100.0

Note: [a] The data for this age group are no longer discernable. Apparently 4.5 percent of Georgia's African American population was 60 years old and over.

The age categories overlap, but these are the categories Du Bois originally provided. Based on the data provided, one discovers that the median age of Georgia's African American population was younger than that for France's general population. The proportion of the population age 30 and under was larger for Georgia's African American population (73.5 percent versus 51.3 percent). On the other hand, the life expectancy of France's general population may be higher. These data for Georgia and France were probably for 1890 or for some year within that decade.

Chart 9 (Page 10): Du Bois frequently employed cross-national comparisons when trying to provide a context for the interpretation of data related to African American quality of life. Given the suppression of the African American family during slavery, Du Bois wanted to demonstrate that current marriage rates among African Americans compared favorably with other racial and ethnic groups. On page ten of the exhibit, Du Bois provided a bar chart comparing the "conjugal condition" of Negroes and Germany's general population. Since this chart appeared in the section of charts addressing Georgia's African American population, it is assumed that the data were for Georgia's African American population. Also neither the year for the data nor the data source was identified.

Conjugal condition (marital status) was operationalized as single, married, and widowed and divorced, and Du Bois provided comparative data for three different age groups. The data for single persons and widowed and divorced persons are no longer discernable on the original chart. However, a table comparing the proportion of persons married for the two population groups by age can be constructed and is provided below. Some of the original variable headings have been altered by the editor.

Table 16.3. Conjugal Condition

Age Group by Race or Ethnicity	Percent Married
15–40[a]	
Germany	37.3
Negroes	54.0
40–60[b]	
Germany	84.9
Negroes	78.5
60 and over[c]	
Germany	62.2
Negroes	54.5

Notes: [a] Under the label Negroes, Du Bois placed an age range in a smaller font. It appears that the age range is 15–40, but the last number is blurred.
[b] The age range for Negroes is 45–64, but the numbers are blurred.
[c] The age range for Negroes is 65 and over, but again the numbers are blurred.

Since the age ranges for the two ethnic-racial groups are not comparable, exact comparisons cannot be made. Among the two older age groups, the percentage of Germans in Germany's total population who were married was only 6.4 percentage points and 7.7 percentage points higher than the rate for African Americans residing in Georgia. How much of the difference in the marriage proportion may be attributed to the difference in the age ranges is not known. Nevertheless, the marriage proportion for the two older age groups is roughly comparable. Provided that the percentages for the two youngest age groups are based on the same age range, younger African Americans residing in Georgia (54.0 percent) were much more likely to be married than Germans residing in Germany (37.3 percent).

Chart 10 (Page 11): This chart contained a line drawing that included four data points. Each data point specified the number of African Americans residing in Georgia in a rural area or cities of varying sizes. These data are now presented in tabular form. The table headings have been added by the editor but are based on information provided by Du Bois. The editor has added the "total" category, and Du Bois' chart title has been retained.

Table 16.4. City and Rural Population, 1890

Geographic Area	Number of Negroes
Country and villages	734,952
Cities from 2,500 to 5,000	97,699
Cities from 5,000 to 10,000	8,025
Cities over 10,000 inhabitants	7,888[a]
Total	848,564

Note: [a] The last three digits of this figure are not clearly discernable.

The total for African Americans in this table is approximately 10,000 persons less than that reported in Table 16.1. The source of the discrepancy is not known. Based on the data provided in the above table, 86.6 percent of Georgia's African American population resided in the rural areas and small villages.

Chart 11 (Page 12): The title of this chart is "Slaves and Free Negroes." The graph is a vertical line graph; however, the headings across the top of the graph are no longer clearly discernable. The figures for the "percent of free Negroes" can be determined for 1790 through 1870, but it is not clear whether these data refer to free African Americans in Georgia or the United States. It is assumed that these data were for the state of Georgia. The following table has been reconstructed by the editor.

16.5. Slaves and Free Negroes

Year	Percent of Free Negroes
1790	1.3
1800	1.7
1810	1.7
1820	1.2
1830	0.8
1840	0.9
1850	0.7
1860	0.8
1870	100.0

Between 1790 and 1860 the percent of free Negroes within the total Negro population ranged from a high of 1.7 percent in 1800 and 1810 to a low of 0.7 percent in 1850.

Chart 12 (Page 13): The data in this chart were originally presented in a bar chart format. These data are now presented in a tabular format preserving the titles and race descriptions Du Bois utilized. The table headings and the "total" line have been supplied by the editor. Neither the year for these data nor the source of these data is known. If these data were based on available census data, these data were probably for 1890.

Table 16.6. Race Amalgamation in Georgia. Based on a Study of 40,000 Individuals of Negro Descent

Color Category	Percent of Persons of Negro Descent
Black i.e., Full-blooded Negroes.	44
Brown i.e., Persons with some White blood or descendents of light colored Africans	38
Yellow i.e., Persons with more white than Negro blood	18
Total	100

Over half (56 percent) of Georgia's African American population at the time these data were collected was of mixed race.

Chart 13 (Page 14): The information presented on this page addressed the issue of literacy and was provided on a decennial basis for 1860 through 1900. The data for 1900 were probably provisional since a question mark was placed beside the date and the percentage in the original bar chart. Although neither the source nor the area covered was stated in this bar chart on "illiteracy," it is assumed that these data literacy data were for African Americans residing in Georgia. Since these data were provided on a decennial basis, census data were probably utilized. The reconstructed table is presented below with variable headings supplied by the editor.

Table 16.7. Illiteracy

Year	Percent of Negroes Illiterate
1860	99.0
1870	92.0
1880	81.8[a]
1890	67.27
1900 (?)	50.0 (?)

Note: [a] This figure is no longer clear.

From 1860 to 1900, it appears that the proportion of African Americans (in Georgia ?) who were illiterate was cut in half.

Chart 14 (Page 15): The next chart displayed African American children's enrollment in public schools from 1860 through 1897. These data were originally presented in a bar chart format. While not specifically identified, these data are for African American children residing in Georgia. These data along with additional data were later presented by Du Bois in the 1901 Atlanta University Conference report, *The Negro Common School*. The enrollment data are now presented in tabular form. The editor has slightly altered the variable headings.

**Table 16.8. Negro Children Enrolled in
the Public Schools**

Year	Number of Negroes Enrolled in Public Schools
1860	7
1870	10,351
1878	72,655
1884	110,150
1888	120,533
1891	156,836
1891	180,565

The number of African American children enrolled in Georgia's public schools increased steadily from 1860 to 1891.

Chart 15 (Page 16): Turning from children's enrollment in public schools, Du Bois documented the number of African American teachers in Georgia's public schools from 1888 through 1897. These data were originally presented within four circles that were vertically aligned. Data were presented for 1888, 1889, 1893, and 1897; however, the figures for 1893 are no longer discernable. These original data are now presented in tabular form minus the data for 1893. The variable headings have been provided by the editor, and Du Bois did not identify the source of these data.

**Table 16.9. Negro Teachers in Georgia
Public Schools**

Year	Number of Negro Teachers in Public Schools
1888	2,512
1889	2,500
1897	3,316

Although falling slightly from 1888 to 1889, the number of African American teachers teaching in Georgia's public schools increased by 32.6 percent from 1888 to 1897.

Chart 16 (Page 17): A bar graph was employed next to document the numbers of African American students enrolled in the different educational courses of study offered by the Georgia public schools. Unfortunately, Du Bois identified neither the year for these data nor the data source. The data are now presented by the editor in tabular form. Again, the total line and some of the variable headings have been added by the editor.

**Table 16.10. Number of Negro Students Taking the Various
Courses of Study Offered in Georgia Schools**

Course of Study	Number of Negro Students Enrolled
Business	12
Classical	88
Professional	152
Scientific	181
Normal	383
Industrial	2,252
Total	3,068

Approximately three-fourths (73.4 percent) of African American students were enrolled in the "industrial" course of study.

Chart 17 (Page 18): Du Bois next turned to African American land ownership and property value. The title of this chart is "Value of Land Owned by Georgia Negroes." The chart contained a vertical series of money bags that were centered on the chart. The money bags varied in size in a manner similar to what one would find in a cartogram. If the value of the land owned for each year was included inside each money bag, it is no longer discernable. Money bags were provided for 1875, 1880, 1885, 1890, 1895, and 1899. The size of the bag steadily increases as one moves from year to year. The source for these data was not provided.

Chart 18 (Page 19): The title of the next chart is "Acres of Land Owned by Negroes in Georgia." These data were presented in a bar chart format for each year from 1874 through 1899. The only year missing was 1881. Even though the number of acres owned by African Americans was not identified for each year, the changing bar lengths indicate that the number of acres of land owned by Georgia's African American community increased steadily from 1874 through 1892. The only exception was 1883. From 1892 through 1899, the number of acres of land owned hovered around the 1892 value. The data source was not identified.

Chart 19 (Page 20): With the next chart, Du Bois provided a county-level map depicting the number of acres owned by Georgia's African American community. The number of acres of land owned by African Americans was placed inside each county's boundaries. Unfortunately, the figures for some of the counties are no longer clearly discernable. The title given to the map is "Land Owned by Negroes in Georgia, U.S.A. 1870–1900." Just to the right of the map, Du Bois placed the phrase, "the figures indicate the number of acres owned in each county in 1899." However, the date given for the year is in question as it is somewhat blurred. Again, the source for these data was not provided.

Chart 20 (Page 21): The title of the next chart was "Valuation of Town and City Property Owned by Georgia Negroes." These data were plotted on a piece of grid paper. A land value scale was provided on the left-hand side of the grid. Each bar represented $100,000, and the scale ranged from $0 to $4,800,000. A time line was provided at the bottom of the grid, and each box represented one year. The scale began with 1870 and ended with 1900. A line graph was drawn within the grid, and labels for six different eras were included within the grid. The six different eras were labeled ku-kluxism (1870–74), political unrest (1874–80), age of the new industrialism (1880–90), lynching (1891–94), financial panic (1894), and disfranchisement and proscriptive laws (1894–1900). These data are now presented by the editor in a tabular format. The source for these data was not stated.

Table 16.11. Valuation of Town and City Property Owned by Georgia Negroes

Time Period	Era	Valuation Ranges for Property Owned by Georgia Negroes
1870–74	Ku-Kluxism	$300,000–$1,200,000
1874–80	Political Unrest	$1,200,000–$1,000,000
1880–90	Age of the New Industrialism	$1,000,000–$3,500,000
1891–94	Lynching	$3,600,000–$4,600,000
1894	Financial Panic	$4,600,000
1894–1900	Disfranchisement and Proscriptive Laws	$4,600,000–$4,300,000

The value of town and city property owned by Georgia's African American community rose substantially from $300,000 in 1870 to 4,300,000 in 1900. The total land value owned peaked at a little over 4,800,000 in 1893, and the total land value owned declined from 1873 ($1,200,000) to 1879 ($1,100,000) and from 1893 ($4,800,000) to 1900 ($4,300,000).

Chart 21 (Page 22): The information in this chart was presented in a pie chart format. The title for the pie chart is "Assessed Valuation of All Taxable Property Owned by Georgia Negroes." It appears that dollar amounts were provided for three time periods: 1875, 1885, and 1900. Unfortunately, the dollar amounts for the total assessed property evaluations are no longer clearly discernable, and Du Bois did not provide a source for these data.

Chart 22 (Page 23): The value of property owned by African Americans residing in two Georgia cities and the number of African American property owners in each city were provided in this graph based on the intersection of two bar charts. The property owners' bar chart runs from left to right, and the property value bar chart runs from top to bottom. The two selected cities, Savannah and Atlanta, are identified in boxes at the bottom of the page. Data were provided for 1880, 1890, and 1899, but the figures for the number of owners and the property value in each city are not distinguishable. Based on a visual inspection of the length of the bars on each graph, it appears that the number of African American property owners was greater in Savannah for each time period, but the total value of the property owned by African Americans was higher in Atlanta for each time period. Again, the sources for these data were not identified.

Chart 23 (Page 24): The "Value of Farming Tools" was presented in the next bar graph. Data were provided for 1879, 1883, 1888, 1893, and 1898. Unfortunately Du Bois did not provide a value scale. The bars are of varying lengths, but it is not possible to determine the value of farming tools for each period. Comparing the changes in bar lengths over time, one can tentatively conclude that the value of farming tools increased steadily from 1879 to 1893 with the largest increase being registered between 1888 and 1893. The 1898 farming tool value was between the 1888 and 1893 values. Since it is not known whether Du Bois adjusted these financial data for fluctuations in the value of the dollar over time, one cannot determine whether the increase in value was based on an increase in the real value of the tools. The source of the financial data was not provided. Although the state is not identified, it is assumed that these data apply to the value of farm tools owned by African Americans residing in Georgia.

Chart 24 (Page 25): The next chart depicts the assessed value of household and kitchen furniture owned by African Americans residing in Georgia from 1875–99. However, the termination date is not clearly distinguishable and could be 1898. The bar graph was originally drawn in a circular manner. The data are now presented by the editor in tabular form. The editor has also supplied the variable headings. Again the source of the data is not identified, and it is assumed that Du Bois did not index the financial data to the value of the dollar for one point in time.

Table 16.12. Assessed Value of Household and Kitchen Furniture Owned by Georgia Negroes

Year	Value of Negro Household and Kitchen Furniture Owned
1875	$21,188
1880	$498,532
1885	$738,170
1890	$1,173,824
1895	$1,322,894
1899[a]	$1,434,875

Note: [a] The date is not clear in the original. It could be 1899 or 1898.

Although constant dollars were apparently not used, one may tentatively conclude that the value of household and kitchen furniture owned by African Americans residing in Georgia increased steadily throughout the period under investigation. It also appears that the greatest percentage increase in assessed household and kitchen furniture value occurred between 1875 and 1880.

Chart 25 (Page 26): The occupations of Georgia's African American male population over age ten for 1890 were presented in a bar chart. Data were supplied for twenty-two occupational categories. These data are now presented by the editor in tabular form. The variable headings have been modified, and the "total" line has been provided by the editor. The source for these data was not identified.

Table 16.13. Occupations of Georgia Negroes, 1890

Occupational Category	Number of Males Over 10
Agricultural Laborers	99,400
Farmers and Planters	83,012
Laborers	28,723
Steam Railway Employees	7,440
Servants	7,000
Draymen, Hackmen	4,390
Carpenters and Joiners	3,761
Saw and Planing Mill Employees	2,471
Messengers	1,870
Wood Choppers	1,399
Blacksmiths and Wheelwrights	1,328
Clergymen	1,277
Masons	1,243
Brick-Makers and Potters	977
Barbers	899
Merchants	837
Painters, Glazers, and Varnishers	676
Boot and Shoe Makers	632
Professors and Teachers	620
Livery Stable Keepers	620
Engineers	520
Gardners and Florists	519
Total	249,614

Consistent with the times, agricultural laborers, farmers and planters, and laborers were identified as the dominant occupational categories. Approximately 84.6 percent of Georgia's male African American workers over ten years of age were employed in these three job categories.

Chart 26 (Page 27): The next chart also addressed the topic of occupations, but now the focus was on the racial differences in the occupational distribution. A pie chart was employed to display this information. The title given to the pie chart is "Occupations of Negroes and Whites in Georgia." Data for African Americans were placed in the top wedge of the pie chart while data for Whites were included in the bottom wedge. Percentage data by race were provided for the following five occupational categories: 1) agriculture, fisheries, and mining; 2) manufacturing and mechanical industries; 3) domestic and personal service; 4) professions; and 5) trade and transportation.

Unfortunately, the percentages associated with each slice of the racial wedge are no longer clearly discernable. It appears that the dominant employment category for African Americans and Whites residing in Georgia was agriculture, fisheries, and mining. One can safely assume that the bulk of the workers for each race were employed in some type of agricultural-related job. The domestic and personal service occupational category percentage was discernable for African Americans. It appears that 28 percent of Georgia's African American working community was employed in this area. Unfortunately, the age range of the working age population was not specified, and Du Bois did not state the year for the data or the data source. Given the terminology associated with the occupational categories, one could assume that these data were obtained from the census and that the year was probably 1890.

Chart 27 (Page 28): The data preserved in this chart were presented in a spreadsheet format. The title given to the spreadsheet is "Occupations." With this chart Du Bois failed to identify the year, the racial group, or the source of these data. It appears safe to assume that the occupational data were for African Americans residing in Georgia, but these data may not apply to all areas of the state. Information was entered into the spreadsheet in either ink or pencil, and the script is cursive.

While the occupational groups are no longer clearly identifiable, information was provided for thirty different occupations. For each occupation line, a single category number or value range could be checked with respect to weekly wages, annual income, and hours (worked) per day. Unfortunately, the writing has faded significantly, and the information provided cannot be clearly delineated.

Chart 28 (Page 29): Similar data were provided in the next chart. The title given to this spreadsheet is "Occupations and Income." The uncertainty surrounding the previous spreadsheet also applies to these data. It is assumed that these data apply to African Americans residing in Georgia, but it does not appear that the data apply to all geographic areas. The source for the data is unknown. Three spreadsheet headings were provided by Du Bois.

The first heading is "Occupations by Sex." Twenty-seven occupational categories were identified for males and four categories were identified for females. Next to the occupational category column was a column labeled "number." Unfortunately, none of the data provided are clearly discernable. The second major heading is "Wages by Sex." Eighteen wage ranges were specified. These ranges were followed by a column for males and another for females. Again, the data are too faded so accurate determinations cannot be made. The final category was "Income by Families." It appears that family size was in the first column, but the heading is unclear. Nine data rows were provided and numbered one through nine. This column was followed by twelve family income columns. The income range cannot be determined, and it appears that Du Bois was documenting the number of families in each income range by the size of the family. A final data column was provided for families for whom the income data were "unknown."

Chart 29 (Page 30?): While the original page number for this chart is no longer clear, the chart addressed debt among tenant farmers in 1898. These data appear to be based on 300 African American farm tenants residing in selected rural areas of Georgia; however, the selected areas were not specified. The original data were presented in a bar chart format with the following title, "Condition of 300 Negro Farm Tenants after 1 Years Toil, 1898." The seven response categories were bankrupt, in debt, cleared nothing, cleared less than $10, cleared $10–25, cleared $25–50, and cleared $50 or more. Percentages were placed within each bar, but they can no longer be determined with certainty. The income categories also overlapped. Measuring the length of all the remaining bars against the longest bar (in debt), it appears that 55–60 percent of the 300 African American farm tenants included in the study were in debt. Although Du Bois did not comment directly on this, these data provided empirical documentation that debt was one of the serious problems associated with the crop-lien system.

Chart 30 (Page 31?): Again, the original page number for this chart was not clearly discernable. While the previous chart addressed the quality of life of 300 African American tenant farmers residing in rural Georgia, this chart and the next two charts documented the quality of life of 150 African American families residing in the city of Atlanta. The title of the first chart is "Income and Expenditure of 150 Negro Families in Atlanta, GA, U.S.A." The date for the annual family income data was not disclosed.

On this particular chart, three graphs were integrated in an adjacent manner. A large darkened circle with the label, "Annual Income" was positioned on the left hand side. This figure could have originally been a pie chart, but the data are no longer available. Just below this figure were two columns of data. The first was labeled "class," and the label for the second column was indistinguishable. It could represent average income for the income class, but this cannot be confirmed. The income ranges included in the class column are $100–200, $200–300, $300–400, $400–500, $500–750, $750–1,000, and $1,000 and over. The income ranges are not mutually exclusive. Du Bois went on to combine several income categories to identify the presence of four distinct African American social classes within the city of Atlanta. Families in the "well-to-do" class had an annual income of $1,000 or more, while families included in the "comfortable" class earned $500 to $1,000 annually. "Fair" class families included families with annual incomes in the $300 to $500 range. Families with annual incomes of $100 to $300 were included in the "poor" class. Du Bois did not indicate how many families were included in each class.

At the top of the graph, Du Bois presented a figure addressing the annual expenditures of these 150 African American families. The expenditure categories described included rent, food, clothes, direct taxes, and other expenditures and savings. The rent box included a picture of a home for a well-to-do African American family. The food box included writing which is no longer discernable. Within the clothing box, pictures of a well-dressed African American male and an African American female were presented. The direct taxes box provided data on the tax rates for the state of Georgia, state and county taxes, and the tax rate for Atlanta. Some of the information is discernable, but too much of the data is

not discernable. The "other expenditures and savings" box included such categories as the high life, religion, art, education, sickness, savings, amusements,
books and papers, and travel.

A bar chart was included just below the expenditure figure. The proportion
of financial resources allocated to each of the five major expenditure categories
was noted within the bar for each of the seven income ranges noted earlier. Unfortunately, the percentage data are now discernable only for the expenditure
categories for "clothing" and "other expenditures and savings." These data are
now provided by the editor in tabular form. The title and headings have been
supplied by the editor.

Table 16.14. Expenditures for 150 Atlanta Negro
Families by Expenditure Type

Income Class	Clothing (Percent)	Other Expenditures and Savings (Percent)
$100–200	28.0	9.9
$200–300	23.0	4.0
$300–400	18.0	8.5
$400–500	15.0	24.5
$500–750	17.0	34.0
$750–1,000	19.0	36.0
$1,000 and over	16.0	50.5

Since clothing is one of life's basic necessities, it is not surprising that families included in the "poor" class allocated a greater proportion of their total expenditures to clothing than did other social classes. Likewise, for "comfortable"
and "well-to-do" families, a greater proportion of their funds were directed toward discretionary spending and savings. Finally, centered at the bottom of the
original chart, Du Bois provided the exhibit viewer with the following instruc-
tions, "For Further Statistics Raise This Frame."

Chart 31 (Page 32): The title of the next chart is "Family Budgets." Budgets
for eight of Atlanta's African American families were presented on this page.
Detailed budgets were supplied for each family. It appears that a standard budget form with twenty-seven categories for responses was utilized, but the responses to the items are no longer completely legible. The occupation of the
family's primary earner and the annual family income are stated below.

- Fireman and Engineer $32 ($320)[2]
- Sash and Blind Maker $360
- Carpenter $360
- Rock Mason $375
- Wheelwright $450

- Barber $400
- Blacksmith $450
- Painter $540

Chart 32 (Page 33): Budgets for eight additional African American families from Atlanta were presented on this chart. Unfortunately, this page has been damaged severely. The labels identifying the occupation of the primary wage earner and the annual family income amount has faded to the point that this information cannot be discerned. The same standardized budget form is used on this page, but the writing is too small and cannot be distinguished clearly. There appears to be a large ink stain in the middle of the chart. The stain could be attributed to water damage.

Chart 33 (Page 34): A grid map of Albany, GA was presented on this chart. African American and White inhabitants were plotted on the map. At the bottom of the map, one has the heading, "Albany, Dougherty County, GA." A legend was placed immediately under this heading. The legend identified the African American inhabitants by social class. The heading for the legend is "Distribution of 2500 Negro Inhabitants." Four social classes were identified and were labeled well-to-do, better class of laborers, poor, and lowest class. A small dot preceded each class. Perhaps these circles were of a different color originally. Given the present condition of the photocopy of the map, the dot system can no longer be accurately employed to identify the African American inhabitants by social class. Following the legend the phrase, "approximate distribution of whites," is placed in parentheses. It appears as if a diamond was used to identify White inhabitants. The copy of the map is so small, that it is no longer possible to distinguish all inhabitants by race or African American inhabitants by social class. Neither the date for the map nor the source of these data was provided by Du Bois.

Chart 34 (Page 35): Similar data for McIntosh County, Georgia are provided in the map preserved on this page of the exhibit. In the lower left-hand corner one has the heading, "McIntosh County, GA" which is followed by two lines of data specifying the population of the county by race for 1890. At this time the county's White population was 1,258 while the African American population was 5,212.[3]

Du Bois stated that the data plotted on the map of McIntosh County reflected the "Distribution of 2000 Negro Inhabitants Outside the Town of Darien." Each dot on the map identified the geographic location of African American residents. The different dot types also signified a different social class. Unfortunately, it is no longer possible to determine which type of dot represented which social class. Du Bois labeled these social classes as the well-to-do, better class of laborers and small farmers, poor, and lowest class. At the end of the legend on African American social class, one has one final dot which was utilized to signify the "Approximate Distribution of Whites." In the far left-hand corner of the graph, Du Bois provided information on the total land area for McIntosh

County, the number of acres of land owned by African Americans as well as three indicators of what may have been different modes of transportation. McIntosh County covered 488 square miles, and African Americans were identified as owning 13,760 acres of land. Roads and railroads running through the country were plotted. A third mode of transportation appears to have been specified, but the exact mode can no longer be identified. Again, the source for these data was not noted.

Chart 35 (Page 36): While McIntosh County's rural population was plotted on the previous map, on the current map Du Bois plotted the geographic location of the African American inhabitants of the city of Darien. The title of the map and the social class legend appeared in the map's top right-hand corner. The title reads, "Darien, McIntosh Co., GA." Underneath the title Du Bois indicated that the dots on the map represented the "Distribution of 1,000 Negro Inhabitants." As before each dot signified a different social class, but it is no longer possible to distinguish the classes clearly on the basis of the dots. The four African American social classes identified in this map resemble the designations utilized in the previous maps. The four African American social classes were the well-to-do, better class of laborers, poor, and lowest class. No data source was provided. This chart was the last of the charts documenting the quality of life of African Americans residing in Georgia.

Chart 36 (Page 37): With this chart Du Bois began his discussion of the quality of life of the African American community in the United States. State-level and small area data were now replaced with data for the country as a whole. From this point forward Du Bois provided an English and a French title for each chart. In this exhibit reconstruction, only the English titles are retained. The title of this introductory chart is, "A Series of Statistical Charts Illustrating the Condition of the Descendants of Former African Slaves Now Resident in the United States of America." The French title is placed underneath the English title.

Next, in the center of a page is a small map of the United States. A symbol was provided to identify the center of the African American population, but the symbol cannot be clearly identified within the map. To the left of the map one has the following statement, "Prepared and executed by Negro Students under the Direction of Atlanta University, Atlanta, GA, United States of America." To the right of the map, the same information is provided in French. In the center of the chart, the viewer was presented with two statements about Atlanta University. The two statements are: "The University was founded in 1867. It has instructed 6,000 Negro students." This same information was then provided in French.

A pie chart identifying the occupations that 330 of Atlanta University's graduates had entered was presented next. The pie chart provided a percentage distribution of these graduates among six different occupational fields. Unfortunately the percentages are no longer clearly discernable, and the source of these data was not provided. The six occupational categories were teachers, ministers, government service, business, other professions, and housewives. This information was also provided in French.

The bottom fourth of the chart was devoted to a summary description of Atlanta University. The information was presented in English and French. Du Bois provided the following statement.

> The University has 20 professors and instructors and 250 students at present. It has five buildings, 60 acres of campus, and a library of 11,000 volumes. It aims to raise and civilize the sons of the freedmen by training their more capable members in the liberal arts according to the best standards of the day. The proper accomplishment of this work demands an endowment fund of $500,000.

Linking African American social uplift with liberal arts education rather than industrial education became a major point of contention between Du Bois and Booker T. Washington. Here one witnesses an early formulation of Du Bois' position.

Chart 37 (Page 38): This chart contained a map of the United States. The title of the map is "Distribution of Negroes in the United States." Neither the date nor the source for these data was specified. A population density legend was placed between the map title and the actual map. The heading reads "Negroes to the Square Mile." Four circles running from left to right were presented in a row above the heading. The density scale is as follows: less than 1, 1–4, 4–8, 8–15, and 15–25.[4] The circles appear to have been color coded, but the difference in color is no longer distinguishable. Consequently, it is not possible to determine where the African American population density was the highest. The dark areas of the map included the South, the Northeast through Massachusetts, and parts of the Central region. The rest of the map was coded in one light color.

Chart 38 (Page number uncertain): A bar chart depicting the growth of the African American population from 1750 to 1890 was presented here. Under the English and French title, Du Bois placed the phrase, "Done by Atlanta University." This acknowledgement accompanied the remaining charts in the exhibit. The editor has reformatted these data in tabular form, provided variable headings, and retained Du Bois' original title. The source of these data was not specified. The data from 1750–1780 appear to have been based on estimates, while the population data for 1790 through 1890 were taken from the U.S. decennial census. These data are reconstructed in Table 16.15.

The African American population in the United States doubled from 1750 to 1770 and then doubled again by 1800, 1830, and 1870. From 1870 to 1890, the African American population increased by 53.5 percent.

Chart 39 (Page number uncertain): A line graph depicting the growth of the White and African American population in the United States was displayed on this exhibit page. Census data were provided for 1790 through 1890. Population size measured in five million population intervals were portrayed on

**Table 16.15. Increase of the Negro Population in the
United States of America[a]**

Year	Negro Population (Number)
1750	220,000
1760	310,000
1770	462,000
1780	562,000
1790	757,208
1800	1,002,037
1810	1,377,808
1820	1,771,656
1830	2,328,642
1840	2,873,648
1850	3,638,808
1860	4,441,830
1870	4,880,009
1880	6,580,793
1890	7,488,788

Note: [a] Data for 1750–80 were based on estimates.

the left-hand side of the graph, and the census years were presented at the bottom of the chart in ten year intervals. There was some writing within the main body of the chart, but there are some smudges on the chart and the information is not clearly discernable.

The population information originally presented in the line graph is now presented by the editor in tabular form. Du Bois' original title has been retained, but the editor has added the variable headings. These data are reconstructed in Table 16.16.

Basing the total U.S. population figure only on the number of Whites and African Americans for each census year, one discovers that in 1790 African Americans comprised 19.3 percent of the total population. This percentage fell to 14.2 percent in 1860 and to 12.0 percent by 1890.

Chart 40 (Page 41?): The page number for this chart is not completely recognizable. On this chart Du Bois provided small maps of ten different countries along with a map of the U.S. The country's name and the total population for the country were placed inside each map. The United States map depicted the total African American population. Since the country maps were portrayed as cartograms, the size of the country map varied by the size of country's total population. Data for Norway, Belgium, Switzerland, and Germany could not be determined with certainty. Neither the date nor the data source for these cross-national data was supplied. The information for seven of the countries is now

Table 16.16. Comparative Rate of Increase of the White and Negro Elements of the Population of the United States

Year	White Population (Number)	Negro Population (Number)
1790	3,172,006	757,208
1800	4,306,466	1,002,037
1810	5,862,073	1,377,808
1820	7,866,797	1,771,656
1830	10,532,060	2,328,642
1840	14,189,705	2,873,648
1850	19,553,068	3,638,808
1860	26,922,537	4,441,830
1870	33,589,377	4,880,009
1880	43,402,970	6,580,793
1890	55,101,258	7,488,788

presented below by the editor in tabular form. Du Bois' original title has been retained, but the editor has supplied the variable headings.

Table 16.17. Negro Population of the United States Compared with the Total Population of Other Countries

Country	Total Population
Spain	17,300,000
Australia	3,224,579[a]
Sweden	4,474,400
Netherlands	4,500,000[a]
United States	7,500,000[b]
Hungary	17,500,000[a]
England	27,500,000

Note: [a] The accuracy of this figure is questionable.
[b] African American population.

These data were probably for the 1890–1900 decade. At this time the African American population in the United States was larger than the total population for Australia, Sweden, or the Netherlands.

Chart 41 (Page 42): On this chart Du Bois placed a map of the United States in each of the page's four quadrants. Each map contained a map of the United States within a map of the United States. The outer map contained a white interior while the smaller map inside the larger map was black. Maps were provided for 1800, 1830, 1860, and 1890. The title given to the chart was "Pro-

portion of Negroes in the Total Population of the United States." As one moved
from 1800 to 1890 the maps became progressively bigger, but the proportion of
the total African American population became progressively smaller. In 1800
African Americans comprised approximately one-fifth of the U.S. population.
By 1830 the African American proportion of the total population dropped to
one-sixth. By 1860 and 1890 the proportions were one-seventh and one-sixth
respectively. See Chart 39 for a discussion of a similar finding.

   Chart 42 (Page 43): The title of the next chart was "Occupations in which
American Negroes are engaged." Along the left margin, the following five occupational categories were identified: 1) agriculture, mining, and fishing; 2)
professions; 3) domestic and personal service; 4) commerce and transportation;
and 5) manufacturing and mechanical industries. The proportion of African
Americans working in each of these occupational categories was presented in a
series of three vertical bar columns. The first column focused on males and females collectively, while the next two columns addressed males and females
separately. If numbers or percentages were utilized to demonstrate level of involvement in each category, these indicators are no longer clearly discernable.
However, it is possible to determine which occupational category attracted the
most persons. Collectively, African American males and females were most
likely to be working in the agriculture, mining, and fishing category. At the turn
of the twentieth century, it would be safe to assume that most African Americans were working in agricultural jobs. When looking at the sexes separately,
one notes that males were more likely to be in agricultural jobs while females
were slightly more likely to be associated with jobs in domestic and personal
service. Neither the date for the information utilized in this chart nor the source
of these data was identified. Based on the occupational categories cited, it appears that census data were employed.

   Chart 43 (Page 44): A pie graph was used in this chart page to document
racial differences in occupational class. Occupational categories similar to those
employed in the previous chart were utilized to identify the various pieces of the
occupational pie. In this graph Du Bois did provide a category for "other occupations," and the agriculture category only addressed agriculture. African American and White pie slices were plotted side-by-side. Unfortunately, Du Bois did
not include a scale to gauge the size of each racial pie wedge. Again, the year for
these data was not specified, and it appears that Du Bois was basing his findings
on census data although this was not formally stated.

   Chart 44 (Page 45): A bar graph was employed next to identify nineteen
different occupational classes in which at least 10,000 African Americans were
employed. The different occupational bars were listed according to descending
size. Du Bois only provided numerical data for the largest and smallest occupational category. The largest and smallest occupational categories were agricultural laborers and hostlers. The number of African Americans employed in each
category was 1,108,728 and 10,500 persons respectively. Although the data
source was not identified, it appears that Du Bois utilized census data, and the

data were probably for 1890. The formal title of the bar chart was "Occupations in which 10,000 or more American Negroes Are Engaged." The nineteen occupational categories are now listed in order of descending size.

- Agricultural laborers
- Farmers
- Servants
- Laborers
- Launderers and Laundresses
- Railroad employees
- Draymen, etc.[5]
- Carpenters
- Barbers
- Sawmill employees
- Porters
- Teachers
- Tobacco factory operatives
- Clergymen
- Other agricultural pursuits
- Seamstresses
- Blacksmiths
- Brickmakers, etc.
- Hostlers[6]

Chart 45 (Page 46): Attention next turned to the topic of education. Du Bois provides a bar chart to document the growth in the number of African American teachers in the United States from 1885 to 1895. The title given to the bar chart is "Number of Negro Teachers in the Public Schools of the United States." Data were provided for 1885, 1888, 1892, and 1895. Unfortunately, Du Bois either did not provide the number of teachers for each bar or the numbers have faded beyond recognition. One is presented with four bars of differing lengths. The general trend is a steady increase in the number of African American teachers in the public schools over the period, and the biggest increase is noted between 1885 and 1888. The source of these data was not identified.

Chart 46 (Page 47): A cross-national comparison of literacy rates was provided in this bar chart. The title of the chart is "Illiteracy of the American Negroes Compared with that of Other Nations." Here the proportion of African Americans in the United States who were illiterate was compared to the proportion of persons judged to be illiterate in nine different countries. It is interesting to note that the proportion of the total population illiterate in Romania, Serbia, and Russia was higher than that for the proportion of African Americans residing in the United States around the turn of the nineteenth century. Unfortunately, there is no way to determine what the length of each illiteracy bar signifies precisely, and Du Bois did not provide the year of or the sources for these data.

Chart 47 (Page 48): African American enrollment in Negro common schools in the former slave states was addressed next. In this bar chart enrollment data were provided for five different years. These data are now presented by the editor in tabular form. The variable headings have been supplied by the editor. It is assumed that students enrolled in the Negro common schools were African American.

**Table 16.18. Enrollment in the Negro Common
Schools in the Former Slave States
of the United States**

Academic Year	Number of African American Students Enrolled
1876–77	571,506
1880–81	802,374
1885–86	1,048,659
1890–91	1,329,549
1895–96	1,429,713

The number of African Americans residing in the former slave states enrolled in Negro common schools rose steadily from the 1876–77 to the 1895–96 school year. The source for these data was not provided.

Chart 48 (Page 49): The title of the next bar chart is "Proportion of Total Negro Children of School Age Who Are Enrolled in Public Schools." Vertical bars were presented for the years 1876, 1886, and 1896. According to the legend provided, each bar documented and distinguished the proportion of African American children enrolled and not enrolled in public schools. Unfortunately, the differences in color codes can no longer be distinguished, and it appears that percentages may not have been inserted within each bar segment. While the length of each bar increased over time, in their present form, these data cannot be used to determine whether or not the proportion of African American children enrolled in public schools increased over the period. Again, Du Bois did not provide the source of these data.

Chart 49 (Page 50): The empirical documentation of African American socioeconomic progress from 1860 to 1890 was addressed next. The title of this exhibit page is "The Rise of Negroes from Slavery to Freedom in One Generation." Two rectangular boxes were placed on this page. One is in the lower right-hand corner of the page and the other is in the upper right-hand corner. The first rectangle has the label "1860" at the top while the other includes the label "1890." Five dashed lines extend from the first rectangle to the second, but the information included inside the two rectangles is no longer discernable. Several statements, in English and French, were included in the top right-hand corner of the page and are legible. They read, "In 1890 nearly one fifth of them [African

Americans] owned their own homes and farms. This advance was accomplished entirely without state aid and in the face of proscriptive laws. In 1860 nearly 90 % of the Blacks were slaves." Du Bois did not provide the source of his information.

Chart 50 (Page 51): This chart addressed the issue of slavery in the United States. The title of the chart is "Proportion of Freemen and Slaves among American Negroes." Data were provided for 1790 through 1870 on a decennial basis. Although Du Bois did not reveal his source, he was relying on U.S. census data. The census years were displayed along the top of a graph, and it appears as if percentages could have been utilized along the left margin. Unfortunately the center of the graph with the data was not reproduced in the material accessed by the editor. The format for the data in the original exhibit is thus unknown.

Since data on African American slavery were collected by the U.S. census bureau, the editor for the most part has been able to replicate what Du Bois intended to portray. The table title, variable headings, and columns depicting actual counts have been provided by the editor.

Table 16.19. Negro Slaves and Freemen in the United States,
**   1790–1860**

Census Year	Negro Slaves		Negro Freemen	Total Negro Population
	Number	Percent	Number	Number
1790	697,681	92.1	59,527	757,208
1800	893,602	89.2	108,435	1,002,037
1810	1,191,362	86.5	186,446	1,377,808
1820	1,538,022	86.8	233,634	1,771,656
1830	2,009,043	86.3	319,599	2,328,642
1840	2,487,355	86.6	386,293	2,873,648
1850	3,204,287	88.1	434,521	3,638,808
1860	3,953,731	89.0	488,099	4,441,830

Source: U.S. Census, 1790–1860. See http://en.wikipedia.org/wiki/ African_American.

The proportion of the African American population in the United States enslaved declined from 92.1 percent in 1790 to 89.0 percent in 1860. Prior to emancipation, the largest proportion of African American Freemen in the total African American population was 13.7 percent in 1830.

Chart 51 (Page 52): Attention next turned to the rural-urban composition of the African American population in the former slave states. Immediately under the title, a key in English and French was provided to allow the viewer to distinguish the rural and urban proportions included in the bar chart. The urban population was operationalized as the "Proportion of Negroes Living in Cities of 8,000 inhabitants or more." The rural population was identified as the "Proportion of Negroes Living in Villages and Country Districts." However, the data in the bar chart appear to have reflected only the percent of African Americans in the former slave states residing in rural areas for the four census years between 1860 and 1890. These data are now presented by the editor in tabular form. Du Bois' original title has been retained, but the variable headings have been supplied by the editor. While these data were probably based on census results, the source was not formally stated.

**Table 16.20. City and Rural Population among
American Negroes in the Former
Slave States**

Year	Percentage of Negroes Living in Villages and Country Districts
1860	95.8
1870	91.5
1880	91.6
1890	88.0

Between 1860 and 1890, the proportion of the African American population in the former slave states residing in villages and country districts declined from 95.8 percent to 88.0 percent. The "Great Migration" of the African American population from the rural South to the urban North took place between 1890 and 1930. Du Bois provided documentation of the first wave of this massive migration stream in the chapter on the sources of Philadelphia's African American population in *The Philadelphia Negro* ([1899] 1996).

Chart 52 (Page 53): African American marital status was addressed next. The title of this chart is "Conjugal Condition of American Negroes According to Age Periods." The headings along all four borders of the chart have been preserved, but the data in the center of the table are no longer discernable. None of the conjugal condition categories were identified in the body of the chart. Age periods are listed along the right border and left border. The age groups are 0–15, 15–20, 20–25, 25–30, 30–35, 35–45, 45–55, 55–65, and ages over 65. The label, "Males," is at the top right-hand side of the chart while "Females" is on the left-hand side. "Percents" appears at the bottom of the chart. The zero value is in the center of the percentage scale at the bottom, but it is not marked. Scales run in ten point intervals from 10 percent to 100 percent from the center to the right margin and form the center to the left margin. Du Bois identified neither the date of the data nor the data source.

Chart 53 (Page 54): A graph similar to an age-sex pyramid was used to portray racial amalgamation over time. The title given to the chart was "The Amalgamation of the White and Black Elements of the Population in the United States." A percentage scale was placed at the base of the pyramid-mound, and four different years throughout the nineteenth century signified the various layers of the mound. Information was provided for 1800, 1840, 1860, and 1890. The proportion of the population that was mixed-race was presented down the middle of the mound. The population that was considered Negro or White was to the left and right respectively but it looks as if part of the chart documenting the White population is missing. Although Du Bois did not formally state the source for his data, he was probably utilizing census data. Even though the figures on racial amalgamation were not distinguishable, the proportion of the population that was mixed-race (i.e., African American and White) steadily increased throughout the nineteenth century.

Chart 54 (Page 55)[7]: African American poverty was addressed in this chart. More specifically, Du Bois' focus was on pauperism and the almshouse. The almshouse was a residence that was provided for the poor and was supported by charity. This chart was comprised of a semi-circle followed by a single horizontal bar. The title of the chart was "Pauperism among American Negroes." Above the semi-circle, Du Bois placed the label, "Proportion of Almshouse Paupers in Every 100,000 Negroes." The number 100,000 was placed at the top of the semi-circle, and the number 476 was placed at the base of the circle. These data suggest that for every 100,000 African Americans in the United States, 476 African Americans were recipients of almshouse support. However, since the number for almshouse paupers was blurred, the pauperism rate stated here could be incorrect. The proportion of African American paupers by sex was signified by the bar underneath the semi-circle. Although no scale is provided, based on the editor's measurement of the bar length, it appears that 55 percent of African American paupers were male and 45 percent were female. Neither the date for these data nor the data source was stated formally.

Chart 55 (Page 56): Du Bois provided some of the earliest demographic studies by a sociologist in the United States (Odum 1951; Wortham 2009b). In this chart he addressed African American mortality. On this page of the exhibit, Du Bois placed five vertical bars. Each bar signified the African American mortality rate for a particular geographic location. The mortality rate was placed at the top of the bar, and the particular location was identified at the bottom of the bar. African American mortality rates were provided for the following areas: the United States as a whole, U.S. cities, and Philadelphia's 5th, 7th, and 30th Wards. The 5th Ward was identified as a "slum" while the 7th and 30th Wards were labeled "mixed class" and "better class" respectively. Although Du Bois did not identify his sources, the African American mortality rates for the country as a whole and the cities were probably taken from the 1890 U.S. census. Du Bois obtained the mortality data for Philadelphia from his study, *The Philadelphia Negro* ([1899] 1996). The death rates for the Philadelphia Wards were for the

1884–90 period. These death rates excluded still-births, and all five mortality rates cited in the chart were per 1,000 African Americans.

The data in the bar chart are now presented as a table. The editor has reformatted the material and supplied the variable headings. Du Bois' original title has been retained.

Table 16.21. Mortality of American Negroes

Geographic Area	Mortality Rate per 1,000 Negroes
United States	32.40
U.S. Cities	33.88
Philadelphia's 5th Ward (Slum)	48.46
Philadelphia's 7th Ward (Mixed Class)	30.54
Philadelphia's 30th Ward (Better Class)	21.74

The mortality rate for African Americans residing in U.S. cities was slightly higher than that for African Americans throughout the United States. The steady decline in the African American mortality rate across the three Philadelphia wards suggests that African American mortality varied inversely by social class. The mortality rate among African Americans residing in the "better class" ward was less than half the rate for African Americans residing in the "slum" ward.

Chart 56 (Page 57): This chart documented African American entrepreneurship. The title given to the chart was, "Negro Business Men in the United States." Eight rectangular figures are displayed throughout the page, and each figure represented a particular business activity. The size of the box signified the number or proportion of African American men involved in each business activity. No numerical identifiers appear to have been used, and if they were, they are no longer identifiable. Neither the date for the data nor the data source was identified.

Du Bois does state that the estimated capital invested by African American men in various business ventures was $8,784,637. The eight most popular business activities listed in order of descending box size were:

- Grocers
- General merchandise stores
- Publishers
- Undertakers
- Druggists
- Building contractors
- Building and loan associations
- Bankers

Grocers were by far the most popular business activity among African American men throughout the United States.

Chart 57 (Page 58): Du Bois considered land ownership to be an important indicator of improvement in African American quality of life. This bar chart documented the extent of land ownership among African Americans residing in nine of the Southern Black Belt states. Each bar was used to distinguish the proportion of African American land owners and tenants in each selected Black Belt state. Only the percentage figure for land owners was visible on the chart.

This bar chart has been reconstructed as a table, and Du Bois' original title has been retained. Each state is listed according to the selected state's proportion of African American land owners. The states were listed in descending order.

**Table 16.22. Negro Landholders in Various States
of the United States**

State	Percentage of Negro Landholders	
	Owners	Tenants
Virginia	27	73
Texas	22	78
Arkansas	21	79
Tennessee	20	80
North Carolina	19	81
South Carolina	18	82
Mississippi	13	87
Georgia	12	88
Louisiana	12	88

The percentage of African American landholders who were owners ranged from a high of 27 percent in Virginia to a low of 12 percent in Georgia and Louisiana. Neither the year nor the source for these data was formally identified.

Chart 58 (Page 59): Du Bois next documented the value of land owned by African Americans in three Southern Black Belt states. Data concerning the date of the property evaluation and the value of the property were provided for Virginia, North Carolina, and Georgia. A total figure for the property value owned by African Americans in these three states was provided also. A square was utilized to portray the information. The data for Virginia were at the top while the information for North Carolina and Georgia were along the left and right side respectively. The total figure was placed at the bottom. Du Bois did not provide a source for these data.

These data have been reconstructed by the editor in tabular form, and as before Du Bois' original title has been retained. The variable headings have been supplied by the editor.

**Table 16.23. Assessed Value of Property
Owned by Negroes in Three
States of the United States**

State / Year	Assessed Property Value in Dollars
Virginia (1895)	$13,933,958
North Carolina (1891)	$8,018,440
Georgia (1895)	$12,941,230
Total	$34,893,684[8]

The assessed value of property owned by African Americans in these three Black Belt states at the end of the nineteenth century was just under thirty-five million dollars. These financial data are slightly distorted since the property assessments were not all for the same year and the value of the dollar fluctuates annually.

Chart 59 (Page 60): The title of this chart was "Crime among American Negroes." Under the title Du Bois cited a national African American crime rate of 3,250 crimes per million African Americans. A diagonal bar was placed in the middle of the chart to distinguish the different types of crimes committed by African Americans. The five crime categories identified in the legend were crimes against government, society, persons, property, and miscellaneous crimes. It is no longer possible to distinguish these crimes along the diagonal bar, and it does not appear that Du Bois provided any numerical benchmarks like number of crimes or proportion of crimes for each crime type. "Crimes against society" is the only visible category along the diagonal, and based on a crude measurement of the length of this bar segment relative to the total bar length, it appears that these crimes accounted for approximately one-ninth of all crimes committed by African Americans.

While Du Bois identified neither the date of nor the source for these data, they were probably derived from the 1890 U.S. census. Du Bois cited the census as a source for his data on crime in two of the annual Atlanta University Conference reports. These reports were *Some Notes on Negro Crime Particularly in Georgia* (1904) and *Morals and Manners among Negro Americans* ([1914] 2010). The first report was edited by Du Bois and the second was co-edited by Du Bois and Augustus Granville Dill. In the latter conference study Du Bois and Dill ([1914] 2010: 41) identified the African American crime rate for 1890 as 3,250 crimes per million African Americans.

Chart 60 (Page 61): In this chart Du Bois documented the number of African American newspapers and periodicals in the United States. The data were presented in a layered pyramid format. These data are now presented in tabular form, and the table headings have been provided by the editor. Du Bois failed to provide the date for or the source of the information; however, he did present the same information in *The Negro in Business*, the 1899 Atlanta University Conference final report.

**Table 16.24. American Negro Newspapers
and Periodicals**

Newspaper / Periodical	Number
Magazines	3
Daily Papers	3
School Papers	11
Weekly Papers	136
Total	153

These data revealed that at the end of the nineteenth century weekly papers accounted for 88.9 percent of all African American newspapers and periodicals.

Chart 61 (Page 62): The last two charts in the exhibit were devoted to religion among African Americans and the Black Church. In this first chart, Du Bois employed a bar graph to distinguish the number of African Americans affiliated with Catholic and Protestant Christianity. Actual numbers were provided for these two designations. With respect to Christian identification, African Americans were shown to be overwhelmingly Protestant. In the second part of the bar graph, Du Bois distinguished among four different Protestant sects. These sects were in order of descending size: Baptists, Methodists, Presbyterians, and Congregationalists. A miscellaneous category was provided also. African American Protestants were primarily Baptist or Methodist. Numerical data were not associated with the variations in bar length on this part of the bar graph, but the miscellaneous category bar was slightly larger than the Presbyterian bar. Data for African Americans affiliated with non-Christian traditions were not provided.

While Du Bois did not identify his data source, he was utilizing 1890 data obtained from the *Census of Religious Bodies*. Du Bois later referenced this data source in *The Negro Church* ([1903b] 2003). This study was based on the topic for the 1903 Atlanta University Conference. Given this data source, the editor is now able to present the data originally provided in the bar chart in tabular form. These data are reconstructed in Table 16.25.

Over ninety-nine (99.5) percent of African American Christians were Protestant, and among African American Protestants the vast majority were either Baptists (52.9 percent) or Methodists (44.7 percent).

Chart 62 (Page 63): The *Census of Religious Bodies* provided detailed data on membership, number of churches, attendance, and value of church property. In the last chart included in "The Georgia Negro: A Social Study," Du Bois provided a few summary statistics concerning the Negro Church in the United

Table 16.25. Religion of American Negroes

Religious Identification	Negro Members
Catholics	14,517
Protestants	2,659,460
Protestant Sects	
Baptists	1,403,559
Methodists	1,187,563
Presbyterians	29,561
Congregationalists	6,908
Miscellaneous	26,880[9]

States. Statistical data were provided for number of organizations, number of church edifices, value of church property (dollars and francs), and number of communicants. In each case, except for the value of church property, Du Bois placed a bar line beside the numerical figure. At the bottom of the chart, two bars were used so that the "number of communicants" could be compared with the "population of New York." Du Bois did not provide a numerical figure for New York's population, but it appears that this bar was approximately three-fourths the length of the communicants bar.

While the data source was not formally identified, it is apparent that Du Bois accessed the 1890 *Census of Religious Bodies* data to construct this final exhibit graph. These data are now presented by the editor in tabular form. The variable headings have been presented by the editor.

Table 16.26. Statistics of Negro Church Organizations

Statistic	Numerical or Dollar Amount
Number of Organizations	23,462
Number of Church Edifices	23,770
Value of Church Property	$26,626,448
Number of Communicants	2,673,977

Based on the communicants and organizations data, the average size of the Negro Church in 1890 was 114 communicants. Looking at the financial and organizational data, the average value of Negro Church property was $1,134.88.

In "The Study of the Negro Problems," Du Bois (1898a) maintained that the social problems impacting African American quality of life could be best investigated from an interdisciplinary perspective. Insights from historical, sociological, statistical, and anthropological analyses could be employed to provide a more comprehensive assessment of the development and contemporary context of a specific social problem. In this exhibit provided for the 1900 Paris Exhibition (*Exposition Universelle*), Du Bois utilized statistical data to empirically document African American social advancement and racial inequality in Georgia and the United States at the end of the nineteenth century. These data provided the rationale for arguing on the exhibit's title page that "the problem of the 20th century is the problem of the color-line."

Notes

1.   *Editor's note*: To view pictures of the original charts, please go to http://129.17 1.53.1/ep/Paris/ html/charts_1.html. The title of the site is "Paris 1900 World's Fair (*Exposition Universelle*) The Georgia Negro Exhibit."

2.   *Editor's note*: The annual family income for the other seven African American families included on this chart page ranged from a low of $360 to a high of $540. The $32 amount for the family headed by a fireman and engineer appears to be a misprint. A more likely annual family income value is $320.

3.   *Editor's note*: According to the 1890 census, the total population of McIntosh County, GA was 6,470. The population figure provided for African Americans in the original exhibit was 522. This is a misprint and the corrected figure (5,212) has been cited in the discussion of this particular chart.

4.   *Editor's note*: The last number in the sequence is unclear. It could represent either 15–25 African Americans or 15–20 African Americans.

5.   *Editor's note*: A drayman was the driver of a horse or mule drawn flat-bed wagon that was used to transport goods. See http://en.wikipedia.org/wiki/Drayman.

6.   *Editor's note*: The hostler was a stable worker whose primary responsibility was to provide care for horses. See http://en.wikipedia.org/wiki/Hostler.

7.   *Editor's note*: It looks as though there were two page 54s in the exhibit. This chart would be the second page labeled as page 54. The next two pages following this chart were numbered 56 and 57 respectively.

8.   *Editor's note*: There is a discrepancy between the total Du Bois provided and the total derived by adding the valuations for the three states. The total valuation figure obtained by the editor was $34,893,628. This represents a discrepancy of $56. Since it was hard to distinguish clearly some of the valuation figures, this factor could account for the observed discrepancy.

9.   *Editor's note*: The total African American membership in the Protestant Sects based on the five categories Du Bois identified is 2,654,471. The membership number cited for all African American Protestants was 2,659,460. This discrepancy could be attributed to undercounting. It is possible that some smaller Protestant denominations were not included in the list used to reconstruct this table.

Editor's Bibliography

"African American." http://en.wikipedia.org/wiki/African_American. Accessed February 11–12, 2011.

Allport, Gordon. *The Nature of Prejudice*. Cambridge, MA: Perseus Books Publishing, LLC, [1954] 1979.

"American Negro Academy–Early Membership, Occasional Papers, Internal Problems, The Nature of the Membership, The Final Years." http://encyclopedia.jrank.org/articles/ pages/5951/ American-Negro-Academy-html. Accessed November 6, 2010.

Aptheker, Herbert. "Editorial Notes." In *Contributions by W.E.B. Du Bois in Government Publications and Proceedings*, edited by Herbert Aptheker, 230. New York: Kraus-Thomson Organization Limited, 1980.

"Articles of Religion." www.anglicanonline.org/basics/thirty-nine_articles.html, 2007. Accessed December 8, 2010.

Binet, Alfred. *Les alterations de la personnalite*. Paris: F. Alcan, [1892]. English translation *Alterations of Personality*, translated by Hellen Green Baldwin with notes and a preface by J. Mark Baldwin. New York: D. Appleton and Company, 1896.

Blum, Edward J. *W.E.B. Du Bois: American Prophet*. Philadelphia: University of Pennsylvania Press, 2007.

Bonacich, Edna. "A Theory of Ethnic Antagonism: The Split Labor Market." *American Sociological Review* 37 (1972): 547–59.

"Boon." http://thesaurus.com/bowse/boon. Accessed February 27, 2011.

Bruce, Dickson D., Jr. "W.E.B. Du Bois and the Idea of Double Consciousness." In *The Souls of Black Folk*, edited by Henry Louis Gates, Jr and Terri Hume Oliver, 236–44. A Norton Critical Edition. New York: W.W. Norton & Company, 1999.

Calloway, Thomas J. "The Negro Exhibit." In *Report of the Commissioner-General for the United States to the International Universal Exposition, Paris, 1900. Volume II*. U.S. Senate Document No. 232 (56th Congress, 2nd. Session), 463–467. Washington, D.C.: Government Printing Office, 1901.

Carroll, Charles. *The Negro A Beast or In the Image of God*. St. Louis: American Book and Bible House, 1900.

Dixon, Thomas. *The Leopard's Spots: A Romance of the White Man's Burden, 1865–1900*. New York: Doubleday, Page & Company, 1902.

"Drayman." http://en.wikipedia.org/wiki/Drayman. Accessed February 11, 2011.

Du Bois, W.E.B. "Strivings of the Negro People." *The Atlantic Monthly* 80 (1897a): 194–98.

____. "The Problem of Amusement." *The Southern Workman* 27 (1897b): 181–84.

____. "The Conservation of Races." American Negro Academy, *Occasional Papers*, No. 2. Washington, DC: American Negro Academy, 1897c.

_____. "The Study of the Negro Problems." *Annals of the American Academy of Political and Social Science* 11 (1898a): 1–23.

_____. "The Negroes of Farmville, Virginia." *Bulletin of the Department of Labor* 3 (1898b): 1–38. Reprinted in *W.E.B. Du Bois and the Sociological Imagination: A Reader, 1897–1914*, edited and introduction by Robert A. Wortham, 233–82. Waco, TX: Baylor University Press, 2009.

_____. "Careers Open to College-Bred Negroes." In *Two Addresses Delivered by Alumni of Fisk University, in connection with the Anniversary Exercises of their Alma Mater, June, 1898*. Nashville,TN: Fisk University, 1898c. Reprinted in *Du Bois Writings*, edited by Nathan Huggins, 827–41. New York: Library of America College Edition (Penguin Books), 1996.

_____. "A Negro Schoolmaster in the New South." *The Atlantic Monthly* 83 (1899a): 99–105.

_____. *The Philadelphia Negro: A Social Study*. Philadelphia: University of Pennsylvania Press, 1899b. Reprinted with an introduction by Elijah Anderson. Same original publisher, 1996.

_____. "The Negro in the Black Belt: Some Social Sketches." *Bulletin of the Department of Labor* 4 (1899c): 401–17.

_____. *The Negro in Business*. Atlanta: The Atlanta University Press, 1899d.

_____. "The Negro and Crime." *Independent* 51 (1899e): 1355–57.

_____. "The Religion of the American Negro." *New World* 9 (1900a): 614–25.

_____. "To the Nations of the World." In *Report of the Pan-African Conference, held on 23rd, 24th, and 25th July 1900, at Westminister Town Hall, Westminister, S.W.* [London], 10–12. Headquarters 61 and 62, Chancery Lane, W.C., London, England, 1900b

_____. "The Georgia Negro: A Social Study." http://129.171.53.1/ep/Paris/html/charts 1. html, 1900c. Accessed May 28, 2010.

_____. "The American Negro at Paris." *The American Monthly Review of Reviews* 22 (1900d): 575–77.

_____. *The College-Bred Negro*. Atlanta, The Atlanta University Press, 1900e.

_____. "Testimony of Prof. W.E. Burghardt Du Bois." In *Report of the Industrial Commission on Education*, 159–75. Washington, DC: United States Industrial Commission Reports, Volume 15, 1900–02.

_____. "The Freedman's Bureau." *The Atlantic Monthly* 87 (1901a): 354–65.

_____. "The Negro as He Really Is." *The World's Work* 2 (1901b): 848–66.

_____. "The Evolution of Negro Leadership." *The Dial* 31 (1901c): 53–55.

_____. "The Relations of the Negroes to the Whites in the South." *Annals of the American Academy of Political and Social Sciences* 18 (1901d): 121–40.

_____. "The Negro Landholder of Georgia." *Bulletin of the Department of Labor* 6 (1901e): 647–777.

_____. "The Spawn of Slavery: The Convict Lease System in the South." *Missionary Review of the World* 24 (1901f): 737–45.

_____. *The Negro Common School*. Atlanta: The Atlanta University Press, 1901g.

_____. "Of the Training of Black Men." *The Atlantic Monthly* 90 (1902): 289–97.

_____. *The Souls of Black Folk*. Chicago: A.C. McClurg & Company, [1903a]. Reprint edited by Henry Louis Gates Jr. with an introduction by Arnold Rampersad. New York: Oxford University Press, 2007.

____. *The Souls of Black Folk*, Jubilee Edition. New York: The Blue Heron Press, Inc., [1903a] 1953.

____. *The Negro Church.* Atlanta: The Atlanta University Press, [1903b]. Reprinted with an introduction by Phil Zuckerman, Sandra L. Barnes, and Daniel Cady. Walnut Creek, CA: AltaMira Press, 2003.

____. "The Talented Tenth." In Booker T. Washington, W.E.B. Du Bois, Paul Laurence Dunbar, Charles W. Chestnut, and others. *The Negro Problem: Centennial Edition*, with an introduction by Bernard R. Boxill, 31–76. New York: Humanity Books, [1903c] 2003.

____. "The Atlanta University Conferences." *Charities* 10 (1903d): 435–39.

____. *Some Notes on Negro Crime Particularly in Georgia.* Atlanta: The Atlanta University Press, 1904a.

____. "The Negro Farmer." In *Negroes in the United States*, by W.E.B. Du Bois, with tables prepared under the supervision of W. C. Hunt, chief statistician and W. F. Wilcox, special agent of the Census Bureau. United States Bureau of the Census, *Bulletin* 8 (1904b): 69–98. Washington, DC: Government Printing Office.

____. "The Atlanta Conferences." *Voice of the Negro* 1 (1904c): 85–89.

____. "Atlanta University." In *From Servitude to Service: Being the Old South Lectures on the History and Work of Southern Institutions for the Education of the Negro*, edited and introduction by Robert C. Ogden, 155–97. Boston: American Unitarian Association, 1905.

____. "Die Negerfrage in den Vereinigten Staaten." *Archiv fur Socialwissenschaft und Socialpolitik* 22 (1906a): 21–79. Translated by Joseph Fracchia and published as "The Negro Question in the United States." *The new centennial review* 6 (2006): 241–90.

____. "Vardaman." *The Voice of the Negro* 3 (1906b): 189–194.

____. "The Sharecropping System of Lowndes County Alabama." U.S. Department of Labor. Unpublished manuscript, 1906–08. (Title suggested by Reiland Rabaka in *Against Epistemic Apartheid: W.E.B. Du Bois and the Disciplinary Decadence of Sociology*. Lanham, MD: Lexington Books, 2010.)

____. *The Negro American Family.* Atlanta: The Atlanta University Press, 1908.

____. *The Quest of the Silver Fleece.* Chicago: A.C. McClurg & Company, [1911a]. Reprint edited by Henry Louis Gates, Jr. with an introduction by William L. Andrews. New York: Oxford University Press, 2007.

____. "The Negro Race in the United States of America." In *Papers on Inter-racial Problems Communicated to the First Universal Races Congress Held at University of London, July 26–29, 1911*, edited by Gustav Spiller, 348–64. London: P.S. King; Boston: World's Peace Foundation, 1911b.

____. *Black Reconstruction in America.* Reprint edited by Henry Louis Gates, Jr. with an introduction by David Levering Lewis. New York: Oxford University Press, [1935] 2007.

____. *The Autobiography of W.E.B. Du Bois: A Soliloquy on Viewing My Life from the Last Decade of Its First Century.* New York: International Publishers, [1968]. Reprint edited by Henry Louis Gates, Jr. with an introduction by Werner Sollors. New York: Oxford University Press.

____. *Prayers for Dark People*, edited by Herbert Aptheker. Amherst, MA: The University of Massachusetts Press, 1980a.

_____. *Contributions by W.E.B. Du Bois in Government Publications and Proceedings*, edited by Herbert Aptheker. New York: Kraus-Thomson Organization Limited, 1980b.

_____. *W.E.B. Du Bois and the Sociological Imagination: A Reader 1897–1914*, edited and introduction by Robert A. Wortham. Waco, TX: Baylor University Press, 2009.

Du Bois, W.E.B. and Augustus Granville Dill. *Morals and Manners among Negro Americans*. Atlanta, The Atlanta University Press, 1914. Reprinted with an introduction by Robert A. Wortham. Lanham, MD: Lexington Books, 2010.

"*Dum vivimus vivamus.*" http://www.merriam-webster.com/dictionary/dum20%vivamus20%vivamus. Accessed February 21, 2011.

Durkheim, Emile. *The Elementary Forms of Religious Life*, translation and introduction by Karen E. Fields. New York: The Free Press, [1912] 1995.

Ellison, Christopher E. and Darren Sherkat. "The Semi-Involuntary Institution Revisited: Regional Variations in Church Participation among Black Americans." *Social Forces* 73 (1995): 1415–37.

"*Exposition Universelle.*" http://en.wikipedia.org/wiki/Exposition_Universelle_(1900), 2011. Accessed January 6, 2011.

"Expressman." http://en.wikipedia.org/wiki/Expressman. Accessed February 22, 2011.

Finke, Roger and Rodney Stark. *The Churching of America, 1776–2005*. New Brunswick, NJ: Rutgers University Press, 2005.

"Fourteenth Amendment to the United States Constitution." http://en.wikipedia.org/wiki/Fourteenth_Amendment_to_the_United_States_Constitution. Accessed February 22, 2011.

Gabbidon, Shaun L. "W.E.B. Du Bois: Pioneering American Criminologist." *Journal of Black Studies* 31 (2001): 581–99.

_____. *W.E.B. Du Bois on Crime and Justice: Laying the Foundations of Sociological Criminology*. Interdisciplinary Research Series in Ethnic, Gender and Class Relations. Burlington, VT: Ashgate Publishing, 2007.

"*Gaucherie.*" http://www.merriam-webster.com/dictionary/gaucherie. Accessed February 22, 2011.

Grossman, Jonathan. "Black Studies in the Department of Labor, 1897–1907." *Monthly Labor Review* 97: 17–27.

"Guerdon." http://thesaurus.com/browse/guerdon. Accessed February 27, 2011.

"Hackmen." http://www.yourdictionary.com/hackmen. Accessed February 22, 2011.

Haveman, Robert and Timothy Smeeding. "The Role of Higher Education in Social Mobility." *The Future of Children* 16 (2006): 125–150.

"Hostler." http://en.wikipedia.org/wiki/Hostler. Accessed February 11, 2011.

"*Ipso facto.*" http://en.wikipedia.org/wiki/Ipso_facto. Accessed February 22, 2011.

James, William. *The Principles of Psychology*. New York: Holt, [1890]. Reprint New York: Cosimo Classics, 2007.

Johnstone, Ronald. *Religion in Society: A Sociology of Religion*, Eighth Edition. Upper Saddle River, NJ: Pearson / Prentice-Hall, 2007.

Lewis, David Levering. *W.E.B. Du Bois: A Biography*. New York: A John Macrae Book. Henry Holt and Company, 2010.

Lewis, Oscar. *La Vida: A Puerto Rican Family in the Culture of Poverty*. New York: Irvington, 1986.

Lincoln, C. Eric and Lawrence H. Mamiya. *The Black Church in the African American Experience*. Durham, NC: Duke University Press, 1990.

"Lotharios." http://thefreedictionary.com/Lotharios. Accessed February 22, 2011.

MacLean, Vicki M. and Joyce E. Williams. "Sociology at Women's and Black Colleges, 1880s–1940s." In *Diverse Histories of American Sociology*, edited by Anthony J. Blasi, 260–316. Leiden: Brill, 2005.

Martineau, Harriet. *Society in America*, Three volumes. London: Saunders and Otley, 1837. Reprint Cambridge: Cambridge University Press, 2009.

McKee, Claude. "Essay on Essential Baptist Principles." http://www.essentialbaptistprinciples.org, 2010. Accessed February 23, 2011.

Melvin, Tasha. "W.E.B. Du Bois: Criminological Thought Prior to the 1920s." Unpublished M.A. Thesis in Sociology, North Carolina Central University, 2010.

Merton, Robert. "Social Structure and Anomie." *American Sociological Review* 3 (1938): 672–682.

"Metayer." http://www.thefreedictionary.com/metayer. Accessed February 22, 2011.

Morris, Aldon D. "Sociology of Race and W.E.B. Du Bois: The Path Not Taken." In *Sociology in America: A History*, edited by Craig Calhoun, 503–34. Chicago: University of Chicago Press, 2007.

"Nous avons changer tout cela." http://www.merriam-webster.com/dictionary/nous%20avons. Accessed February 22, 2011.

Odum, Harold. *American Sociology: The Story of Sociology in the United States through 1950*. New York: Longmans, Green, 1951.

Park, Robert, R.D. McKenzie, and Ernest Burgess. *The City: Suggestions for the Study of Human Nature in the Urban Environment*. Chicago: University of Chicago Press, 1925.

"Peculium." http://www.thefreedictionary.com/peculium. Accessed February 22, 2011.

Portes, Alejandro. "The Social Origins of the Cuban Enclave Economy of Miami." *Sociological Perspectives* 30 (1987): 340–372.

"Pro Archia Poeta." http://en.wikipedia.org/wiki/Pro_Archia_Poeta. Accessed February 23, 2011.

Provenzo, Eugene F., Jr. *The Illustrated Souls of Black Folk*. Boulder, CO: Paradigm Publishers, 2005.

Saari, Mindy Meyer. "W.E.B. Du Bois and E. Franklin Frazier: Pioneering Figures in the Sociology of the African American Family." Unpublished M.A. Thesis in Sociology, North Carolina Central University, 2010.

"Scab." http://en.wikipedia.org/wiki/Scab. Accessed February 22, 2011.

Shaw, C.R. and H.D. McKay. *Juvenile Delinquency in Urban Areas*. Chicago: University of Chicago Press, 1942.

Smith, Shawn Michelle. *Photography of the Color Line: W.E.B. Du Bois, Race, and Visual Culture*. Durham, NC: Duke University Press, 2004.

Sutherland, Edwin and Donald Cressey. *Principles of Criminology*, Eleventh Edition. Lanham, MD: AltaMira Press, [1934] 1992.

"Tertium quid." http://en.wikipedia.org/wiki/Tertium_quid. Accessed February 21, 2011.

"The Thirty-Nine Articles." http://en.wikipedia.org/wiki/Thirty-Nine_Articles, 2010. Accessed December 8, 2010.

"Toto caelo." http://www.merrian-webster.com/dictionary/toto20%coelo. Accessed February 21, 2011.

Washington, Booker T. *Up from Slavery*. Reprinted edition with an introduction by James Robinson. New York: Barnes and Noble, Inc., [1901] 2003.

Washington, Booker T. and W.E.B. Du Bois. *The Negro in the South*. Philadelphia: George W. Jacobs, 1907.

Weber, Max. *The Protestant Ethic and the Spirit of Capitalism*, edited by Richard Swedberg. A Norton Critical Edition. New York: W.W. Norton & Company, [1904–05] 2009.

Wilson, William Julius. *More Than Just Race: Being Black and Poor in the Inner City.* New York: W.W. Norton & Company, 2009.

Wimberley, Ronald C. and Libby V. Morris. *The Southern Black Belt: A National Perspective.* Lexington, KY: TVA Rural Studies. The University of Kentucky, 1997.

Wortham, Robert A. "Du Bois and the Sociology of Religion: Rediscovering a Founding Figure." *Sociological Inquiry* 75 (2005): 433–52.

_____. "W.E.B. Du Bois and the Scientific Study of Society: 1897–1914." In *W.E.B. Du Bois and the Sociological Imagination: A Reader, 1897–1914*, edited and introduction by Robert A. Wortham, 1–20. Waco, TX: Baylor University Press, 2009a.

_____. "W.E.B. Du Bois and Demography: Early Explorations." *Sociation Today* 7.1 (2009b): http://www.ncsociology.org/sociationtoday/v71/phila.htm.

_____. "*Morals and Manners*: Editor's Introduction." In *Morals and Manners among Negro Americans*, edited and introduction by Robert A. Wortham, ix–xxxvii. Lanham, MD: Lexington Books, 2010a.

_____. "Prayer as Social Commentary in W.E.B. Du Bois' *Prayers for Dark People*." Paper presented at the annual meeting of the Society for the Scientific Study of Religion, 2010b.

Wright, Earl II. "Beyond W.E.B. Du Bois: A Note on Some of the Little Known Members of the Atlanta Sociological Laboratory." *Sociological Spectrum* 29 (2009): 700–717.

"Zeitgeist." http://en.wikipedia.org/wiki/Zeitgeist. Accessed February 27, 2011.

Zuckerman, Phil, Sandra Barnes, and Daniel Cady. "The Negro Church." In *The Negro Church*, edited by W.E.B. Du Bois, vii–xxvi. Walnut Creek, CA: AltaMira Press, 2003.

Bibliography of W.E.B. Du Bois'
Early Sociological Studies: 1897–1902

1897

"A Program of Social Reform." *The College Settlement News* 3.3 (March 1897): 4.

"Strivings of the Negro People." *The Atlantic Monthly* 80 (August 1897): 194–98.

"The Problem of Amusement." *The Southern Workman* 27 (September 1897): 181–84.

"The Conservation of Races." American Negro Academy, *Occasional Papers*, No.2. Washington, DC: American Negro Academy, 1897.

"A Program for a Sociological Society." W.E.B. Du Bois Papers, Department of Special Collections and University Archives, W.E.B. Du Bois Library. University of Massachusetts at Amherst, Unpublished Manuscript.

1898

"The Study of the Negro Problems." *Annals of the American Academy of Political and Social Science* 11 (January 1898): 1–23. Reprinted in *W.E.B. Du Bois and the Sociological Imagination: A Reader, 1897–1914*, edited and introduction by Robert A. Wortham, 33–50. Waco, TX: Baylor University Press, 2009.

"The Negroes of Farmville, Virginia." *Bulletin of the Department of Labor* 3 (January 1898): 1–38. Reprinted in *W.E.B. Du Bois and the Sociological Imagination: A Reader, 1897–1914*, edited and introduction by Robert A. Wortham, 233–82. Waco, TX: Baylor University Press, 2009.

Some Efforts of American Negroes for Their Own Social Betterment, edited by W.E.B. Du Bois. Atlanta: The Atlanta University Press, 1898.

"Careers Open to College-Bred Negroes." In *Two Addresses Delivered by Alumni of Fisk University, in connection with the Anniversary Exercises of their Alma Mater, June, 1898.* Nashville,TN: Fisk University, 1898c. Reprinted in *Du Bois Writings*, edited by Nathan Huggins, 827–41. New York: Library of America College Edition (Penguin Books), 1996.

1899

"A Negro Schoolmaster in the New South." *The Atlantic Monthly* 83 (January 1899): 99–105.

"The Negro and Crime." *Independent* 51 (May 1899): 1355–57.

"The Negro in the Black Belt: Some Social Sketches." *Bulletin of the Department of Labor* 4 (May 1899): 401–17.

The Negro in Business, edited by W.E.B. Du Bois. Atlanta: The Atlanta University Press, 1899.

The Philadelphia Negro: A Social Study. Philadelphia: University of Pennsylvania Press, 1899. Reprinted with an introduction by Elijah Anderson. Philadelphia: University of Pennsylvania Press, 1996.

"The Suffrage Fight in Georgia." *Independent* 51 (November 1899): 3226–28.

1900

"The Problem of Negro Crime." *Bulletin of Atlanta University* (February 1900): 3.

The College-Bred Negro, edited by W.E.B. Du Bois. Atlanta: The Atlanta University Press, 1900.

"The Twelfth Census and the Negro Problems." *The Southern Workman* 29 (May 1900): 305–9.

"To the Nations of the World." In *Report of the Pan-African Conference, held on 23rd, 24th, and 25th July 1900, at Westminister Town Hall, Westminister, S.W.* [London], 10–12. Headquarters 61 and 62, Chancery Lane, W.C., London, England, 1900b.

"The Georgia Negro: A Social Study." http://129.171.53.1/ep/Paris/html/charts 1. html, 1900.

"The American Negro at Paris." *The American Monthly Review of Reviews* 22 (1900): 575–77.

"The Present Outlook for the Dark Races of Mankind." *Church Review* (October 1900): 95–110.

"The Religion of the American Negro." *New World* 9 (December 1900): 614–25.

"Post-Graduate Work in Sociology at Atlanta University." W.E.B. Du Bois Papers, Department of Special Collections and University Archives, W.E.B. Du Bois Library. University of Massachusetts at Amherst, Unpublished Manuscript.

"Testimony of Prof. W.E. Burghardt Du Bois." In *Report of the Industrial Commission on Education*. Washington, DC: United States Industrial Commission Reports, Volume 15 (1900–1902): 159–75.

1901

"The Freedman's Bureau." *The Atlantic Monthly* 87 (March 1901): 354–65.

The Negro Common School, edited by W.E.B. Du Bois. Atlanta: The Atlanta University Press, 1901.

"The Negro as He Really Is." *The World's Work* 2 (June 1901): 848–66.

"Results of the Ten Tuskegee Conferences." *Harper's Weekly* 45 (June 1901): 641.

"The Evolution of Negro Leadership." *The Dial* 31 (July 1901): 53–55.

"The Burden of Negro Schooling." *Independent* 52 (July, 1901): 1667–68.

"The Negro Landholder of Georgia." *Bulletin of the Department of Labor* 6 (July 1901): 647–777.

"The Relations of the Negroes to the Whites in the South." *Annals of the American Academy of Political and Social Sciences* 18 (July 1901): 121–40.

"The Savings of Black Georgia." *Outlook* 69 (September 1901): 128–30.

"The Spawn of Slavery: The Convict Lease System in the South." *Missionary Review of the World* 24 (October 1901): 737–45.

"The Freedmen and Their Sons." *Independent* 53 (November 1901): 2709.

The Black North in 1901: A Social Study. A series of articles originally published in *The New York Times*, November–December 1901. Reprinted in book form. New York: Arno Press, 1969.

"The Social Training of the Negro." *Scroll* 6 (December 1901): 19–23.

"The Problem of Housing the Negro." *The Southern Workman* 30 (July, September, October, November, December 1901): 390–95, 486–93, 535–42, 601–14, 688–93; *The Southern Workman* 31 (February 1902): 65–72.

1902

"The Work of Negro Women in Society." *Spelman Messenger* 18 (February 1902): 1–3.

The Negro Artisan, edited by W.E.B. Du Bois. Atlanta: The Atlanta University Press, 1902.

"Of the Training of Black Men." *The Atlantic Monthly* 90 (September 1902): 289–97.

"Hopeful Signs for the Negro." *Advance* 44 (October 2, 1902): 327–28.

"Crime and Our Colored Population." *The Nation* 75 (December 1902): 499.

Index

Abolition movement, 22

African American: business men, xxviii–xxxiii, 87–101; college education, xxxvii–xxxviii, 45–46, 88; college graduates, 79, 81; crime, xiv, xxviii, xxxi–xxxiii, xxxv, 47–48, 66–67, 103–5, 192; debt, 42–43, 47–48; education, xiv, xvii–xviii, xxv–xxvi, xxix, 9–16, 67–68, 73–83, 108, 121–31, 140, 143–62; family, xli–xlii, 44–45, 143–62; homes, 43–44, 143–62; landholding, 51–52; literature and art, 109, 116; migration, 49, 134, 148, 166; mobility, xxviii; newspapers and periodicals, 116, 192–93; religion, xviii, 12–25; savings, 98; social class, xlii, 46, 50, 138, 143–62, 179, 189–190

African American demographics, Georgia: age distribution, 166–67; conjugal condition, 167–68; debt and income, 176–77; economic assets, 172–74, education, 170–72; family expenditures, 177–78; occupations, 174–76; race amalgamation, 169; rural and urban population, 168; size, 164–65; slaves, 168–69

African American demographics, United States: business, 190–91; conjugal condition, 188; crime, 192; density, 181; education, 185–86; land and property ownership, 191–92; mortality, 189–90; occupations, 184–85, poverty, 189; racial amalgamation, 188–89; rural-urban population, 187–88; size, 164, 181–84; slavery, 186-87

African American occupations, 92–98, 143–62: business enterprise, 151; common and domestic labor, 150; farmer, 126, 129, 150; merchants, 126–27, 129; professionals, 127–30, 151; scientists and artists, 129–30; unemployed and criminal classes, 151–52

African Methodist Church, xix, 21, 56, 99

African Methodist Zion Church, 99

African slave trade, 164

Albany, GA, 41–42, 179

Allport, Gordon, xxiv

Alterations of Personality, xvi

American Freedmen's Union, 28

American Missionary Association, 28, 156

American Negro Academy, xvii, xxxiv, xxxvi–xxxvii, 116–19, 119n1

The American Negro at Paris, 107–10

amusements, xviii, xxxviii, 99–100, 133–42, 157

The Annals of the American Academy of Political and Social Sciences, xxiii, 71n1

assimilation, xxiii

Athens, GA, xxxix, xli, 157–60

Atlanta, GA, xliii, 70, 173, 177–79

Atlanta Baptist Seminary, 156

Atlanta Compromise, xxiii, 56

The Atlanta Constitution, 103–4